Kevin Cripe

The Learning Spiral: A New Way to Teach And Study Chess

MONGOOSE
Press

BOSTON

Publisher: Mongoose Press
1005 Boylston Street, Suite 324
Newton Highlands, MA 02461
info@mongoosepress.com
www.MongoosePress.com

ISBN: 978-1-936277-88-9
Library of Congress Control Number: 2018941682

Distributed to the trade by National Book Network
custserv@nbnbooks.com, 800-462-6420
For all other sales inquiries please contact the Publisher.

Layout: Stanislav Makarov
Editor: Jorge Amador
Cover Design: Alex Krivenda
Printed in the United States of America

First English edition
0 9 8 7 6 5 4 3 2 1

Table of Contents

*Failures, repeated failures, are finger
posts on the road to achievement.
One fails forward toward success.*
– attributed to C.S. Lewis

Foreword

I was a teacher of upper elementary students in 1972 when Bobby Fischer and Boris Spassky fought for the World Championship in Iceland. It was my first year of teaching and I was a novice and naïve, but I knew how to have fun with the students (and hoped that they would learn too). We painted all the desks in the 64 squares, made pieces, and waited every morning for the latest game. The whole class moved the pieces as did the grandmasters, and we discussed, analyzed, and tried to predict the next move. Every student learnt from this daily routine (we played previous games on rest days and were disappointed when the championship ended after 21 games), and it made for much excitement and perhaps even for great learning.

Chess only requires two people, one board, 64 squares, 16 pieces each, up to 4^{76} possible moves in a game – and so much intrigue, sophistication, fun, and analyses can accrue. Chess has been around in various forms for millennia and many have tried to teach the basics, guide the novice through to a proficient level, and developed the proficient to expert level. This book is aimed at the first levels, and it is written by a master teacher – one who knows how to intrigue the student, create fun, and guide the player into the depths and alleyways of this great game. I have come to know Kevin over the past few years: his passion and skill come through on every page of this book.

Many claims have been made about how chess makes you smarter and increases achievement. Indeed, the European Parliament expressed its favorable opinion on using chess courses in schools as an educational tool aiming to enhance thinking skills, transferring them to math and reading achievement, and increasing a love of schooling (Binev, Attard-Montalto, Deva, Mauro, & Takkula, 2011). Recently, Sala and Gobet (2016) completed a meta-analysis of 24 articles based on 5,221 students. The overall effect was .34 and it was noted that longer training had slightly higher effects (> 25 hours = .43, < 25 hours = .30), and the effects were higher in math (d=.38) than in reading (.25). This effect is just below the average of all possible influences (d=.40, Hattie, 2009) and the authors concluded "that chess instruction is no more effective in enhancing children's cognitive and academic skills than many (at least more than 50%) other possible educational interventions." Much of the effect, they suggested, could be due to the instructors' passion rather than to chess itself; and it is possible that students who play chess start off with higher abilities. This passion is a key, and turning students on to the teacher's passion is one of the gifts of teaching.

The Learning Spiral

We asked many adults who their best teacher was and why. Turning students on to a passion, and seeing something in students that they might not see in themselves, were the major reasons for nominating the best and most impactful teacher. Does it matter that chess may not translate into higher scores in math or reading, if the love of strategy, intrigue, mastery, and skill are the outcomes? Bring on more chess in school if is taught well!

Aha, *taught well*. The lack of passion, skill, and understanding of teaching can kill a great subject. For example, a randomized control trial of 4009 Year 5 students in the United Kingdom found no evidence that the chess intervention (of 30 hours' instruction) had an impact on math (d=.01), science (d=-.01), or reading (d=-.06; Jerrim et al., 2016). However, the teachers and students were very positive about the intervention (53% liked playing very much) and their favorite parts were playing mini-games, learning a new challenging skill, and playing with friends. The greatest barrier, noted the evaluators, was the quality of the teachers (most were teaching assistants or had no training in teaching). Why kill a topic with poor teaching? And thus the power of this book.

The book is full of strategies, trials, ideas, evaluations, checkmates, stale-mates, pins, skewers, deflections, promotions, endgames, and replays and ideas from the best. In many senses, the skills, content and understanding outlined throughout this book mirror much of what we found in our recent synthesis of studies relating to "how we learn." Our results were based on a model with three major student inputs and outputs – the skills students bring to the task, the will in terms of the students mind frames about learning (e.g., resilience, resourcefulness, reflection, or relating), and the thrill (the motivations for learning, such as mastery, completing tasks to please others, or love of challenge). We then made distinctions between when a student is first exposed to a new task like chess – where they need to work out the highlights, the outlines of the bigger picture, and acquire some basic skills. The all-important phase of learning is the consolidation or "over-learning" of these basic ideas. This is where deliberate practice, practice testing over time, seeking help, and reviewing past trials are much needed. Then on to the deeper levels of learning where ideas are combined, where knowing when "good is good enough," when planning and predicting and working out errors and learning from productive failure are developed. Consolidating this deeper learning is optimally accomplished from thinking aloud with peers and teachers, and this all then leads to transferring the surface learning and deeper learning to new situations. The most powerful way to accomplish such transfer is to first see the similarities and differences in the problems before attempting to solve them (Hattie & Donoghue, 2016). All these phases are outlined in this book – the skills, the patterns, the deliberate practice opportunities, the error detection, the thinking aloud, and best of all the detecting of similarities in board positions before making a move.

Foreword

It is also worth noting that so much of the research on expertise owes much to chess, from the earliest studies of individual differences (Binet, 1893) to the more recent models of expertise. De Groot (1978) noted that players asked to think out loud did not think further ahead than less skilled practitioners, but that they did have superior memories for chess patterns. It is the patterning, not the algorithmic differences, that explain how experts choose better moves. Chase and Simon (1973a, b) reinforced that it was "pattern recognition" that matters – there were no differences between skilled players and novices when the chessboard was displayed in random patterns.

Skilled chessplayers think in "chunks" (groupings of pieces on given squares) and, considering that there are so many viable patterns, these players have a greater memory of possible patterns; they visually encode more of the board; they focus on more relevant moves and sequences of moves; and they can better (and faster) choose between moves in a more parallel than serial manner, knowing the possible implications of their next move. The experts could thus "look ahead" more by taking these patterns into account, and could more readily store these chunks in memory. Simon and Gilmartin (1973) estimated that chess masters could acquire 10,000-100,000 patterns and modern chess-playing computer programs can acquire 300,000, although experts rarely visit more than 100 patterns before selecting a move. It is pattern recognition that underlies chess skill. Hence, this book is based on learning "chunks" and patterns, provides ample opportunities for deliberate practice, invites the reader to predict ahead, and invokes a progressive deepening of the searches and moves for the player.

I recently received two emails from students from that 1972 class – they remembered the fun of the chess, the painted tables, and the love of learning a skill. Whether it helped them to become scientists or novelists matters not; it was the love of learning, the passion of discovery, and the sense of growing as a learner that counted. It was hard work, it stretched their thinking, caused collaboration with others, and was a shared journey of discovery. Thanks, Kevin. Be challenged. Persevere with the deliberate practice. Enjoy.

John Hattie
Director, Melbourne Education Research Institute
University of Melbourne, Victoria, Australia
December 2017

References

Binet, A. (1893). Mnemonic virtuosity: A study of chess players. *Revue des Deux Mondes, 117,* 826-859.

Binev, S., Attard-Montalto, J., Deva, N., Mauro, M., & Takkula, H. (2011). Declaration of the European Parliament, 0050/2011.

Chase, W. G., & Simon, H.A. (1973a). Perception in chess. *Cognitive Psychology, 4,* 55-81.

de Groot, A.D. (1978). *Thought and choice in chess* (2nd ed.). The Hague: Mouton.

Gobet, F., & Charness, N. (2006). *Chess and games. Cambridge handbook on expertise and expert performance* (pp. 523-538). Cambridge, MA: Cambridge University Press.

Hattie, J.A.C. (2009). *Visible learning: A synthesis of 800+ meta-analyses on achievement.* Oxford, UK: Routledge.

Hattie, J.A.C., & Donoghue, G. (2016). Learning strategies: A synthesis and conceptual model. *Nature: Science of Learning.* 1. doi:10.1038/npjscilearn.2016.13. http://www.nature.com/articles/npjscilearn201613

Jerrim, J., Macmillan, L., Micklewright, J., Sawtell, M., & Wiggins, M. (2016). *Chess in Schools. Evaluation Report and Executive Summary.* Education Endowment Foundation. Available online at: https://educationendowmentfoundation.org.uk/public/files/Projects/Evaluation_Reports/EEF_Project_Report_Chess_in_Schools.pdf

Sala, G., & Gobet, F. (2016). Do the benefits of chess instruction transfer to academic and cognitive skills? A meta-analysis. *Education Research Review, 18,* 46–57.doi: 10.1016/j.edurev.2016.02.002

Simon, H.A., & Gilmartin, K.J. (1973). A simulation of memory for chess positions. *Cognitive Psychology, 5,* 29-46.

Note to Students, Teachers, and Parents

This book can be used by school-age chess learners, either alone or with the help of a parent or teacher/coach. If you are a student, you may want to skip the Introduction and "Watching Children Learn," and go straight to Chapter 1. If you are an adult (whether a chess teacher or a chess novice), you may wish to read these two sections in order to understand the theory behind the teaching method in this book.

Introduction

This is a book for smart students. You might ask, "What makes me smart?" Smart is developing a consistent practice schedule. Smart is not quitting when things get hard or when losses hurt. Smart is learning from your mistakes and listening to people who give good advice.

Some people think "smart" is about how your brain functions or how quickly neurons fire. I'll be honest, that is part of it. There are plenty of people who have brains that can perform very complicated tasks effortlessly, but who have no chance at becoming great chessplayers. For whatever reason, they don't put in the work, and they don't persevere through hard times.

Smart is made up of many different things. My students once told me, "Mr. Cripe, your Spanish is terrible... but your dancing is worse." Part of being smart is to know what you are not good at. ☺

This book is put together differently from most books, and that's because I have witnessed many children who knew nothing about chess learning the foundations of the game fairly quickly.

Now, you will not become a great chessplayer overnight. Great chessplayers have to memorize many problems. They have to see things instantaneously and know what to do. Some of the learning can be fun, but some of it is just plain work.

This book has plenty of chess problems. Most chess books have problems in them. This one is premised on the idea that a child can learn and process new information quicker than adults. So, concepts are grouped with other concepts.

Children's brains learn information a little differently from those of adults. Here is a model of how to learn something:

The Learning Spiral

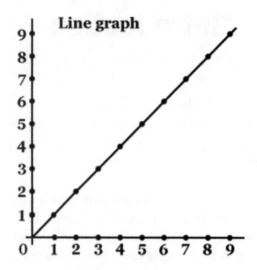

If, one at a time, you learn knight forks and then pins and then one-move checkmates, you will get better at chess. If you stay with it, you may be successful. I have no argument with that. As I have watched children learn, though, this is what I observe:

The Learning Spiral

It is what is known as a three-dimensional Fibonacci sequence: you start with simple and easy information at first, and it should get more complex and diverse as learning occurs. That is the very definition of rigor.

Let me give an example of this idea. Several years ago, I taught my fourth-graders how to perform double-digit multiplication in their heads (no pencils and no paper). It was a struggle at first, but by the end of the second day, 70% of the class had mastered the idea. They had fun doing it.

Introduction

I choose to teach children in a way that acknowledges their natural curiosity and interest in puzzles and challenges. Each chapter of this book is deliberately designed to have very simple problems to moderately difficult problems of varying themes in it. In most chapters, there will be a problem or two that is completely unrelated but not too difficult.

Really bright people can disagree as to what learning is or how it happens. I like this diagram:

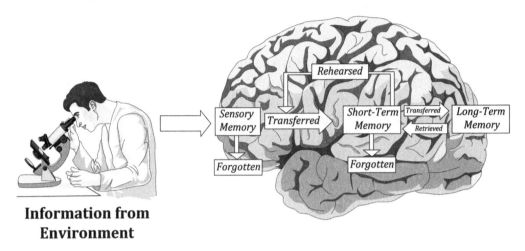

**Information from
Environment**

What is happening? We get information in from our senses. It can get to short-term memory and, with practice, it gets stored in long-term memory. Imagine that we look at a chess problem and solve it. Is that information in long-term memory?

Here is a test. Can you say the answer quickly and explain it to someone else?

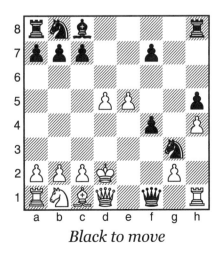

Black to move

The Learning Spiral

Imagine that this is the problem. I can define learning this way. I present a lesson on one-move checkmates where this is the fourth problem in a set of 20. Students practice and can say all the answers to the problems in under a minute. Do they "know" it?

First, they have two big cues: they know that the set is one-move checkmates, and they know that this is the fourth problem.

Both of those cues make it easier to memorize and will make it less usable in a real game.

But what if that problem is within a set of 20 randomly ordered cards? Some are one-move checkmates, some are pins, and a couple others involve new ideas. The student who can know the answers to those questions, no matter how they are randomized, has a much better chance of finding that idea in a game because a game of chess is a sort of random variety of tactics and ideas that can arise. What does the thinking process look like when the concepts are randomly placed?

The way you learn complex information is the way you will process that information.

Paz y esperanza,
Kevin Cripe

Watching Children Learn

The Idea

The student population I teach is about eighty percent English Language Learners (mostly Spanish-speaking) and about 98% receive lunch for free or at reduced prices. In teacher parlance, our student population is an inverted "Response to Intervention" (RTI) pyramid. In the traditional RTI model, some 70-80% of students are "Tier 1," meaning that they need very little support. Then there are about 15-25% in Tier 2, which means they need some extra support. Tier 3 is supposed to be about 5% of the student population; these are students who need serious interventions.

At schools with demographics like mine, that pyramid gets inverted – that is, from 60 to 70% of the students need Tier 3 interventions. This not only puts an enormous strain on resources, but it also brings to the forefront the question, "What can we do to fix things?"

There is an analogy which will be useful in understanding how well-intentioned ideas can go very wrong.

Imagine that I was going to teach children at my school how to make a 5-foot putt using the approach that we use to teach subjects like math and reading to students at schools like mine. First, there would be an assumption that these children just can't learn how to putt a golf ball like other children. Children from demographics like this don't have much experience with golf. A fair amount of blame would be placed on parents in anticipation of failure and – more importantly – a fear of failure.

We need to slow things down and not move forward until they master or show mastery of each step. They would spend weeks learning how to hold a putter. When they actually started putting, they would work on 1-foot putts, and only after making the prerequisite 97% of putts from that distance would they move on.

This, of course, would eventually create a gap between themselves and children from other schools whose parents had all the right types of golf equipment and spent time at all the right golf courses. There would be something called the "achievement gap" and serious thinking people would write volumes discussing "What can we do to close this achievement gap?"

The Learning Spiral

Back at school, after about 3 or 4 months of practice the students would work up to 2-foot putts. More well-intentioned people would come in and say, "We need to stop all learning while we give meaningless tests for a couple of days." We will call this, "progress monitoring."

Many of these students would drop out of golf altogether, and more experts would come in and write more volumes about the dropout rate.

Think about it: the children are 97% successful every step of the way and yet they fall further and further behind.

Why not try the following instead?

Start students blindfolded 10 feet from the hole, trying to make putts. They won't make very many of them – at first. Have some kind of song or funny thing that happens during the learning process. Reward effort, improvement and success equally. Be positive when they fail and point out how much better they are getting. As they try 10-foot putts with and without blindfolds, move them closer to the hole, eventually getting to 5 feet. This will be the easiest thing they do.

By approaching the task this way, a couple of very important things have happened. First, the second group will have a great deal more confidence because they have experienced failure and overcome it. There will come a point when the 97%ers fail and it will destroy many of them. Never allowing a child to fail in a structured environment with love and support, so that they learn how to respond to failure, is dooming that child to fail on a huge scale later in life.

From a learning perspective, there is one other very important thing which happens: the children who start out with the 10-foot putt and work backwards are going to make much faster progress in getting to 15- and 20-foot putts. They will be used to challenges.

Will the 97%ers learn how to make a 5-foot putt? Yes – only much more slowly and with much less growth potential than the group which has been challenged.

This leads to Rule #1 in teaching children: "Engaged challenge in rigorous activities produces the most growth... even if there is initial failure."

Someone might ask, "Well, if a 10-foot putt is good for teaching a 5-foot putt, why not start with a 100-foot putt?" The simple answer is because the 100-foot putt is so unlike a 5-foot putt that a child would not necessarily see or experience a connection. Teaching math facts is a good thing. Using fact families to help in understanding math facts is a good thing. But using physics to teach math facts may not have a great effect on learning outcomes.

How the Idea Works: Collocating Information

One day during report-card time, I was called into the office and asked to explain the reading scores on the report cards for my second-graders. I had watched children learn for many years, taught chess for a long time, and had tried some things that seemed to produce a great deal of success with students. I was told that students could not learn information that fast, and that English Language Learners could not make the growth that my students made. There was an argument, which lasted about two months, and at the end of the day, the powers-that-be decided that the English-only students could keep their scores and that the English Language Learners would have the score on their report cards literally whited out and left blank... sigh.

You might ask, "What were you doing that was causing those children to learn so fast?" and/or, "Are you sure you were right?"

When you are teaching groups of children who are behind, and you are trying to get them to catch up, doing what everybody else does will not help anything. If you use the exact same materials in the same way as students who are more advanced, your students will learn, and the more advanced students will learn faster. It is not the information you present, it is how it is presented and the degree to which you integrate rigor and challenge into it. I felt there were two ways to approach how to create the most efficient language-processing schema for English Language Learners. First, you can assume that because ELLs tend to come in behind, they cannot learn information as quickly as other children. If you think that, you should give up and try another profession, or at least don't teach ELLs.

The other view is that a child's brain responds uniquely to challenge. The more creative and engaging you can make something, the more you can increase the level of complexity and rigor. It isn't that all children are geniuses, it's that if you treat a child like he or she is smart, you will find many more smart children in your classroom. The key word is "collocation," or how you group ideas and words together. Here are two ways to teach language:

The Learning Spiral

Would you want your child taught a language this way?

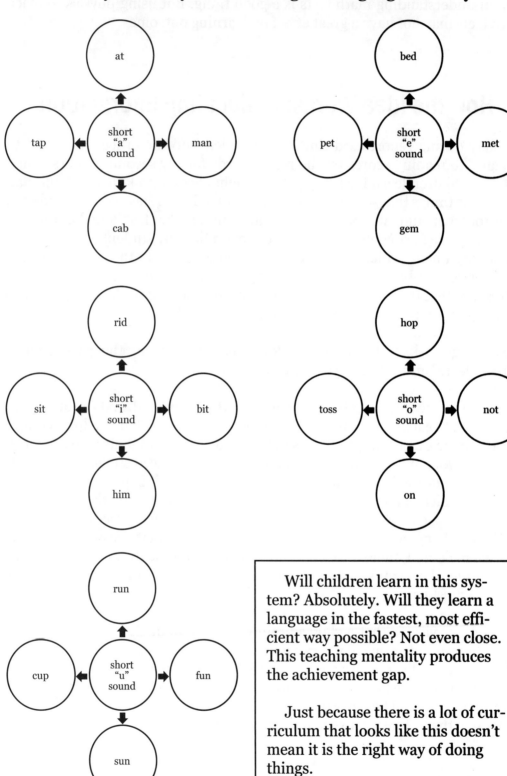

Will children learn in this system? Absolutely. Will they learn a language in the fastest, most efficient way possible? Not even close. This teaching mentality produces the achievement gap.

Just because there is a lot of curriculum that looks like this doesn't mean it is the right way of doing things.

Watching Children Learn

A collocation of ideas for ELLs and short vowel sounds

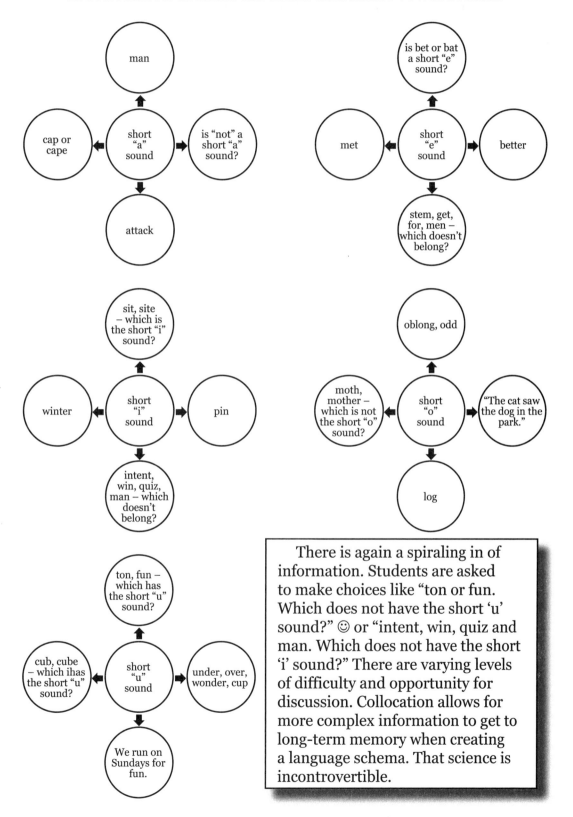

There is again a spiraling in of information. Students are asked to make choices like "ton or fun. Which does not have the short 'u' sound?" ☺ or "intent, win, quiz and man. Which does not have the short 'i' sound?" There are varying levels of difficulty and opportunity for discussion. Collocation allows for more complex information to get to long-term memory when creating a language schema. That science is incontrovertible.

The Learning Spiral

These are overly simplistic diagrams, but the science is on the side of the integration of ideas and concepts and showing how things are related or not related.

As education theorist Mohammed Rhalmi puts it:

> Language is not learned by learning individual sounds and structures and then combining them, but by an increasing ability to break down wholes into parts. We can also use whole phrases without understanding their constituent parts.

The acquisition of language, especially a second language, is a very complex thing. The way to teach children to learn that language will not be as simple as "Short a + short e + short i + short o + short u + long a + etc., etc., etc. + diagraphs + prepositions + etc., etc., + grammar + syntax = fluency and comprehension."

Words are at the heart of this. Take the word "bridge." Suppose I say a bridge is something to cross, "Here is a picture of a bridge" and now on to the word "ridge," and then "smidge," and so on. Learning will happen – just not very quickly.

The concept of "collocation" can be found in Michael Lewis's *The Lexical Approach* (Language Teaching Publications, 1993), a groundbreaking work that discusses how to group things together to make the learning of a language most efficient.

What was the terrible idea I tried that caused such a problem on the report cards? I decided to try something with my second-graders to see if I could use simple collocations of words so that students could master challenging texts. I didn't realize it was collocation at the time, but my thought was that it was the best way to accomplish the task at hand.

What I felt, at the time, was that if I grouped words in a variety of ways, then the level of challenge would go up and so the level of interest would go up, too.

The core issues seemed to be the lack of foundational information and the speed at which it was being processed. So I tried something: I took my second-grade ELLs and tried to teach them a sixth-grade reading selection by finding the key words and having them memorize the words.

Here is the passage, from *The Six-Minute Solution* (Sopris West, 2003):

Cells: Basic Units of Life

Cells are **considered** to be the **basic units** of **life** itself. All **living** things are made up of cells. A tree is made up of cells, as is an **alligator.** Some living things only have one cell, such as **bacteria.** Other living things, such as **humans,** have **trillions** of cells in their **bodies.** It wasn't until the early 1600's that the **existence** of cells was **discovered**. An **English scientist, Robert Hooke, built** an early **microscope.** He placed a thin slice of **cork** under the microscope, **magnified** it, and made **observations. Imagine** his **surprise** when he saw many squares in the cork. Robert Hooke thought the small squares **resembled** the tiny rooms in which **monks** lived. Robert Hooke named his discovery after these rooms, which were called cells.

As microscopes improved, scientists made important discoveries about cells. They observed that there are many kinds of cells and that these cells are very complicated. Scientists discovered that all cells do not look alike. Many cells apparently **specialize** in **performing** a **certain** kind of **function.** These cells have shapes that help them do their jobs. For **example,** muscle cells are **elongated.** These cells have the ability to expand and contract. **Narrow** white blood cells have a rounded shape. Their shape **assists** them in better flowing through veins. Cells that make up the eye are **sensitive** to light, as is the eye itself.

Microscopes have greatly improved, so much so that Robert Hooke would not believe his eyes if he looked through one today. Scientists' **knowledge** of cells and their functions have advanced **considerably** as well. Scientists are **continually** studying and discovering more each day about cells. One important area of research on cells is how to stop **dangerous** cells, such as cancer cells, from growing. What started with Robert Hooke and a slice of cork is ongoing, with the **health** and well-being of humankind as the **ultimate** goal.

Here is the word list I created:

cells, cider, cede
considered, considering
basic, music, fantastic
unit, unicorn, unilateral
life, lives, living
alligator, crocodile
bacteria, virus
human, human-kind

trillions, millions, billions
body, bodies, embodies
exist, existence, existing
for, from, form
even, ever, every
discovery, discovered
English, Spanish, French
scientist, science
Robert Hooke
built, build, building
microscope, microscopic
cork, fork, stork, pork
magnify, magnifying
observe, observations
imagine, imagination
surprise, surprising
resemble, resembling
monks, junk, trunk, chunk
apparent, apparently
special, specialize
perform, performing
certain, certainly
function, junction
example, ample, sample
elongated, elongate
narrow, wheelbarrow
assists, assisting, assist
sensitive, insensitive
knowledge, college
consider, considerably
continual, continually
danger, dangerous
health, healthy, wealth
ultimate, ultimately

I embedded the list of words needed in a bigger list of words that rhyme, that share similar prefixes or suffixes, or that were antonyms, and told the students they had to say all the words accurately in less than 1 minute. We practiced them in order and sometimes out of order.

About 80% of the second-graders were eventually able to say all the words in less than 1 minute. They were able to read the passage fluently and to pass a quiz about what happened in the passage.

Watching Children Learn

There was one other thing happening that year, which contributed to their success. Every day, we partner-read a page from the book *Myths, Legends, Neat Things* (Instructional Fair, 1990) for grades 3 to 5. After reading the selection, they would work with their partner to answer questions about details and sequencing.

At first it was not easy, but at some point it simply became part of what we did. There came a point when there were no more reading selections (we finished the book). What to do? *What to do?* I had the 5th-to-8th-grade copy of *Myths, Legends, Neat Things* which I used when I taught upper grades and I thought, "Let's try this and see how it goes." The first few days, my second-grade ELLs struggled with 5th-to-8th-grade level material, but at some point they just decided, "This is what we do every day, we might as well learn it."

It wasn't a big surprise to me when they could read 100+ words in under a minute. It didn't surprise me when they understood the passage. It surprised me when I had to sit in the principal's office and watch as their reading scores were whited out.

A child's brain is very different from an adult's brain in at least one very important respect: it doesn't comprehend limits. We place artificial limits on how much a child can learn and, for the most part, they rise or descend to our level of expectation. The process by which most children can achieve great things is to assume, as a teacher, that great things are possible.

How does that relate to chess? I have looked at many books designed for children to learn chess (I have not seen all of them). For the most part, there is a similar path: Pins + knight forks + skewers + back-rank checkmates + etc., etc., etc. = efficient initial chess thought schema. Really?? Does the science of how children actually learn support that model, or is it just the way it has always been done?

When your son or daughter plays chess, do they sit down and think, "Every time my knight moves it will successfully fork something," or "Every time my bishop moves it will pin something," or "The rook is always worth 5 points"? Those are simple ideas for a complex thought process and your child is smart. What do you want for your child?

The Learning Spiral

The traditional structure of chess books for **children**

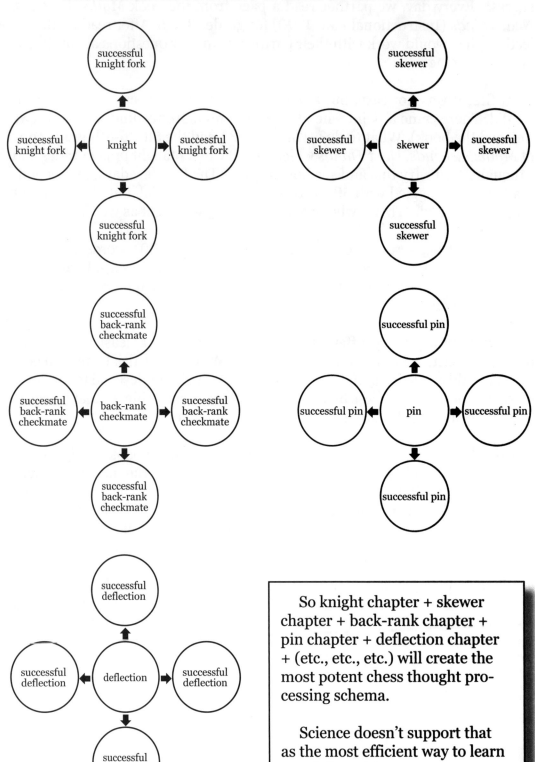

So knight chapter + skewer chapter + back-rank chapter + pin chapter + deflection chapter + (etc., etc., etc.) will **create the** most potent chess thought processing schema.

Science doesn't support that as the most efficient way to learn new information.

Collocation of chess problems as a structure for learning

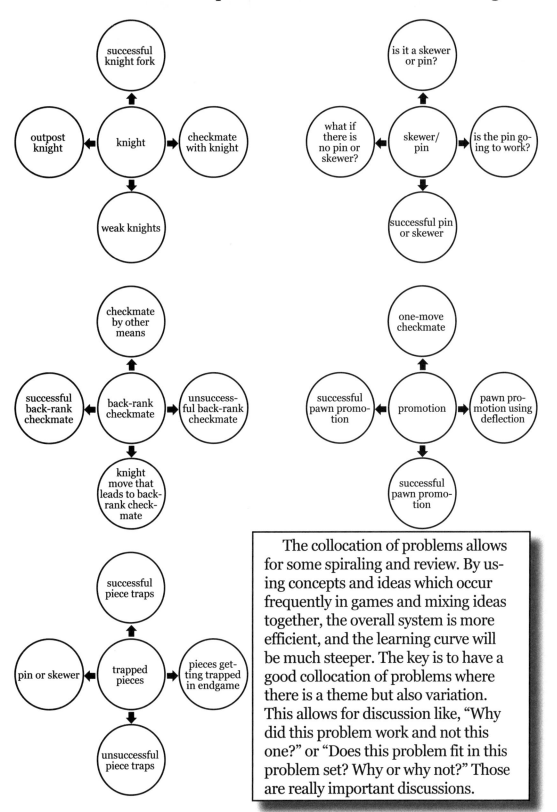

The collocation of problems allows for some spiraling and review. By using concepts and ideas which occur frequently in games and mixing ideas together, the overall system is more efficient, and the learning curve will be much steeper. The key is to have a good collocation of problems where there is a theme but also variation. This allows for discussion like, "Why did this problem work and not this one?" or "Does this problem fit in this problem set? Why or why not?" Those are really important discussions.

The Learning Spiral

I am not a research scientist. I have spent years observing children learn things and asking myself, "How could they learn information faster and more efficiently?" I will try things that work and sometimes things that won't work. You may notice, as your child weaves his or her way through this book, that there are many problems that involve pieces getting trapped. Why? Trapping pieces seems to me to be one of the most complex ideas for a beginner to learn. Start with the concept early.

Does the book have faults? Yes! One fault it has is the same one found in many other books: the problems occur in sequence. That is the nature of books and pages. In my chess club, I tend to use flashcards. That randomization is a better way of doing things. However, it is an impossible process to recreate in a chess book.

I have no doubt that, over time, some of the problems in this book might change. Even how the chapters are structured could be changed. This is an attempt to create an initial chess thought-processing schema using real science. I'm not talking about science by being able to say, "Adriaan de Groot, *Thought and Choice in Chess*" in a single breath.

I am a public-school teacher. If I had a dime for every time I heard the phrase, "research says" at a meeting, I could have retired years ago. To say, "We do it this way because we have always done it this way" moves you closer to the Flat Earth Society than the direction in which rules of scientific inquiry and observation will take us.

Really, which would be more fun – having a child receive high marks in a system that is so simple everyone can get high marks in it, or sitting in an office, listening to a principal say, "There is no way your child could have achieved at this level," while they are trying to make the chess trophies your child just won disappear by pouring gallons of white correction fluid on them?

> *"You shall know a word by the company it keeps."*
> J.R. Firth, 1957

> *"You shall know a chess piece by the company it keeps."*
> Kevin Cripe, 2017 ☺

Chapter 1

The Pieces and How They Move

This chapter is about learning how the pieces move and what they can and cannot do. Look carefully at problems where there is a choice. Chess is a game of choices; you can be winning a game and make one bad choice and then lose. The sign "#" means checkmate. The game ends with checkmate.

The "+" sign means "check," and the king must always move out of check. There are three ways to get out of check, and you will learn that.

When you start to play chess, you should always try to take notation (write down your moves). The main reason for this is that after the game, you can go over it with a stronger player and learn from your mistakes.

Chapter 1

Bishops

The bishop is worth 3 points and moves diagonally.

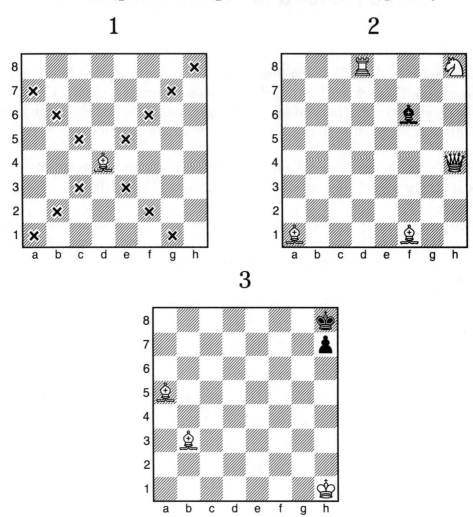

Questions about bishops:

In Diagram 1, how many squares can the bishop move to?

In Diagram 2, what is Black's best move? Why?

In Diagram 3, what is White's best move? Why?

Rooks

The rook is worth 5 points and moves horizontally and vertically.

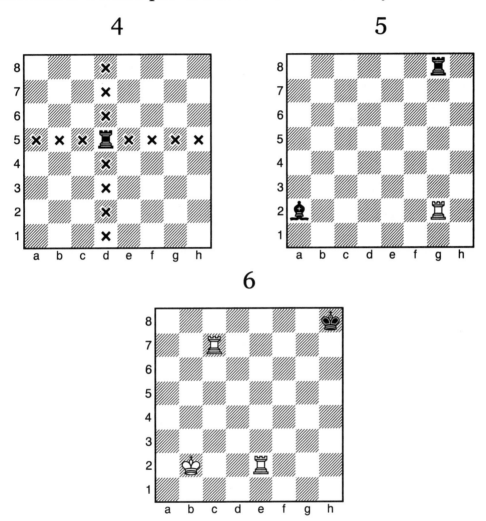

Questions about rooks:

In Diagram 4, how many squares can the rook move to?

In Diagram 5, which move is better: 1.RxB(a2) or 1.RxR(g8) ? Why?

In Diagram 6, which move is better: 1.Rh2 or 1.Re8 ? Why?

Chapter 1

Kings

The king can move one square in any direction.

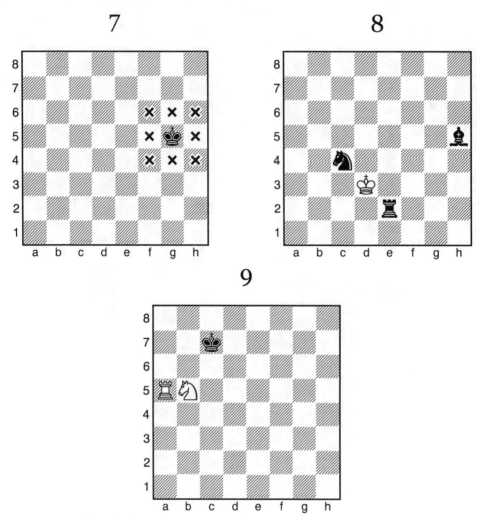

Questions about kings:

In Diagram 7, how many squares can the king move to?

In Diagram 8, which is possible – 1.Kxe2(R) or 1.Kxc4(N) ?

In Diagram 9, where should the king move to get out of check?

The Pieces and How They Move

The king must always get out of check: There are three ways to get out of check:

1. Move the king out of check
2. Take the piece which is giving check
3. Block the check (interpose)

It is very important to know how pieces check the king and how the king gets out of check. There are problems on pages 51 and 52 under the heading, "Block, capture, or move?" Study those problems.

Chapter 1

Queens

The queen is worth 9 points and moves diagonally, horizontally, and vertically (like a rook and bishop put together).

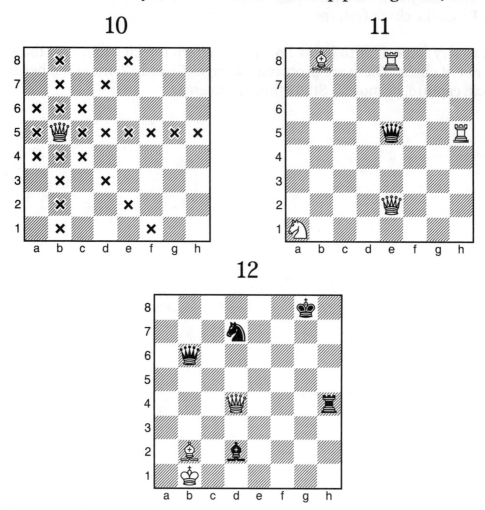

Questions about queens:

In Diagram 10, how many squares can the queen move to?

In Diagram 11, which piece should the black queen capture?

In Diagram 12, what is the white queen's best move? Why?

General question about the queen:

Why is the queen worth more than any other piece?

Knights

The knight is worth 3 points and is the only piece which can hop over other pieces. Its move is shaped like a capital "L."

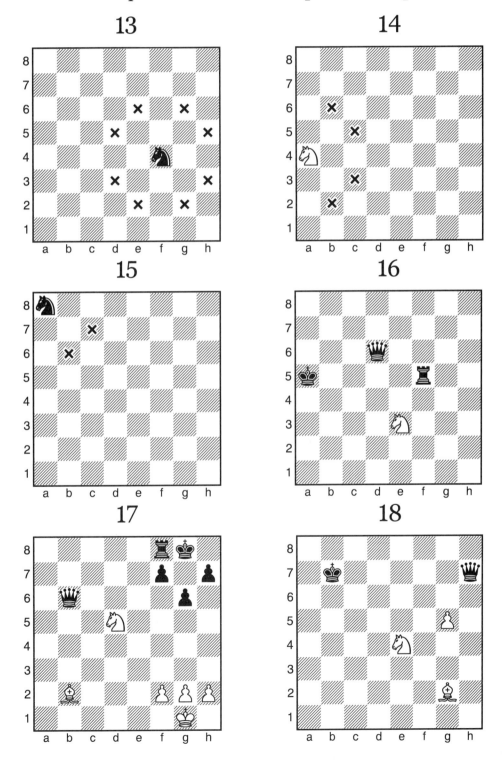

Chapter 1

Questions about knights:

Look at Diagrams 13, 14, and 15. What do you learn about knights?

In Diagram 16, is there a better move than 1.Nxf5 ?

In Diagram 17, is there a better move than 1.Nxb6 ?

In Diagram 18, what is the best square for the knight to move? Why?

With knights, there is something called the Knight's Tour which might help you to quickly master how the piece moves.

Knight's Tour

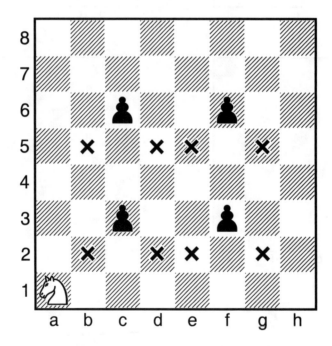

The goal is to move the knight from square a1 to b1 to c1 and so on across and up the board. However, in the tour the knight may not land on any square that the pawns control (marked with an X) and cannot take a pawn. The knight can hop to c2, then to a3, and to b1.

From b1 it needs to go to c1. (This is a tough one and requires five moves.) The knight can get to c1 from three entry squares: d3, b3, and a2. There are several five-move combinations that work. Starting from b1, move to a3 (only move), then move to c4, a5, b3, and c1.

You move horizontally across the board to h1. Then go up to h2 and move horizontally back across to a2. Then move up to a3 and move horizontally across to h3.

Use three minutes as a reasonable time standard. With practice, over time it's possible to go from a1 and finish at a8.

It's a great way for a student to come to understand how the knight moves.

Chapter 1

Pawns

The pawn is worth only 1 point – but if it can make it safely to the last row, it can become a queen.

A pawn captures pieces that are one square in front of it diagonally.

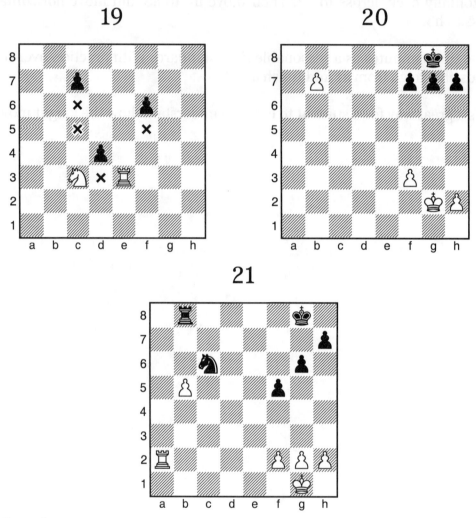

Questions:

In Diagram 19, the pawn on c7 can move one or two squares. The pawn on f6 can move one square. The pawn on d4 can take the rook or the bishop or move to d3. What is the best move for the pawn on d4?

In Diagram 20, with White to play, what is the best move? Why?

In Diagram 21, can White play 1.bxc6 ? Is it a good move?

The Pieces and How They Move

True or false: As a pawn moves "safely" down the board, it becomes stronger. Explain your reasoning.

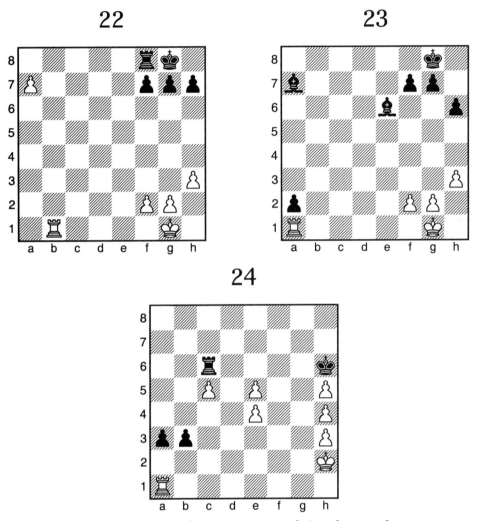

22

23

24

In Diagram 22, is 1.a8Q the best move? Explain why or why not.

In Diagram 23, what move can Black make to help the pawn on a2 to queen?

In Diagram 24, it is Black to move. Who has better pawns? Black can play 1...Rxc5 winning a pawn, or 1...Kxh5 winning a pawn. Are there any other moves which are better? Explain why.

Chapter 1

Answers

Bishops

The bishop is worth 3 points and moves diagonally.

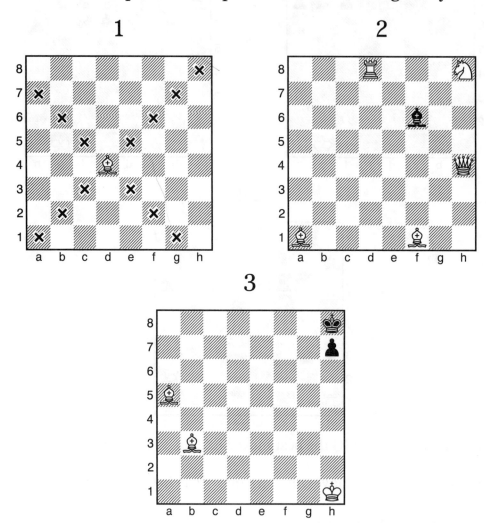

Questions about bishops:

In Diagram 1, how many squares can the bishop move to? – *13*

In Diagram 2, what is Black's best move? Why? – *The queen is worth 9 points and it is unprotected. 1...Bxh4 wins the queen.*

In Diagram 3, what is White's best move? Why? – *There are many bishop moves. However, 1.Bc3# (checkmate) is the best one because it ends the game.*

Rooks

The rook is worth 5 points and moves horizontally and vertically.

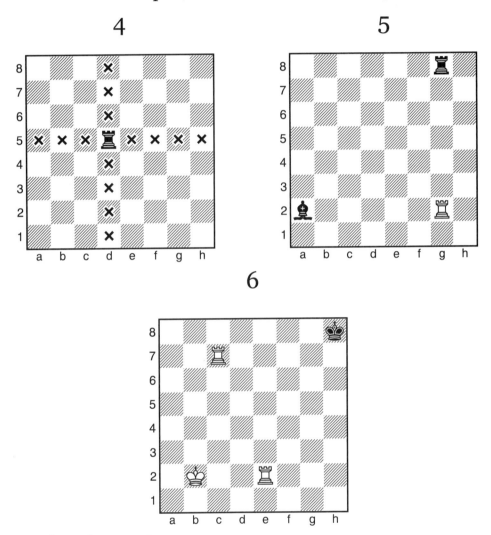

Questions about rooks:

In Diagram 4, how many squares can the rook move to? – *14*

In Diagram 5, which move is better – 1.Rxa2 or 1.Rxg8 ? Why? – *Black's rook is worth 5 points and the bishop is worth 3, but the bishop protects the rook. If White plays 1.Rxg8, then Black plays 1...Bxg8 and it's an even trade.*

In Diagram 6, which move is better – 1.Rh2 or 1.Re8 ? Why? – *1.Rh2 is just a check. The king can go to g8 (1...Kg8). 1.Re8# is checkmate and wins the game at once. So 1.Re8# is the best move.*

Chapter 1

Kings

The king can move one square in any direction.

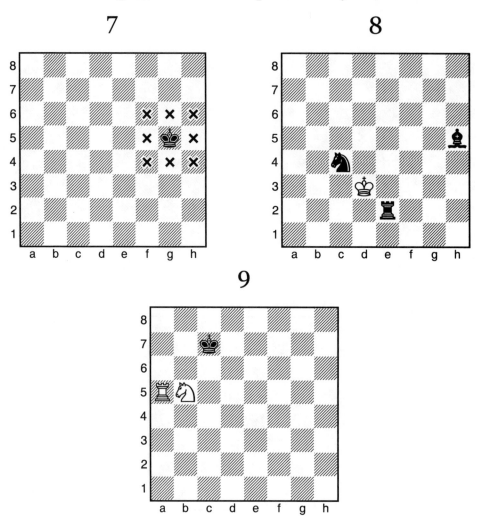

Questions about kings:

In Diagram 7, how many squares can the king move to? – *8*

In Diagram 8, which move is possible, 1.Kxe2 or 1.Kxc4 ? – *The rook is worth 5 points and the knight is worth 3 points, but Black's bishop protects the rook. 1.Kxc4 wins the knight for free.*

In Diagram 9, where should the king move to get out of check? – *There are 7 legal squares to move to. There is one good move: 1...Kb6 is a king fork and Black will win one of White's pieces.*

The Pieces and How They Move

The king must always get out of check. There are three ways to get out of check:

1. Move the king out of check
2. Take the piece which is giving check
3. Block the check

Chapter 1

Queens

The queen is worth 9 points and moves diagonally, horizontally, and vertically (like a rook and bishop put together).

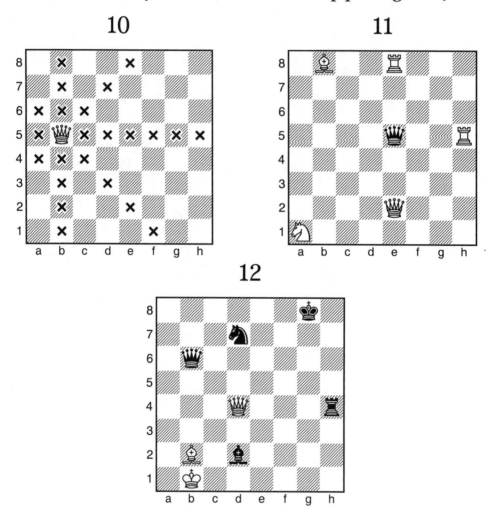

Questions about queens:

In Diagram 10, how many squares can the queen move to? – *23*

In Diagram 11, which piece should the black queen capture? – *There are many options. What about 1...Qxe2? Then 2.Rxe2 and it is an even trade. Which white piece is unprotected? The knight. Thus 1...Qxa1 is the best move.*

In Diagram 12, what is the white queen's best move? Why? – *There are many moves here. There are a free rook, a free knight, and a free bishop. Remember this: "When you find a good move, take your time and find a better one."*

The Pieces and How They Move

White's queen and bishop make a battery. The bishop protects the queen. 1.Qg7# (checkmate) wins the game.

General question about the queen:

Why is the queen worth more than any other piece? – *Because it can move to more squares than any other piece.*

Chapter 1

Knights

The knight is worth 3 points and is the only piece which can hop over other pieces. Its move is shaped like a capital "L".

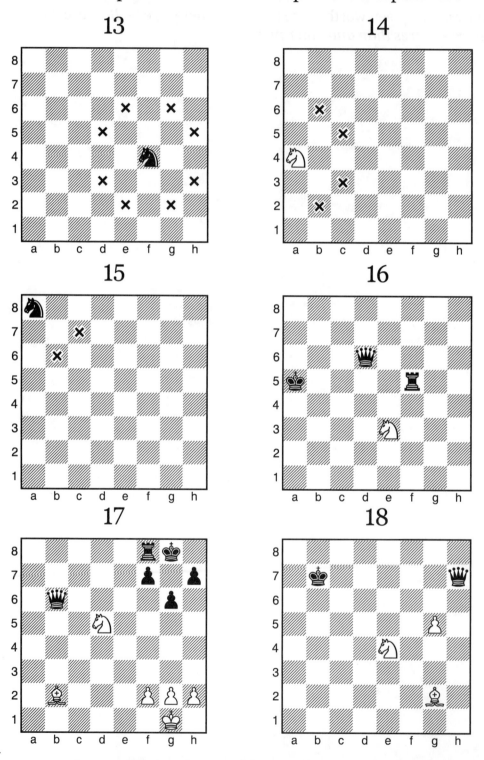

Questions about knights:

Look at Diagrams 13, 14, and 15. What do you learn about knights? – *Knights have fewer squares to move to as they get closer to the edge and the corner of the board.*

In Diagram 16, is there a better move than 1.Nxf5 ? – *Yes: 1.Nc4+ forks the king and queen. The king must move out of check and then White can take the queen for free.*

In Diagram 17, is there a better move than 1.Nxb6 ? – *Yes: 1.Ne7# wins the game.*

In Diagram 18, what is the best square for the knight to move to? Why? – *1.Nf6+ puts the king in check by the bishop (discovered check or discovered attack), and after the king moves, White can take Black's queen.*

Chapter 1

Pawns

The pawn is worth only 1 point – but if it can make it safely to the last row, it can become a queen.

A pawn captures pieces that are one square in front of it diagonally.

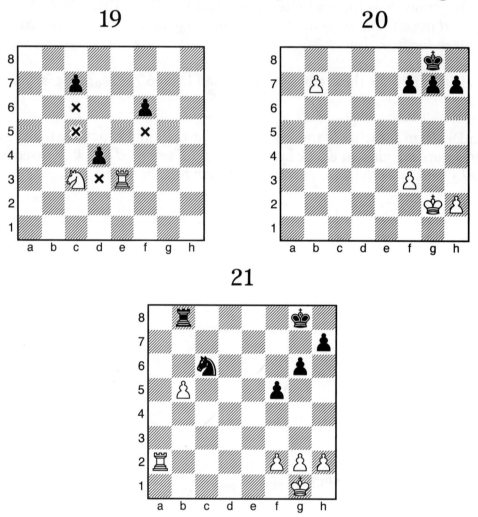

19

20

21

Questions:

In Diagram 19, the pawn on c7 can move one or two squares. The pawn on f6 can move one square. The pawn on d4 can take the rook or the bishop or move to d3. What is the best move for the pawn on d4? *Take the rook: 1...dxe3.*

In Diagram 20, what is the best move? Why? – *1.b8Q# is the best move because it is checkmate. It could also become a rook , knight, or bishop, but of these only the rook would still allow it to be checkmate.*

The Pieces and How They Move

In Diagram 21, can White play 1.bxc6 ? Is it a good move? – *No! After 1.bxc6, Black can play 1...Rb1#. Therefore, the pawn is said to be "pinned."*

True or false: as a pawn moves "safely" down the board it becomes stronger. Explain your reasoning. – *As long as the pawn is safe, it becomes stronger and more valuable because it gets closer to turning into a queen.*

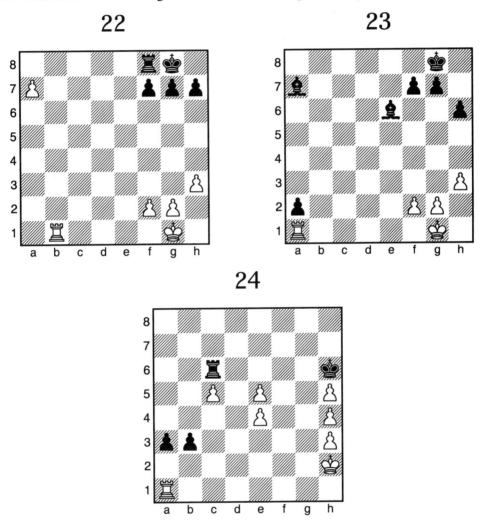

In Diagram 22, is 1.a8Q the best move? Explain why or why not. – *It is not a good move, because the black rook can take it for free. But if White plays 1.Rb8, the pawn will queen. It is a good idea to control the square in front of the pawn.*

In Diagram 23, what move can Black make to help the pawn on a2 to queen? – *1...Bd4 attacks the rook, and then either the rook moves and the pawn queens or the rook stays there and gets taken (and the pawn will still queen).*

In Diagram 24, it is Black to move. Who has better pawns? Black can play 1... Rxc5 winning a pawn, or 1...Kxh5 winning a pawn. Are there any other moves which are better? Explain why. – *White's pawns are isolated and defenseless. They are easily stopped. Black's two pawns will queen if one of them is pushed. After 1...a2, White can move anywhere and then Black plays 2...b2. On the next move, one of the pawns will queen. Connected passed pawns are very powerful and can defeat a rook.*

En passant

There is a very unique pawn move in chess called *"en passant"* (that's French for "in passing"). The sooner you learn about it, the better.

Look at these examples:

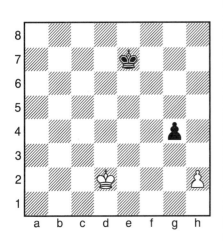

Imagine it is White's move in this position. For some reason, White plays 1.h4. On the very next move, Black has the option to play 1...gxh3 as if White's pawn had gone to h3. This would be terrible for White because Black's pawn would queen. Black has the option to capture on the next move only. *En passant* (usually shown as *e.p.*) is not always the best move but it is something to think about when the possibility happens.

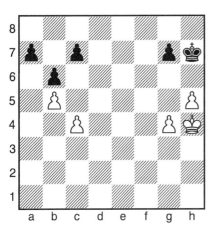

In this position Black thought, "I will play 1...a5 because White's king cannot stop the pawn from queening." Was that a good plan? *No!* On the very next move, White could play 2.bxa6 *e.p.* and get a pawn on a6. White would win because Black's king is too far away. If White were to forget and not take the pawn, then White could no longer capture it on a later move.

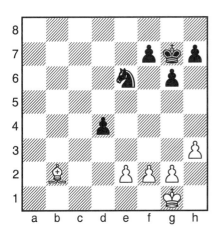

White plays 1.e4. Can Black play 1...dxe3 *e.p.?* No, because Black would be moving into check. You are never allowed to move into check. In a tournament, Black would have to put the pawn back on d4 and move something else. Black touched the piece but cannot move it legally. If Black's king were on g8, then Black could play 1...dxe3 *e.p.*

Chapter 1

Two Problem Sets

The end of this chapter has two different problem sets. The first one is about how to get out of check. There are three different ways to get out of check: you can block the check, take the piece giving check, or move the king away. Most problems will give you two options and you have to choose the best one. That is the nature of chess.

The second set of problems is about how the pieces move.

The best way for a beginner to learn chess is to memorize certain ideas. It's OK to not understand a problem and get it wrong. Do not spend more than one or two minutes on any problem. If you don't know it, look at the answer in the back. Make sure you understand the answer. Go through these until you know the answer quickly. Always have a reason for your answer, and if you are working with a partner, have them ask you why you think your answer is right.

Talking about and discussing problems is a good idea. Problems 25 to 28 are a little bit harder and take a little longer to solve them. Look at the ideas and see how the problem works.

Block (interpose), capture, or move?

BCM 1

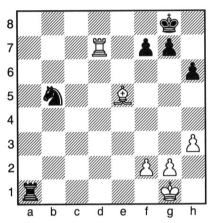

How should White
get out of check?

BCM 2

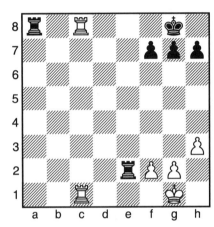

How should Black
get out of check?

BCM 3

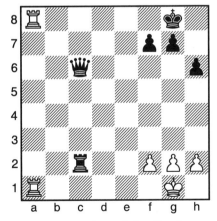

How should Black
get out of check?

BCM 4

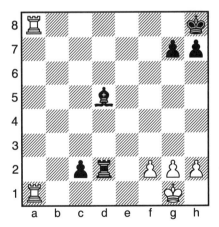

How should Black
get out of check?

BCM 5

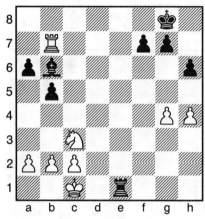

How should White
get out of check?

BCM 6

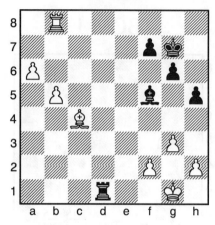

How should White
get out of check?

BCM 7

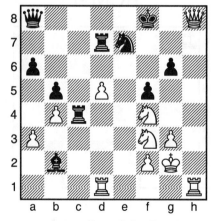

How should Black
get out of check?

BCM 8

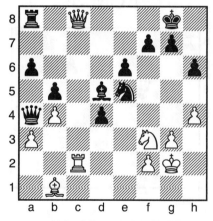

How should Black
get out of check?

Answers

BCM 1

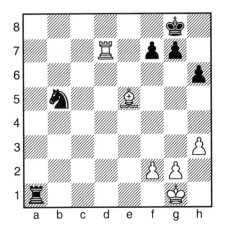

How should White
get out of check?

Let's look at the three choices:

1.Rd1 Rxd1+ and White loses a
rook for no reason.

1.Kh2 is a safe move (h2 is a
flight square).

1.Bxa1 wins the rook and stops
check. It is the best choice in this
position.

BCM 2

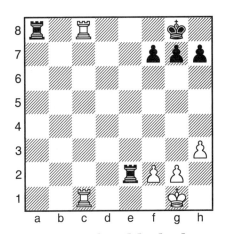

How should Black
get out of check?

Black has only two choices:

1...Rxc8 2.Rxc8+ Re8 3.Rxe8#.
That didn't go well for Black...

1...Re8 and White has no im-
mediate threats.

BCM 3

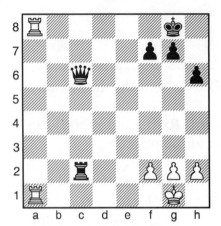

How should Black
get out of check?

This is a good example of what happens if you carelessly grab a piece. Chess is "touch move." What happens after 1.Ra8+ and Black touches the queen???

The queen would have to take the rook or play 1...Qc8 or (even worse) 1...Qe8. Remember, you must get out of check.

If Black plays 1...Kh7, though, Black is still winning. Look at all possibilities and be careful.

BCM 4

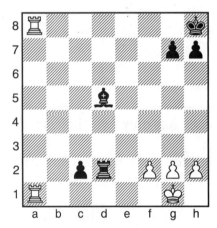

How should Black
get out of check?

Black has two choices and one move wins while the other one loses.

1...Bxa8 leads to 2.Rxa8 + Rd8 (forced) 3.Rxd8#. White wins.

1...Bg8 (blocking or interposing) and now White is stuck: Black threatens 2...Rd1+ which could lead to checkmate. If White makes a flight square with (1...Bg8) 2.h3, then 2...Rd1+ 3.Kh2 c1Q should win for Black.

BCM 5

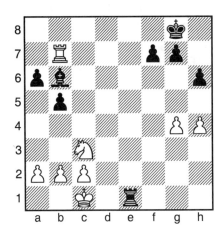

How should White
get out of check?

White has two choices. One
move loses and the other doesn't:

1.Nd1 (blocking or interposing)
and then 1...Be3+ 2.Kb1 (the only
move) 2...Rxd1# and Black wins.

1.Kd2 (Black needs to be a little careful here, as the rook and
bishop are under attack). However, 1...Re6 keeps things even for
the time being.

BCM 6

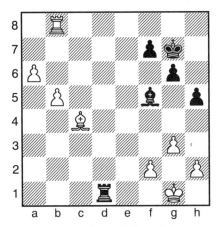

How should White
get out of check?

White has two choices: one will
win and one will lose. White is
clearly winning at the moment.

1.Bf1 Bh3 and now 2...Rxf1# is
unstoppable. Black wins.

1.Kg2 Be4+ 2.f3 Rd2+ 3.Kf1
and now the king is safe. The
a- and b-pawns can safely move
forward and queen.

BCM 7

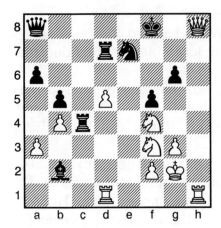

How should Black
get out of check?

Black has three choices. One of them wins and the other two lose:

1...Kf7 2.Rh7#. (Did you think 2.Qxa8? When you have a good move, take your time and find a better one!)

1...Ng8 2.Qxb2, realizing the mistake and winning a piece (there are other wins).

1...Bxh8!. Look at the entire board on every move!

BCM 8

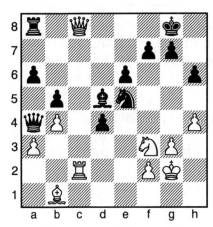

How should Black
get out of check?

Black has two choices; one move wins and the other one loses.

1...Rxc8 2.Rxc8#. The bishop on b1 covers the flight square. White wins.

1...Kh7. This allows a discovered check, but none of White's 10 possible rook moves does anything. Imagine 2.Re2+ g6 (blocking the check). Now White's queen is under attack, the knight on f3 is attacked twice, and Black's queen can get to d1. It is hopeless for White.

Bishops

Diagram 1

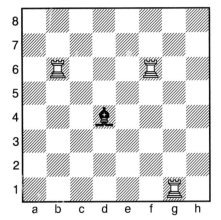

Which rook should Black take?

Diagram 2

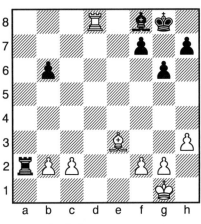

White to move

Diagram 3

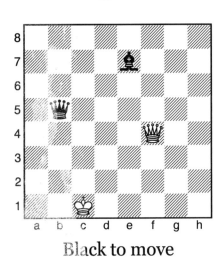

Black to move

Diagram 4

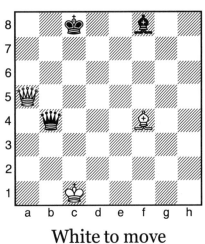

White to move

Rooks

Diagram 5

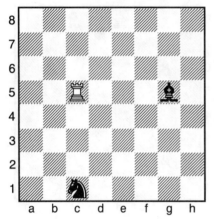

Which piece should White take?

Diagram 6

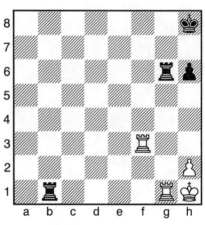

Black to move

Diagram 7

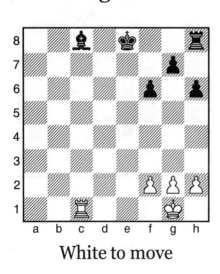

White to move

Diagram 8

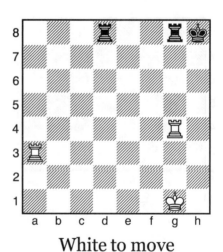

White to move

Queens

Diagram 9

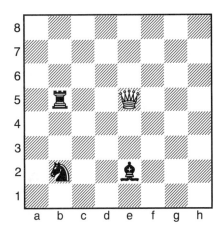

What piece should White take?

Diagram 10

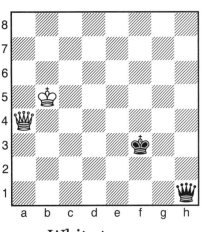

White to move

Diagram 11

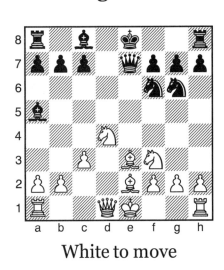

White to move

Diagram 12

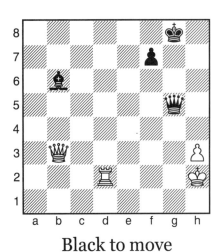

Black to move

Knights

Diagram 13

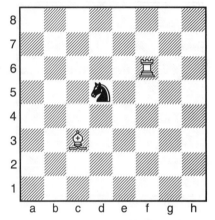

What piece should be taken?

Diagram 14

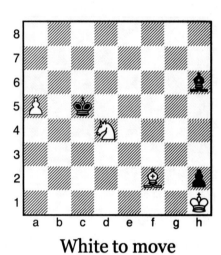

White to move

Diagram 15

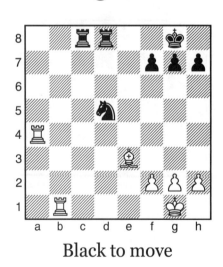

Black to move

Diagram 16

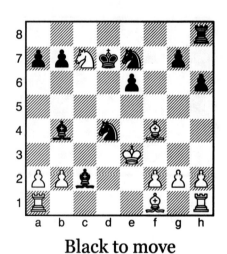

Black to move

Kings

Diagram 17

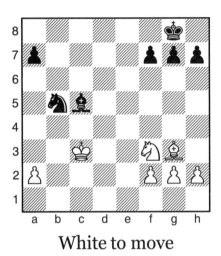

White to move

Diagram 18

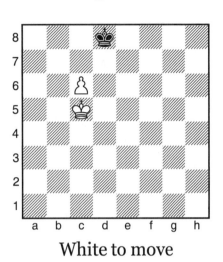

White to move

Diagram 19

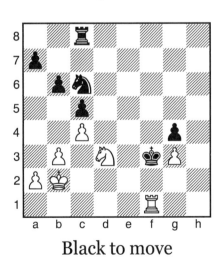

Black to move

Diagram 20

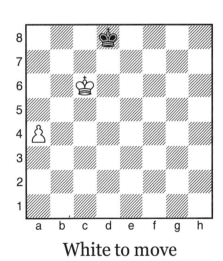

White to move

Pawns

Diagram 21

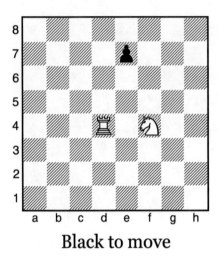

Black to move

Diagram 22

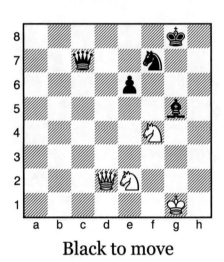

Black to move

Diagram 23

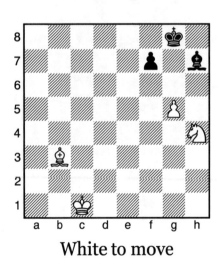

White to move

Diagram 24

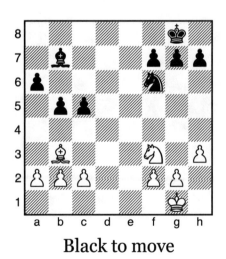

Black to move

Pieces working together

Diagram 25

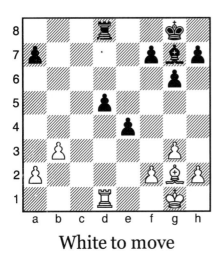

White to move

Diagram 26

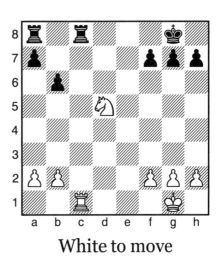

White to move

Diagram 27

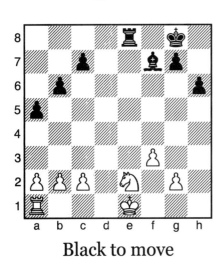

Black to move

Diagram 28

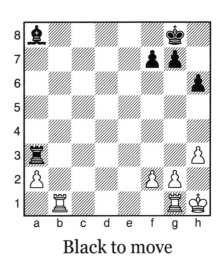

Black to move

Answers

Diagram 1

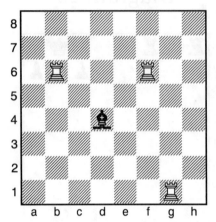

The rooks on f6 and b6 protect each other, and so if the bishop were to take the rook on f6 then the rook on b6 would take back.

Black would win 2 points. The rook on g1 is free. 1...Bxg1 wins 5 points.

Which rook should Black take?

Diagram 2

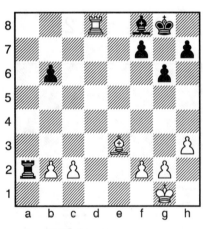

White to move

This problem has three ideas: back-rank weakness, pin, and flight square. White should play 1.Bh6. Why? It attacks the bishop on f8 and 2.Rxf8# is unstoppable. The bishop on f8 is pinned. Imagine that White's pawn on h3 were on h2. Then 1.Bh6 would be terrible. Why? Because Black could move 1...Ra1+. After 2.Bc1 Rxc1+ 3.Rd1, 3...Rxd1# is checkmate. White has to interpose, but those moves are useless.

Diagram 3

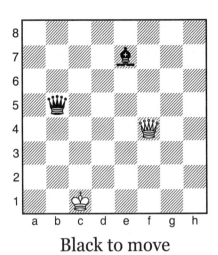

Black to move

Black has 32 moves and one really good move. The idea is pinning. Black plays 1...Bg5. Why? First, the queen protects it. More importantly, White's queen is now pinned to the king. It can only legally move to e3 and d2 (or capture the bishop), but either way Black will win the queen.

Diagram 4

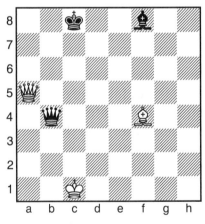

White to move

White has 28 different moves and one really good move. 1.Qxb4 will be a draw after 1...Bxb4. Look at the squares around the king. Is there a square where both the queen and the bishop can move to? Yes, c7 is that square. 1.Qc7# (checkmate) wins the game on the spot.

Diagram 5

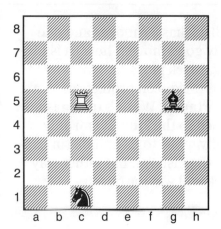

It is a simple choice: should White take the rook or the knight? What could be the difference? Black's bishop protects the knight. If White plays 1.Rxc1, then the bishop can take the rook. With 1.Rxg5, though, the bishop is captured for free. 1.Rxc1 loses 2 points and 1.Rxg5 wins 3 points.

Which piece should White take?

Diagram 6

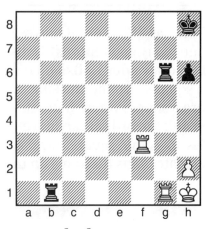

Black has two good moves. Either rook can take the rook on g1, and it's checkmate. The rooks protect each other, and the king cannot take them.

Black to move

Diagram 7

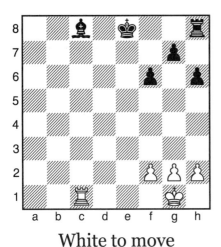

White to move

If you saw 1.Rxc8+ winning 3 points, that is good. What happens after that is important. Black's king is in check. When it moves, you can play 2.Rxh8. This tactic is called a "skewer."

Diagram 8

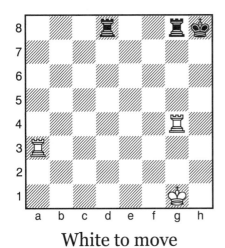

White to move

White has 20 legal moves. The rook on g4 cannot move sideways because the king would be in check. What is the best move?

1.Rh3#. Black's king is trapped on the side of the board and has no moves or interposes.

Diagram 9

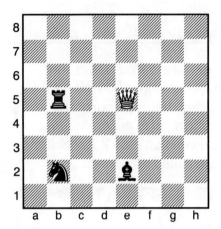

Only one of Black's pieces is not protected. 1.Qxb5 is bad because of 1...Bxb5. 1.Qxb2 is bad because of 1...Rxb2. The only safe piece to take is 1.Qxe2, winning 3 points.

Which piece should White take?

Diagram 10

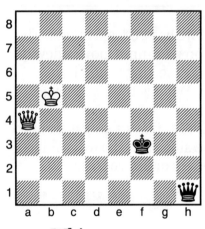

White has 7 king moves and 17 queen moves. Which move is best? Look at Black's king and queen. They are on the same diagonal. What move takes advantage of that? 1.Qa8+. Black's king moves away and then White wins the queen with 2.Qxh1. This is called a skewer.

White to move

Diagram 11

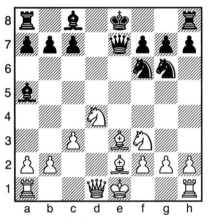

White to move

This is a tricky one. One thing to do before you make your move is see if your opponent has unprotected pieces. Which black piece is unprotected? The bishop on a5. What can White do to take advantage of that? 1.Qa4+. There are several moves to get out of check, but then White will play 2.Qxa5, winning 3 points.

Diagram 12

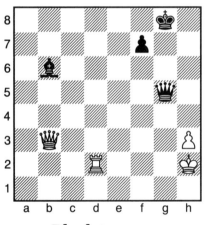

Black to move

Did you say 1...Qxd2 ? If you did, you were wrong!

When you have a good move, take time and find a better one.

1...Qg1# ends the game. Checkmate is the best move!

Diagram 13

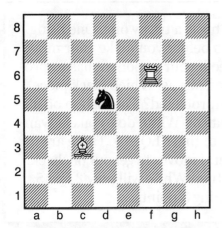

The question is, "How do White's pieces protect each other?" If 1...Nxf6, then 2.Bxf6 wins 2 points. The bishop is unprotected, so 1...Nxc3 instead wins 3 points. With all the pieces on the board, you will need to see if there are other factors, but 3 is more than 2.

Which piece should Black take?

Diagram 14

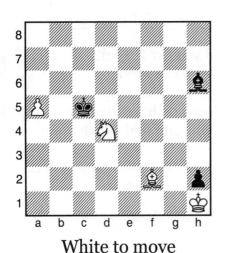

When the knight moves, it will be check. Where is the best place for the knight to move? 1.Nf5+ and the king must move. Then 2.Nxh6 wins the bishop. This is called a "discovered check." For fun, ask yourself, "What if it's Black's move?"

White to move

Diagram 15

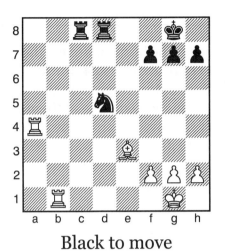

Black to move

Black could play 1...Nxe3. After 2.fxe3, there is no advantage. 1...Nc3 is called a "knight fork." Both of White's rooks are under attack; when one of them moves then Black can take the other one.

Diagram 16

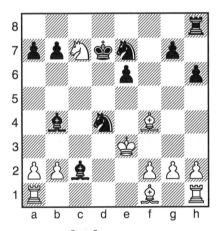

Black to move

I count 47 possible moves for Black here. You probably know it's a knight move. Which one? 1...Ne7f5# is checkmate. The king has no squares to move to. Game over.

Diagram 17

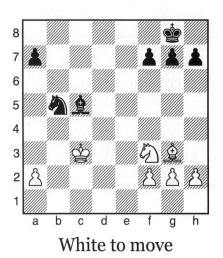

White to move

What is the best square for the king? Think about 1.Kc4: the king attacks both the knight and the bishop, and will win one of them. Kings are powerful pieces near the end of the game. It's always better to have an active king in the endgame.

Diagram 18

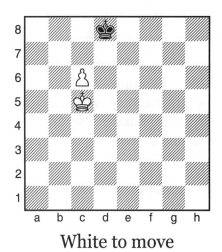

White to move

The big idea here is the "opposition." The idea is to be able to force Black's king out from in front of the pawn. White can play 1.Kd6 (1.Kb6 also works in this example). Black moves 1...Kc8 and then White moves 2.c7. Black must now play 2...Kb7. Then, after 3.Kd7, the pawn will queen.

Diagram 19

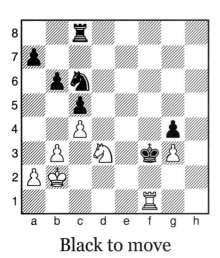

Black to move

Black could play 1...Kxg3 and likely win.

When you see a good move, take your time and find a better one.

1...Ke2 attacks the rook and the knight. White will lose one and then Black should go take the pawn on g3 and queen the black g-pawn.

Diagram 20

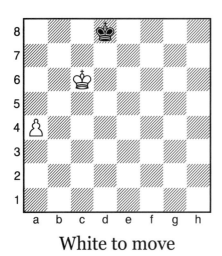

White to move

If White carelessly plays 1.a5, Black can reply 1...Kc8, then on 2.a6 Kb8 and the king will forever block the pawn and the game will be a draw. However, if White plays 1.Kb7 first, then Black's king is cut off from stopping the pawn. Then White can push the pawn and queen it.

Diagram 21

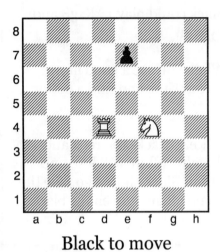

Black to move

Black moves the pawn to e5 (1... e5) attacking both the rook and the knight. It is a pawn fork.

Diagram 22

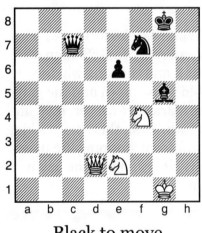

Black to move

This one is a little tricky. Look at the knight on f4 and the queen on d2. What happens if the knight moves? Black will play ...Bxd2. This means it is a bad idea for the knight to move (it is pinned). So, 1...e5 and the pawn attacks the knight. When you see a pinned piece, see if you can attack it. In this case, Black will win either the knight or the queen.

Diagram 23

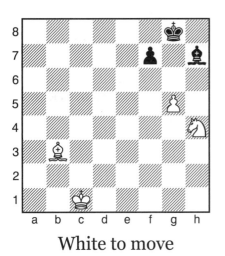

White to move

Which of Black's chessmen are pinned? The pawn on f7 cannot move because it would be check. White can play 1.g6 and attack the bishop. Black cannot play 1...fxg6, but if Black plays 1...Bxg6 then White can take back 2.Nxg6 with complete safety. Remember, the pawn on f7 cannot move.

Diagram 24

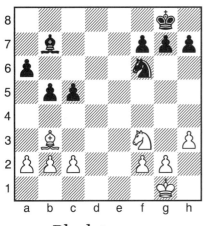

Black to move

Black has a lot of moves. 1...Bxf3 breaks up White's pawns so they can't defend each other, but it doesn't win any material. Think about 1...c4. White's bishop will be trapped. The best it can do is 2.Bxc4 and then Black replies 2...bxc4. Pawns can do an enormous amount of damage.

Diagram 25

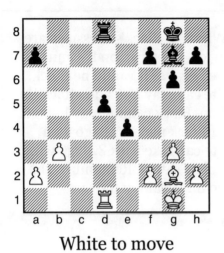

White to move

The key to this position is to look at the rooks. Black's rook is unprotected. What sits between the rooks? A black pawn. White can play 1.Bxe4 because if Black replies 1...dxe4, White will play 2.Rxd8+. The pawn on d5 is pinned. It could take the bishop, but that is a bad move.

Diagram 26

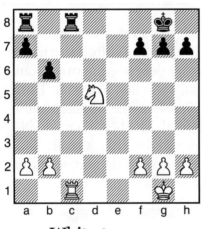

White to move

White has two moves that will produce the same results (sometimes that happens). The key move is the knight fork with Ne7+. White can play 1.Rxc8+, then Black plays 1...Rxc8 and now there's 2.Ne7+ followed by 3.Nxc8. Also 1.Ne7+ and 2.R(N)xc8 will win a rook. Be careful when two moves seem the same.

Diagram 27

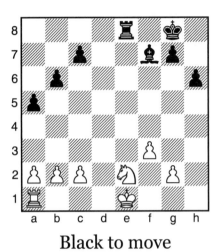

Black to move

Look at Black's rook and White's king. What piece stands between those two pieces? The knight. The knight is pinned and cannot legally move. How do you take advantage of that? 1...Bc4 attacks the pinned piece a second time and there is no way to protect it twice. Whatever move White makes, Black can play 2...Rxe2.

Diagram 28

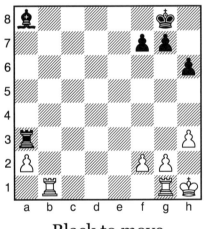

Black to move

Look at White's king and Black's bishop. What piece is between them? The pawn on g2. But the pawn is pinned by the bishop and can't move. How do you take advantage of that? 1...Rxh3# is checkmate. Surprised? The pawn on g2 cannot take it. Look at the entire board. The rook and bishop can have a big effect on the game from across the board.

Chapter 2

Checkmate or Stalemate

By the end of this chapter, you should be able to recognize the difference between checkmate and stalemate.

Before you begin this chapter, you should know how all the pieces move and what squares they cover.

When you win a game in a tournament, you get 1 point. When you draw a game in a tournament, you get ½ point. When you lose a game in a tournament, you get 0 points.

Checkmate/stalemate 1   Checkmate/stalemate 2

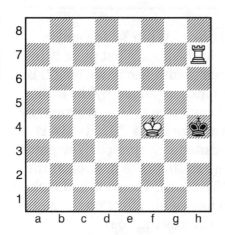   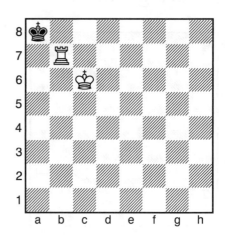

In Diagram 1, White has checkmated Black. 1 point for White.

In Diagram 2, it is stalemate. ½ point for each player.

Let's look at this a little deeper. Juan is winning his game and has reached this position:

Checkmate/stalemate 3

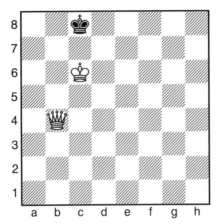

He is thinking of three different moves: Qd6, Qe7, and Qf8. What do you think is the best move? _____ Why? _____

1.Qd6 is a terrible move because it is stalemate. The black king has no legal moves and is not in check. Juan would only get ½ point for a game when he could have gotten 1 point.

1.Qe7 is not a terrible move. Black must play 1...Kb8 and then hopefully Juan will play 2.Qb7# (checkmate). There is a saying in chess: *When you find a good move, take your time and find a better one.*

1.Qf8 is checkmate. Game over. Juan would get 1 point for winning. Juan plays 1.Qf8#. His friend David comes by and says, "1.Qb8 was checkmate, too." Is David right or wrong? Why?

David is very wrong! 1.Qb8 loses the queen. That would be a draw because K vs. K is a draw. Juan would get ½ point.

Isabel is playing Black and has reached this position:

Chapter 2

Checkmate/stalemate 4

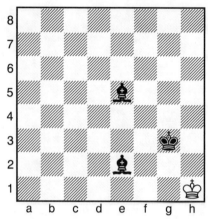

She thinks, "I'll play 1...Bd4 and then White's king cannot go to g1."

Is she right? _____ Why or why not? _____

_____

She is wrong. After 1...Bd4, white's king has no moves, and it's stalemate. What's interesting is that her dark-squared bishop can move to *any* other square, and she should win. Imagine she plays 1...Bh8. White's king has to move to g1 and then Isabel can play 2...Bd4+ 3.Kh1 Bf3#.

When you are winning, make sure that you win. That seems easy enough, but your opponent will be trying to get half a point instead of 0 points. White would be very happy to see Isabel play 1...Bd4 first.

When it gets to the end of a game and your opponent can only move the king, make sure that the king has at least one square to move to. Pawns don't count if they cannot move.

Roberto has reached this position:

Checkmate/stalemate 5

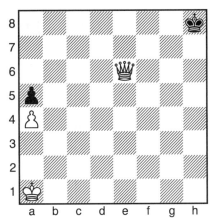

He thinks, "I will trap Black's king in the corner and walk my king across the board and checkmate him." Would 1.Qf7 or 1.Qe7 be better?

Checkmate/stalemate 6

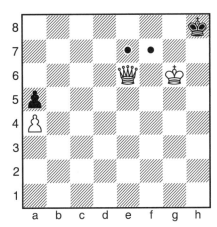

In his mind, he moved his king across the board to g6. Should his queen be on f7 or on e7? _____ Why? _____

1.Qf7 will be stalemate, but with 1.Qe7 his plan works.

Diagram 29

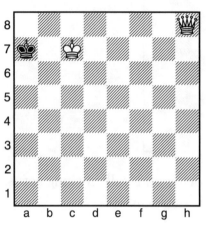

Is 1.Qc8 a good move?

Diagram 30

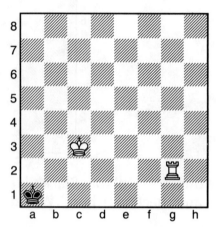

Which is better, 1.Kb3 or 1.Rb2 ?

Diagram 31

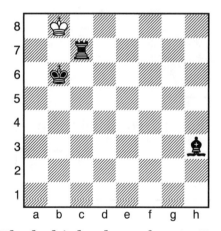

Black thinks that, after 1...Bg2,
White's king has no moves.
Is that right?

Diagram 32

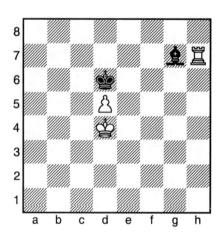

Black played 1...Bg7+. Should
White play 2.Rxg7 ?

Diagram 33

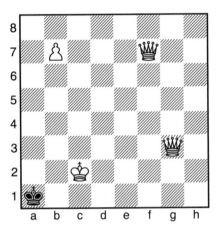

White is winning easily.
Should White play 1.b8Q ?

Diagram 34

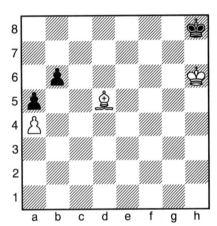

White has played 1.Bd5.
Was that a good move?

Diagram 35

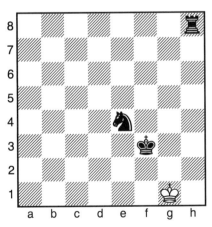

Is 1...Nd2 a good move?

Diagram 36

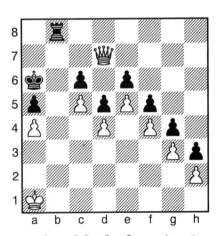

Should Black resign?

Answers

Diagram 29

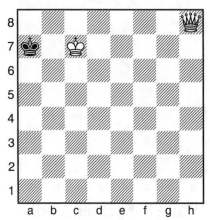

1.Qc8 is a bad move because Black's king is not in check and has no moves. That is stalemate. 1.Qa1 would be checkmate.

Is 1.Qc8 a good move?

Diagram 30

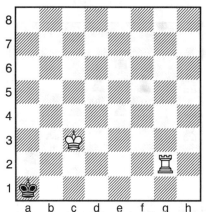

1.Rb2 is bad because Black's king has no moves and isn't in check. That's stalemate. 1.Kb3 forces Black to play 1...Kb1 and then 2.Rg1# (checkmate). Getting your king across from your opponent's king is important.

Which is better, 1.Kb3 or 1.Rb2 ?

Diagram 31

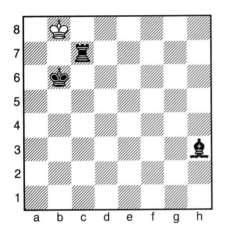

1...Bg2 is a terrible move because White's king has no moves and is not in check. That's stalemate.

What would be a better move?

1...Rc8 is checkmate. The bishop protects the rook.

Black thinks that after 1...Bg2 White's king has no moves. Is that right?

Diagram 32

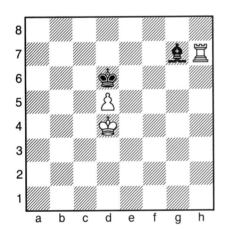

Black played a smart move. If White plays 2.Rxg7 to get out of check – it's stalemate. White cannot take the bishop. White can play 2.Ke4 or 2.Kc4 and still win by trying to queen his pawn.

Black played 1...Bg7+. Should White play 2.Rxg7 ?

85

Diagram 33

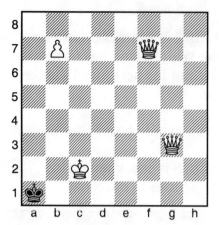

NO!!!

You have enough queens already and have a one-move checkmate. Don't get unnecessary queens. 1.b8Q is stalemate. Instead, 1.Qa3# wins.

Should White play 1.b8Q ?

Diagram 34

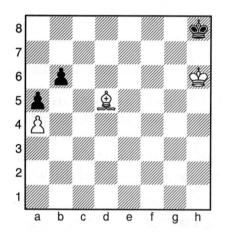

Yes, it is a good move. Black has to push the b-pawn. The game would go like this: 1.Bd5 b5 2.axb5 a4 3.b6 a3 4.b7 a2 5.b8Q#.

Black has to make all those pawn moves because his king has no legal moves.

Was 1.Bd5 a good move?

Diagram 35

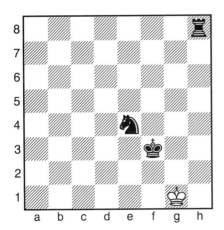

Is 1...Nd2 a good move?

1...Nd2 is a terrible move. Why? White's king has no moves and is not in check: stalemate!

What would be a better move? If Black moves the rook to h7, h6, h5, h4, or h3, then White has to play 2.Kf1. Then Black can play 2...Rh1#.

Diagram 36

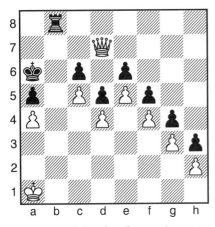

Should Black resign?

Things look bad for Black. White might play 1.Qxe6 and get another queen. What can Black do?

Black has no king moves and no pawn moves... hmmm...

Black plays 1...Rb1+. If the king takes the rook, it's stalemate. So 2.Ka2 Rb2+ 3.Ka3 Rb3+. Black keeps checking the king, and it's a draw by perpetual check.

Chapter 3

Pins and Skewers

Look at the two diagrams below. The diagram on the left is a simple pin, and the one on the right is a simple skewer.

Pins/skewers 1

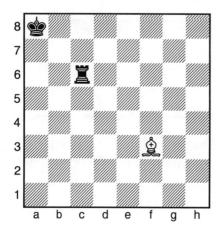

Pins/skewers 2

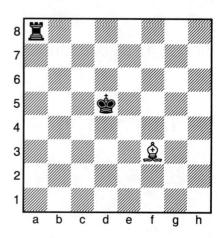

In the left-hand diagram, it is illegal for the rook to move. Why? The king would be in check. This is called an absolute pin. You can never move into check.

In the right-hand diagram, the king is in check and must move out of check. When it does move, the bishop will take the rook. This attack is called a skewer.

In both diagrams, White wins the rook thanks to the bishop attacking along the h1 to a8 diagonal. What's the difference?

In the left diagram, the pin binds or ties the rook to the d4 square. In the right diagram, the king must move and allow the bishop to take the rook on a8.

Let's look at a couple more examples.

Pins/skewers 3

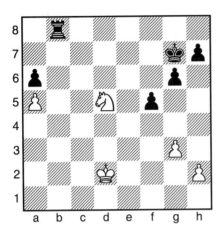

Pins/skewers 4

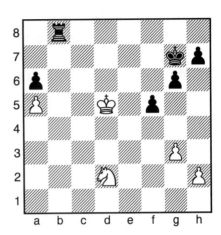

The effect of 1...Rd8 is the same in both diagrams. Black is going to win White's knight. After 1...Rd8 in Diagram 3, it is illegal for the knight to move. The pin is absolute. In Diagram 4, after the skewer 1...Rd8+ the king is in check and must move and then Black will play 2...Rxd2.

Both the pin and the skewer are called "tactics." In some games of chess, tactics are easy. In the diagram on the left above, 1...Rd8 is an easy move to find. All you need to do is ask yourself, "What can the knight do?" The diagram on the right is the same thing. The question is, "What happens after the king moves out of check?" The answer is, "I win the knight."

Most of the time, tactics are not that easy. Now we will look at two diagrams where there is only one difference, but a very important one.

Pins/skewers 5

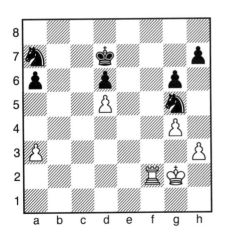

Pins/skewers 6

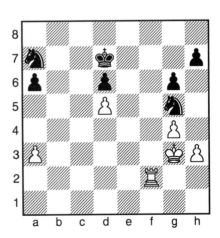

White has this thought about both diagrams: "If the knight on g5 has to move, I can move Rf7+ and skewer the king and win the knight on a7. The knight on g5 guards the f7 square where my rook wants to go. So, I will play 1.h4 and attack the knight. The knight moves away and then I play 2.Rf7+."

If White plays 1.h4 in both diagrams, he will likely win one game and lose one game. What's the difference?

Important chess rule:

Before you make a move, write your move down and ask yourself, "What will my opponent do if I make my move?" (Look at every square.)

What if Black moves 1...Ne4? In Diagram 5, it is harmless. But in Diagram 6, 1...Ne4+ is a knight fork that wins White's rook.

Think before you move!

The same idea is found in the next two diagrams.

Pins/skewers 7   Pins/skewers 8

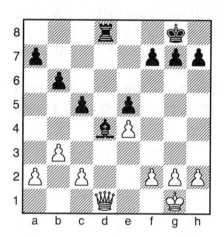

White has this thought about both diagrams: "If I push the pawn to c3, one of two things will happen. First, Black might not move his bishop, and then I will play 2.cxd4 next and win the bishop. Secondly, he might move his bishop somewhere, and then I will play 2.Qxd8#."

Like 1.h4 in the last set of diagrams, 1.c3 is a great move in one diagram but a terrible move in the other. What's the difference? Remember this important chess guideline:

Pins and Skewers

Before you make a move, write your move down and ask yourself, "What will my opponent do if I make my move?" (Look at every square.)

Look especially for your opponent's checks. In Diagram 7, Black has no checks and should lose. In Diagram 8, Black can play 1...Bxf2+ and White's queen will be lost (that tactic is called "discovered attack").

In the next 20 problems, you must decide whether there is a useful pin or a useful skewer, or if something might go wrong. Be careful.

Diagram 37

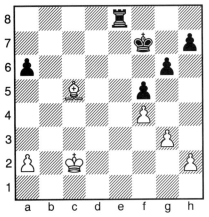

What is Black's best move?

Diagram 38

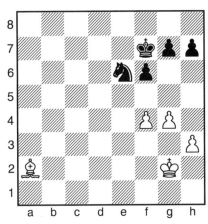

What is White's best move?

Diagram 39

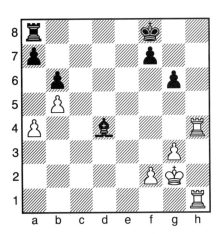

Is 1.Rh8+ a good move?

Diagram 40

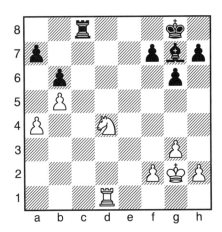

Is 1...Bxd4 the best move for Black?

Diagram 41

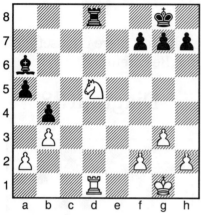

Is 1...Bb7 a good move?

Diagram 42

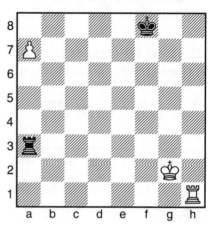

Is 1.a8Q+ a good move?

Diagram 43

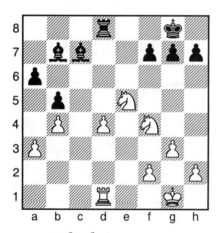

Black to move.
What tactic is used here?

Diagram 44

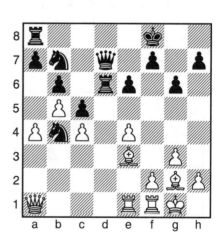

White to move.
What tactic is used here?

Diagram 45

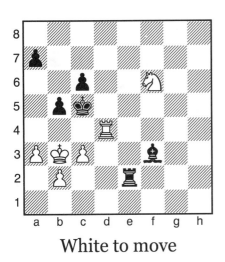

White to move

Diagram 46

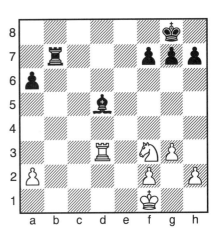

What is Black's best move?

Diagram 47

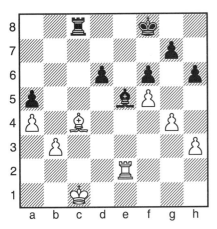

What is Black's best move?

Diagram 48

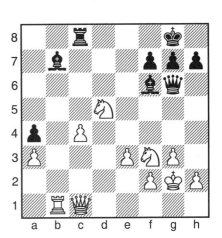

Black sees 1...Bxd5 2.cxd5
and then 2...Rxc1.
Is that right or wrong?

Diagram 49

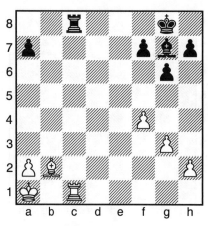

Black to move.
What tactic is used?

Diagram 50

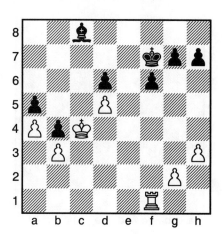

Black to move.
What tactic is used?

Diagram 51

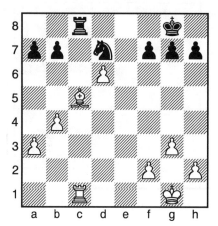

Is 1...b6 a good move for Black?

Diagram 52

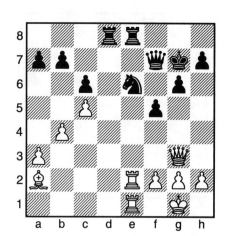

Can White play 1.Rxe6 Rxe6
and then 2.Rxe6 ?

Diagram 53

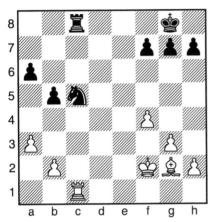

Should White move 1.b4 ?

Diagram 54

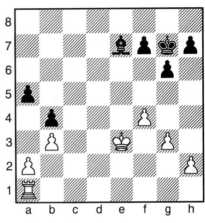

Is 1.Kd4 good?

Diagram 55

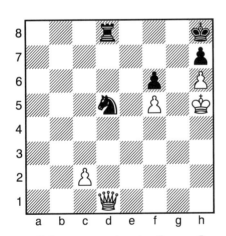

White sees 1.c4, then the
knight moves and 2.Qxd8#.
Is that right?

Diagram 56

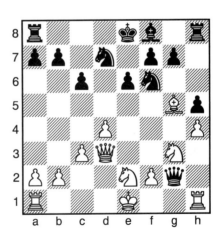

White to move. Very tricky.

Chapter 3

Answers

Diagram 37

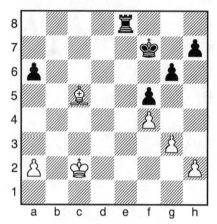

What is Black's best move?

Black's best move is 1...Rc8. Why?

It pins the bishop to the king and after any move by White, Black will play 2...Rxc5. The bishop cannot legally move.

Diagram 38

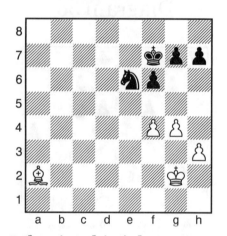

What is White's best move?

1.Bxe6+ Kxe6 doesn't do much. The knight is pinned, though. A good rule is to attack a pinned piece. Pawns can be very effective at this.

1.f5 attacks the knight and should win the game. In the end-game, pawns become very important.

Diagram 39

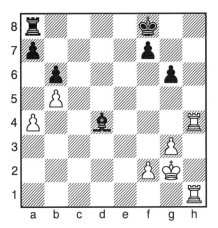

Is 1.Rh8+ a good move?

Let's think through this: 1.Rh8+ and then what? Did you see 1...Bxh8?

...Hmm, did you? What happens next? 2.Rxh8+. Now the king must move and you play 3.Rxa8. You win a rook and bishop for a rook. It is a good move. Be careful to look at all your opponent's pieces, though.

Diagram 40

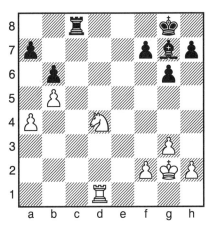

Is 1...Bxd4 the best move?

After 1...Bxd4, White will play 2.Rxd4 and the game seems even. Think about 1...Rd8. What happens if the knight moves? Then 2...Rxd1 wins. What if he doesn't move the knight? Then 2...Rxd4 and you win the knight.

Attack a pinned piece.

Diagram 41

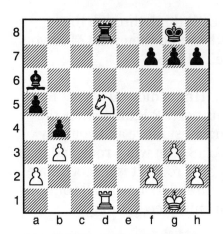

Is 1...Bb7 a good move?

Should you "attack a pinned piece?"

The question you need to ask yourself is, "What can White do?" The knight can legally move, so what are the options? He has two good moves, 2.Nf6 + and 2.Ne7+. Whatever Black does, White will play 3.Rxd8+ next.

Think about your opponent's moves.

Diagram 42

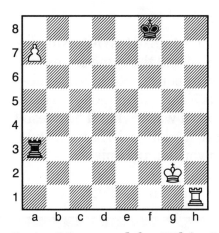

Is 1.a8Q+ good for White?

It doesn't seem good at first. On 1.a8Q+ Black can play 1... Rxa8.

But now look at Black's king and rook. A skewer is possible: 2.Rh8+, Black's king moves away, and then White plays 3.Rxa8. White should win, but you need to practice this and be able to do R+K vs. K in less than a minute.

Diagram 43

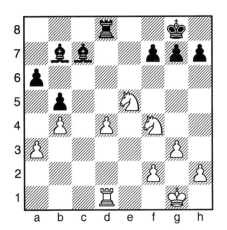

Black to move.
What is the tactic used here?

Look at the rooks. What is in-between the rooks? A pawn. What is the pawn doing? Protecting the knight. But, is it really? Black can play 1...Bxe5 and if 2.dxe5 then Black replies 2...Rxd1+, winning a whole rook.

That tactic is called a "pin." The pawn is said to be "pinned."

Diagram 44

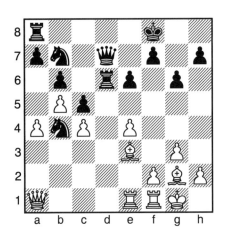

White to move.
What tactic is used here?

There are many pieces on the board. You need to look at each one and look at the entire board. Some beginners will only look at part of the board. When you look everywhere, you can see 1.Qh8+, which is called a skewer. You win a rook.

Diagram 45

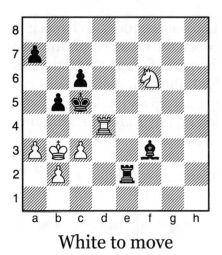

White to move

Look and look and look. There is no pin. There is no skewer. However, in a game of chess, many different kinds of moves are possible. In this book, every now and then, a problem will have a new idea. What's the idea? A one-move checkmate: 1.Nd7# and the game is over!

Diagram 46

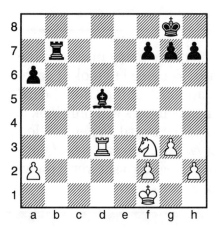

What is Black's best move?

I would ask my students, "What do you notice about this position?" When they see the king and the rook on the same diagonal, they will see the right move. 1...Bc4 pins the rook to the king. Black will win at least a rook for the bishop. That tactic is called a pin.

Diagram 47

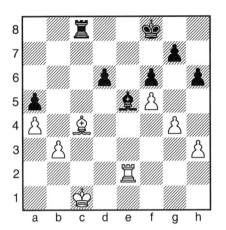

What is Black's best move?

Look at Black's rook and White's king. What is between them? A bishop. The bishop is pinned. How do you take advantage of that?

The answer is: Attack a pinned piece. Move 1...d5 and remember that the bishop cannot take it because it is pinned to the king. On the next move, Black will play 2...dxc4.

Diagram 48

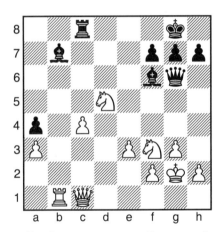

Black sees 1...Bxd5 2.cxd5 and then 2...Rxc1.
Is that right or wrong?

It does look like the pawn is pinned: 1...Bxd5, then 2.cxd5 and 2...Rxc1. That would be good, right?

Look at Black's king. It has no escape/flight squares. After 2...Rxc1, White moves 3.Rb8+ and two moves later it's checkmate. That is called a back-rank checkmate.

Diagram 49

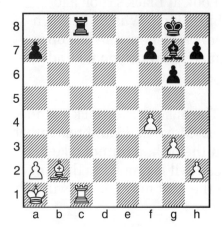

Black to move.
What tactic is used?

This is an example of making sure you look all the way across the board. It looks like White's bishop protects the rook. Does it? Black can move 1...Rxc1# (yes, it's checkmate). The bishop can move along the a1/h8 diagonal, but it cannot move to a3 or c1. This is a one-move checkmate.

Diagram 50

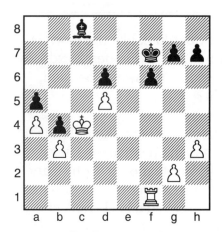

Black to move.
What tactic is used?

Imagine that White just moved 1.Kc4. If White can play 2.Kb5, he will take Black's a- and b-pawns and win easily. Sadly, though, the king and rook are on the same diagonal. 1...Ba6+ and now it's Black who should win. White didn't think about what Black could do. Think about your opponent's moves.

Diagram 51

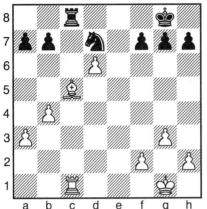

The rooks sit across from each other. The bishop is in the middle. 1...b6 attacks a pinned piece, doesn't it? The question is, "What can White do?" White can play 2.Be3 and that will protect the rook. 1...b6 doesn't win anything. It just pushes away the bishop.

Is 1...b6 a good move for Black?

Diagram 52

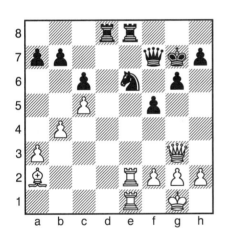

This is like Problem 48. It looks like White will win material, as 3 pieces attack the knight and only 2 defend it. The knight is pinned.

If 1.Rxe6 Rxe6 and now 2.Rxe6, then Black will move 2...Rd1+ and White will be checkmated. White's best move? 1.h3 (flight square) and only then Rxe6.

Can White play 1.Rxe6 Rxe6 and then 2.Rxe6 ?

Diagram 53

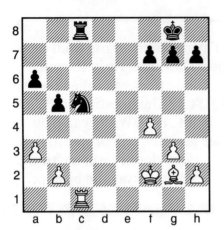

Should White play 1.b4 ?

Before you make a move, what should you do? Think about what your opponent might do! After 1.b4, Black's knight has seven moves. Six of those moves lose. One of them wins: 1...Nd3+ (knight fork), and White loses his rook and likely the game. 1.b4 is a terrible move.

Diagram 54

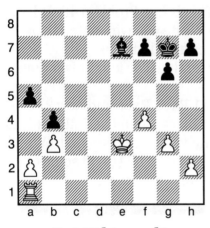

Is 1.Kd4 good?

This is like Problem 50. White is moving his king over to Black's a- and b-pawns. That's a good thing. You can do the right thing the wrong way. What happens after 1.Kd4? 1...Bf6+, skewering the king and winning the rook. Think about what your opponent can do!

Diagram 55

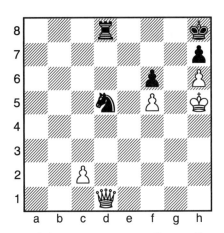

What should White think first? Think, "What can my opponent do after 1.c4?" There are seven knight moves. Six of these moves will lose. However, 1...Nf4+ and White loses his queen. It looked like a pin, but it was really a discovered attack. All White needs to do is move 1.Kh4, and only then play 2.c4.

White sees 1.c4, then the knight moves and 2.Qxd8#. Is that right?

Diagram 56

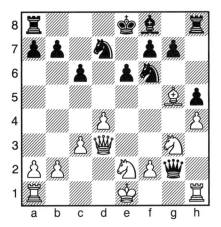

There is no skewer, and there is no pin. What black piece looks most out of place? The queen is on g2 and is surrounded by White's pieces. What should White do? 1.Nf4 and Black's queen is trapped. There are no safe squares.

White to move. Very tricky!

Chapter 4

Knight Moves and Back-Rank Problems

When beginners play chess, they can miss very simple ideas, like giving up a piece for free and missing a one-move checkmate. Tactics often occur in combination with other ideas. Here is a simple problem. Black to move:

Knight fork/back rank 1

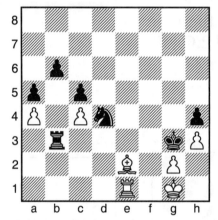

Someone starting out at chess might think, "1...Nxe2+ then 2.Rxe2" and it's even. That's not quite true. The knight can take the bishop for free because White cannot take back. His back rank would not be guarded and if White played 2.Rxe2, then 2...Rb1+ would follow and after 3.Re1 Black could play 3...Rxe1#.

So simple ideas like Black's king being strongly placed and Black's rook being much more aggressively placed are important to understanding what tactics might be involved in the position.

There is an important cognitive problem with giving children a set of problems arranged by theme and where every problem "works." It goes like this:

I teach knight forks and we do 5 to 10 problems related to knight forks. In every problem there is a successful knight fork. Then they play a game and get to a position like the following.

Knight fork/back rank 2

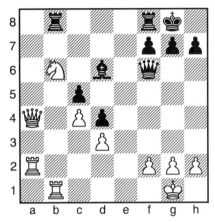

White to move. 1.Nd7 (knight fork)? Yes, it is a knight fork, but it loses at once to 1...Rxb1+.

When tactics are taught in isolation and when every problem is a success, you are giving a student a false sense of what happens in a game of chess.

In this book, each chapter about tactics will have at least two ideas and some problems where the idea doesn't work. That's how chess works in the real world.

Diagram 57

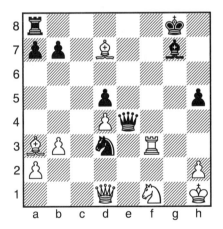

What is Black's best move?

Diagram 58

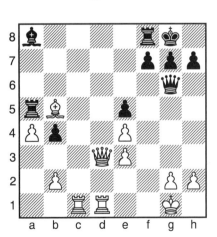

What is White's best move?

Diagram 59

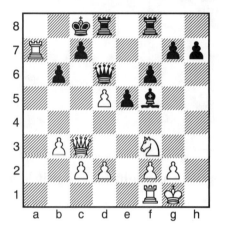

Is 1.Qc6 a good move for White?

Diagram 60

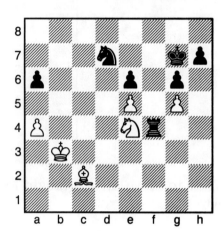

Is 1...Rxe4 a good move for Black?

Diagram 61

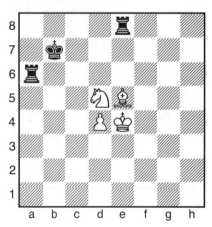

Is 1.Nc7 a good move for White?

Diagram 62

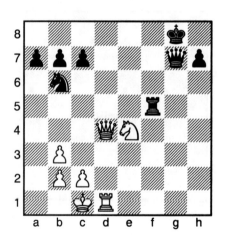

Is 1.Rg1 a good move for White?

Diagram 63

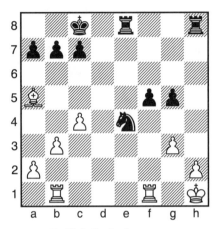

Which is better,
1...Nd2 or 1...Nxg3+ ?

Diagram 64

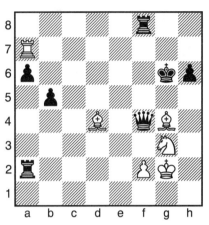

What is White's best move?

Diagram 65

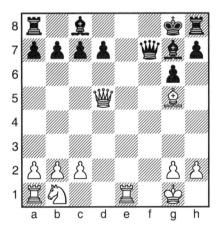

What is White's best move?

Diagram 66

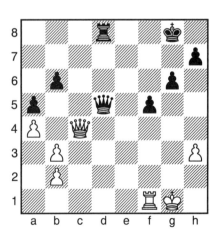

Should White play 1.Rd1 ?

Diagram 67

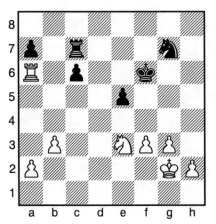

What is White's best move?

Diagram 68

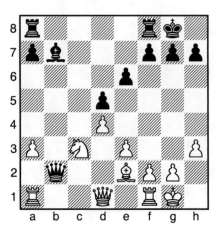

What is White's best move?

Diagram 69

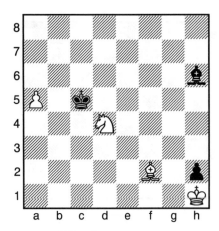

Black to move.
What should happen? Why?

Diagram 70

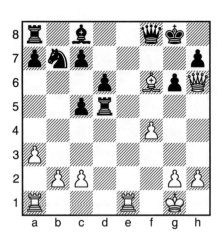

Is 1.Re8 a good
move for White?

Diagram 71

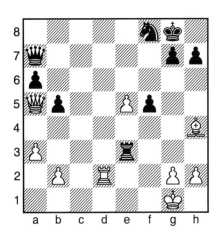

Is 1.Bf2 a good move for White?

Diagram 72

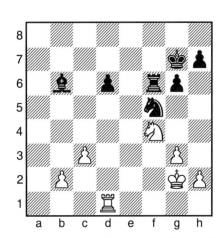

Is 1.Nd5 a good move for White?

Diagram 73

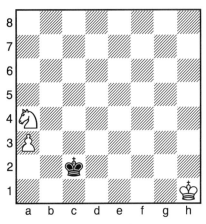

What is White's best move?
Why?

Diagram 74

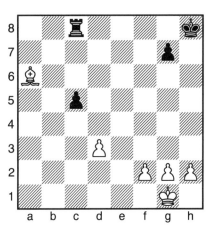

What is Black's best move?

Diagram 75

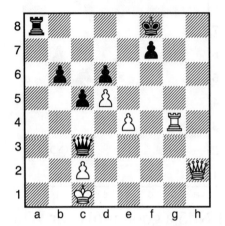

Is 1.Qh8+ White's best move?

Diagram 76

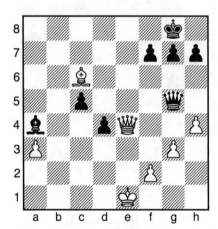

What is Black's best move?

Answers

Diagram 57

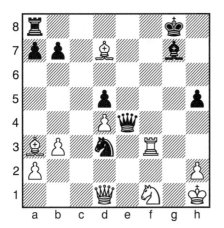

What is Black's best move?

Here is an example of tactics working together. Look at Black's queen and White's king. See White's rook in between? It is pinned and it cannot move. How does that help?

Think about 1...Nf2+. The rook cannot take it, and after the king moves Black will play 2...Nxd1 (knight fork).

Diagram 58

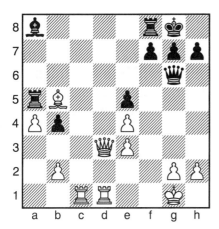

What is White's best move?

This one is hard. The key is in how well White's pieces can work together. Think about 1.Qd8!. If 1...Rxd8, then 2.Rxd8#. What else does 1.Qd8 do? The queen attacks the unprotected rook on a5. What if Black moves 1...Ra7? White replies 2.Rc8! and it's hopeless. Black had problems on the back rank.

Diagram 59

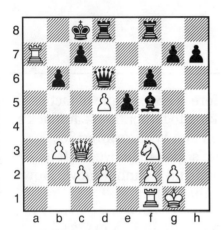

Many beginners won't like playing 1.Qc6 because Black can trade queens. Imagine the board after 1.Qc6 Qxc6 2.dxc6. What are White's threats? 3.Ra8 is checkmate. What can Black do? 2...Kb8 is the only move. Then White moves 3.Rfa1 and it's unstoppable checkmate.

Is 1.Qc6 a good move for White?

Diagram 60

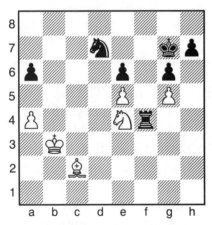

If we are thinking only one move ahead, then 1...Rxe4 looks bad: 1...Rxe4 and then 2.Bxe4. Take time and think, "What could happen after that?" 1...Rxe4 then 2.Bxe4 and now 2...Nc5+ (knight fork). Black will be a full knight ahead and should win easily. (Hint: stop White's a-pawn from queening.)

Is 1...Rxe4 a good move?

Diagram 61

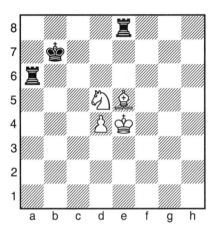

Before White moves 1.Nc7, he/she should think, "What will my opponent do?" Black has 5 king moves and 24 rook moves. There is one really good rook move, 1...Rxe5+. Either the pawn or the king can take the rook, but then Black plays 2...Kxc7 and Black should win. (Hint: stop the pawn from queening.)

Is 1.Nc7 a good move for White?

Diagram 62

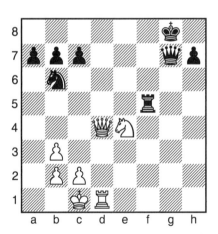

Before White plays 1.Rg1 he/she should think, "What will my opponent do?" 1.Rg1 seems to pin Black's queen to the king. Does it?

No!! Black can play 1...Rf1+ and if White plays 2.Rxf1, then Black captures 2...Qxd4. Or if the king moves (2.Kd2) then 2...Rxg1 wins a whole rook.

Is 1.Rg1 a good move for White?

Diagram 63

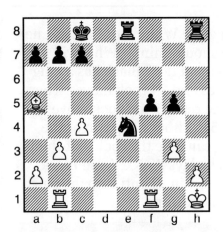

Which is better,
1...Nd2 or 1...Nxg3+ ?

Before you make either move, what is the important thought? It is, "What can my opponent do?" 1...Nd2 seems to be a knight fork... except that bishops get to move backwards: 2.Bxd2 and the knight is lost. How about 1...Nxg3+? Can White reply 2.hxg3? No, the pawn is pinned and on the next move Black can play 2...Nxf1. What two tactics worked together? A pin and a knight fork.

Diagram 64

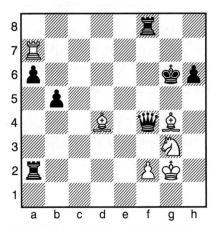

What is White's best move?

You can look for a while and there are no knight forks. The king isn't on the back rank, either.

1.Rg7#. It's a one-move checkmate. Beginners sometimes give up hope when they don't have a queen. There are many ways to checkmate with the other pieces.

Diagram 65

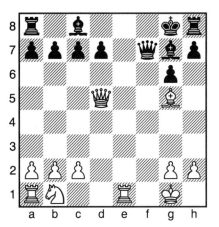

A beginner might think, "I have to move my queen or trade queens." Think about all your checks. What about 1.Re8+ ? The queen cannot take it. Black's only move is 1...Bf8. Hmmm... Then White moves 2.Bh6 and it's an unstoppable checkmate. Black's back rank was very weak.

What is White's best move?

Diagram 66

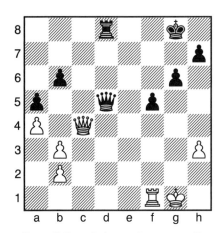

What should you think before you play 1.Rd1 ? "What can my opponent do?" Can the queen take the rook? No, the queen is pinned. What happens if Black plays 1...Qxc4 ? The game will be won or lost with your decision: 2.Rxd8+ makes the king move and then you take the queen. This is called an "in-between move."

Should White play 1.Rd1 ?

Diagram 67

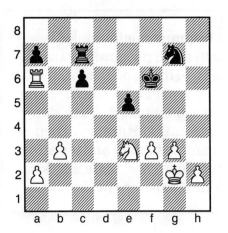

What is White's best move?

White is winning, but we should always look for the fastest and best way to win. Which knight move is the best? Did you think about 1.Nd5+ ? If you thought about it and went, "The pawn can take me," you missed something. The pawn can't take you – it's pinned. Tactics work together. This is a knight fork and a pin on a pawn.

Diagram 68

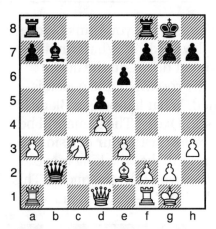

What is White's best move?

Do you remember in Chapter 3's problems there was one where Black's queen was deep in White's position? Be alert when that happens. Is Black's queen in danger? Did you find 1.Na4 ? Black's queen is trapped. There is not a single safe square for the queen to go to.

Diagram 69

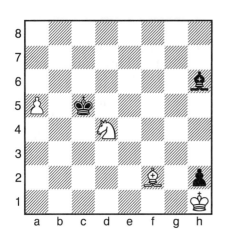

Black to move.
What should happen? Why?

First, think about every possible move for Black's bishop. If it moves to f8, g7, g5, or f4, then 2.Ne6+ wins the bishop. On 1...Bd2 or 1...Bc1, 2.Nb3 + wins the bishop.

King moves? 1...Kd6 then 2.Nf5+. On 1...Kd5, 1...Kc4, or 1...Kb4 White pushes the pawn and it queens. What tactics are used? Discovered attack, knight fork, promotion, and *Zugzwang* (see Chapter 7). That's four!

Diagram 70

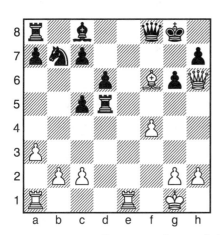

Is 1.Re8 a good move for White?

What is the question we should ask? "What will my opponent do?" Black never developed the bishop on c8. After 1.Re8, what will Black do? 1...Qxh6 is impossible.

What about 1...Qxe8 ? Then White plays 2.Qg7#. This tactic is called deflection. After 1.Re8, 2.Qg7 is an unstoppable checkmate.

Diagram 71

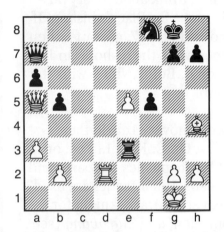

The most important question is, "What will my opponent do?" 1.Bf2 looks like it pins the rook to the queen. The rook can legally move, and where might it move to? After 1.Bf2, 1...Re1 is checkmate. The bishop is pinned. Lesson: *"Think about what your opponent can do!"*

Is 1.Bf2 a good move for White?

Diagram 72

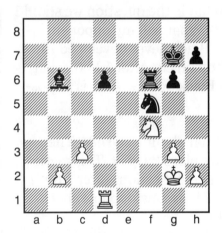

What will Black do after 1.Nd5 ? He/she could panic and try to move a bishop or rook. Then they would likely lose. Take your time and explore all your options. What about a knight move? 1...Ne3+ forces White to play 2.Nxe3 and there is no more threat after 2...Bxe3. So 1.Nd5 wasn't good or bad, White just took a chance and it didn't work.

Is 1.Nd5 a good move for White?

Diagram 73

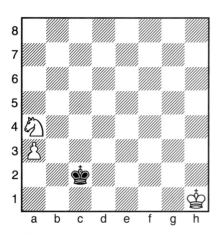

What is White's best move?

If it were Black's move, 1...Kb3 would be played and White would lose the pawn and any chance to win. There is only one square for the knight. Think about 1.Nb2... Now if 1...Kb3, then White can move 2.a4 and will have all day to walk his king over to help the pawn. Black's king cannot take the knight because of a4-a5 and the pawn queens.

Diagram 74

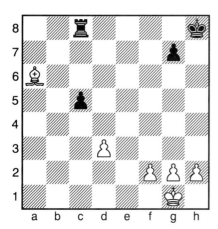

What is Black's best move?

The secret to this one: look at White's king. It is trapped behind its own pawns. There is a back-rank weakness. What should Black do?

1...Ra8 pins the bishop. What is it pinned to? The a1 square. White must make a flight square and lose the bishop.

Diagram 75

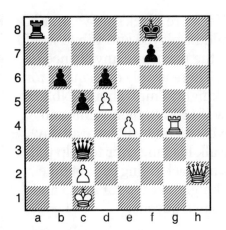

Is 1.Qh8+ White's best move?

No, it's a terrible move. Sometimes students get excited and move too quickly. The fail to ask themselves, "What can my opponent do?" White thought "Qh8+, Ke7 and Qxa8." White didn't see 1.Qh8+ then 1...Qxh8, you lose. But sadly for Black, White has 1.Qxd6+ Ke8 and then 2.Rg8# .

Be careful! Don't turn a win into a loss.

Diagram 76

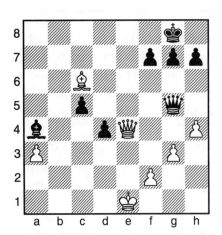

What is Black's best move?

What should Black do? If it's White's move, then 1.Qe8#. Should Black play 1...Bxc6 (threatening White's queen and stopping checkmate)? First, calculate all the checks. You will soon focus on 1...Qc1+. What happens next? White moves 2.Ke2. Then what? For a beginner, this is a hard pattern to visualize: 2...Qd1# and the game is over. In an open board, take your time and calculate.

Chapter 5

Deflections and Promotions

What we will see again in this chapter is that tactics can either work by themselves or work with other tactics. In most games, the tactics that are decisive are those that work together. Look at the diagram below:

Deflections/promotions 1

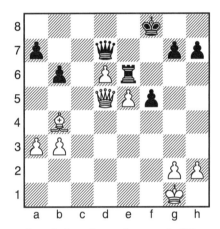

It is White to move: 1.Qxe6 Qxe6, and now 2.d7+ and the pawn queens. Do we name that "pawn promotion," "discovered check," "clearance sacrifice," or "deflection"? These are simply words trying to describe an idea. Different books will use different terms to describe the exact same position. Ultimately, as long as you know the idea, you can use whatever word you want.

When we try to promote or queen a pawn, there will be many deflecting moves. However, deflection has more practical uses than just for queening pawns. Look at the diagram below:

Chapter 5

Deflections/promotions 2

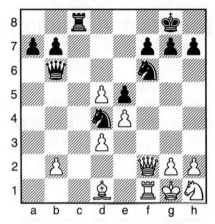

It is Black to move. White's king and knight are poorly placed. There seems to be a lot happening on the g1-a7 diagonal. Here is a hint: Black would like to play 1...Ne2+, but can't because of the bishop. What should Black do, then? 1...Rc2!. White either must take the rook with the bishop or the queen, or move the queen. Then 2...Ne2#. White does have other moves, but then Black just takes the queen.

In this chapter, pawns will turn into queens and pieces will be moved all around. Of course there will be a couple of problems that are just thrown in to mix things up a bit.

Have fun!

Diagram 77

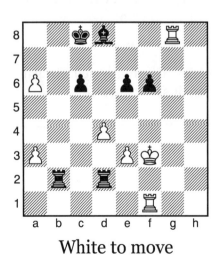

White to move

Diagram 78

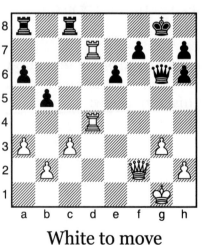

White to move

Diagram 79

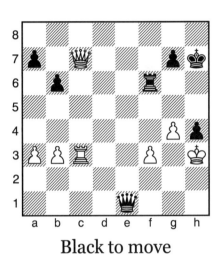

Black to move

Diagram 80

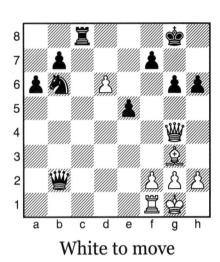

White to move

Diagram 81

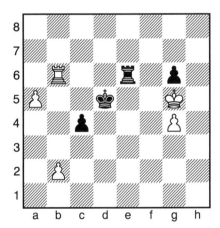

Should White play 1.Rxe6 ?

Diagram 82

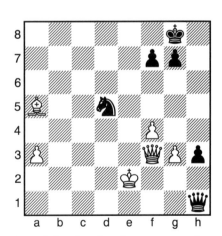

Should Black play 1...Qxf3+ ?

Diagram 83

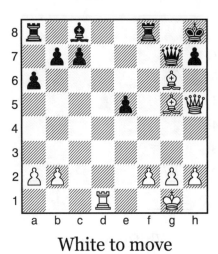

White to move

Diagram 84

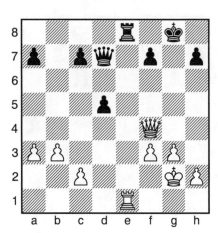

Should White play 1.Rxe8+ ?

Diagram 85

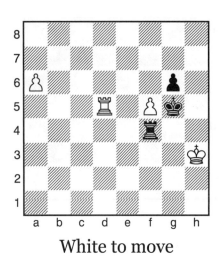

White to move

Diagram 86

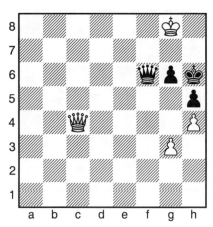

Should White play 1.Qf4+ ?

Diagram 87

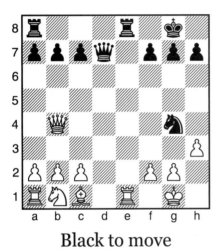

Black to move

Diagram 88

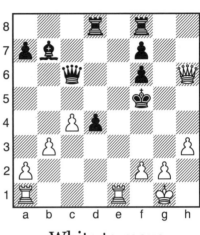

White to move

Diagram 89

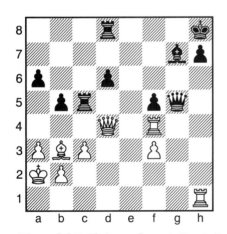

Should White play 1.Qe3 ?

Diagram 90

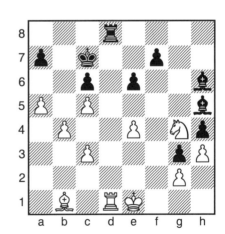

Should Black play 1...Rxd1+ ?

Diagram 91

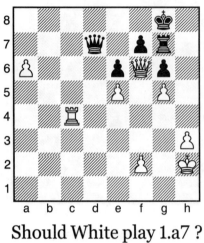

Should White play 1.a7 ?

Diagram 92

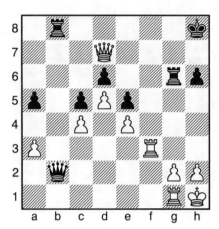

Should Black play 1...Rbg8 ?

Diagram 93

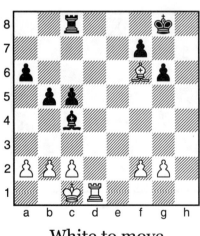

White to move

Diagram 94

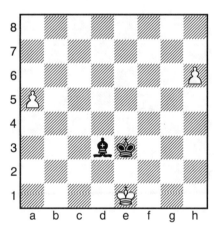

Should White play 1.h7, or 1.a6 ?

Diagram 95

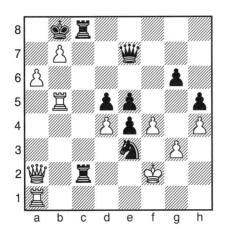

Should White play 1.Kxe3 ?

Diagram 96

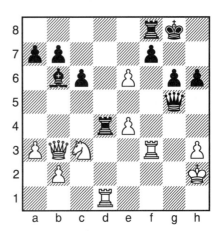

Should Black play 1...Rxd1 ?

Answers

Diagram 77

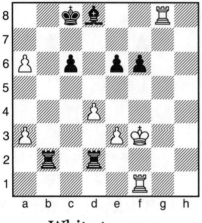

White to move

White could win back the bishop by playing 1.a7. Then 1...Kb7 2.Rxd8 and 2...Kxa7. When you have a good move, take your time and find a better one: 1.Rxd8+ (deflection) 1...Kxd8, and now with 2.a7 Black can't stop the pawn from queening.

Diagram 78

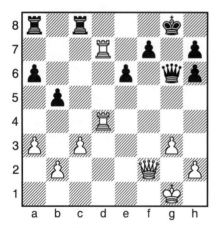

White to move

Imagine Black's queen standing on g5. What would White do? White would play 1.Qxf7+ Kh8 and then 2.Qh7#. Black's queen must protect f7. What can White do about it? 1.Rg4!. Black will either lose the queen or get checkmated (deflection).

Diagram 79

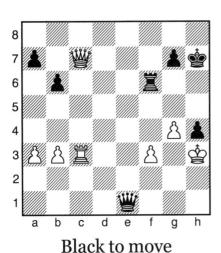

Black to move

What two things is White's queen doing?

1. It protects the rook.

2. It stops ...Qh1 and ...Qg3 from being checkmate. How can Black take advantage of that? 1... Rf7!. If 2.Qxf7, then White gets checkmated. But if the queen tries to stay on the h2-b8 diagonal, then the rook on c3 is lost.

Diagram 80

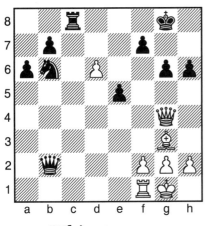

White to move

White is down two pawns, and you would think Black could stop the d6-pawn from queening. What should White do? 1.Qxc8+!. The important idea is that, after 1... Nxc8, White plays 2.d7 and Black cannot stop both the threat of 3.d8Q and the threat of 3.dxc8Q. White wins a rook.

Diagram 81

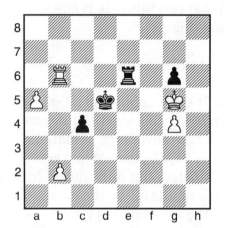

Should White play 1.Rxe6 ?

The answer is yes, and this is the reason: When Black plays 1...Kxe6, the king cannot stop the pawn from queening. White plays 2.a6 and the king is too far away to catch the pawn. There will be more on this later, but it is called "the rule of the square."

Diagram 82

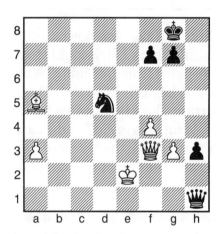

Should Black play 1...Qxf3+ ?

The question is, "What happens after 1...Qxf3+ ?" White will play 2.Kxf3, and then what? If White gets to play g3-g4, the king will be able to take the h-pawn and White will win. So Black plays 2...Ne3!. If 3.Kxe3, then 3...h2 and the pawn will queen. After 2...Ne3, the pawn gets to queen no matter what.

Diagram 83

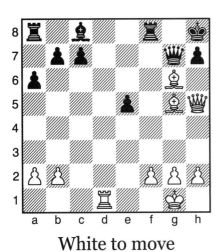

White to move

One of the keys to this problem is Black's bishop on c8. It isn't developed. White plays 1.Bf6! (deflection). If 1...Qxf6, then 2.Qxh7#.

What about 1...Rxf6 ? In that case, White plays 2.Rd8+ Rf8 3.Rxf8+ (deflecting the queen), and after 3...Qxf8 White plays 4.Qxh7# (two deflections).

Diagram 84

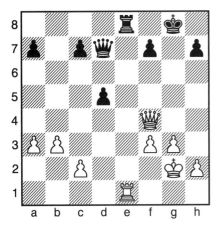

Should White play 1.Rxe8+ ?

Let's see: if 1.Rxe8+, then 1...Qxe8 and maybe 2.Qg5+ and, after Black moves, 3.Qxd5. White is two pawns ahead. When you find a good move, take your time and find a better one. 1.Qg4+, and what happens after the reply 1...Qxg4 ? The in-between move 2.Rxe8+. Black's king moves and then 3.gxf4. White wins a rook and has an easy win.

Diagram 85

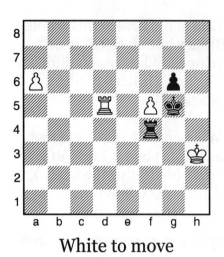

White to move

If you move 1.a7, Black simply moves 1...Ra4 and the pawn is stuck. However, if White moves 1.Ra5 first, Black cannot stop the pawn from queening. Rooks belong behind passed pawns.

Diagram 86

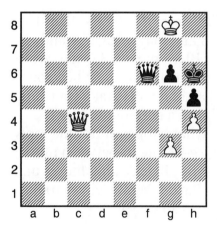

Should White play 1.Qf4+ ?

Visualize the position after 1.Qf4+ Qxf4 2.gxf4. Is it stalemate? No.

Black must move 2...g5. Then White will play 3.fxg5+ (not 3.hxg5+ because then Black's h-pawn queens). After 3.fxg5+, Black plays 3...Kg6, then 4.Kh8 Kf7 5.Kh7 and the pawn will queen.

1.Qf4 created *Zugzwang*.

Diagram 87

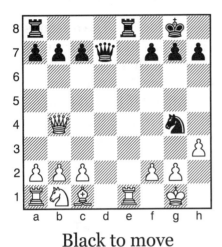

Black to move

Black is a piece down, but way ahead in development. Think about 1...Qd6. White's queen has big problems. If 2.Qxd6, then 2...Rxe1#. If 2.Qc3 or 2.Qd2, then Black plays 2...Qh2+ followed by 3...Qh1#. Notice that if White tries Rxe8+, after Black replies ...Rxe8 nothing has changed.

Diagram 88

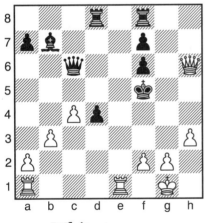

White to move

How long did it take you to find 1.g4# ? One-move checkmate!

Diagram 89

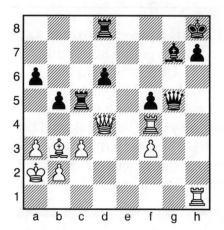

Should White play 1.Qe3 ?

It seems logical. The queen is under attack and 1.Qe3 protects the rook. But there is a much stronger move. Did you think about 1.Rfh4 ? If 1...Bxd4, then 2.Rxh7#. Of course Black can play 1...Qxh4, but after 2.Qxh4 White is threatening the rook on d8 and also checkmate on h7. It's hopeless for Black.

Diagram 90

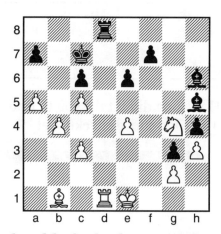

Should Black play 1...Rxd1+ ?

This is a little tricky. 1...Rxd1+ and then 2.Kxd1. What happens next? 2...Bxg4+ and 3.hxg4. Then 3...h3 and a pawn will queen. Notice that the bishop on b1 can't help, and the first move (1...Rxd1+) pulled the king away from the g- and h-pawns. Sort of like Problem 81.

Diagram 91

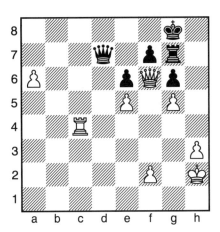

Should White play 1.a7 ?

You should see that after 1.a7 Black's queen takes the pawn. Then it's game over after 2.Qd8+ Kh7 3.Rh4#.

The promoting pawn was used for deflection. The queen doesn't have to take the pawn, but 1... Qe8 will be followed by 2.Rb4 and then 3.Rb8 and the pawn will queen.

Diagram 92

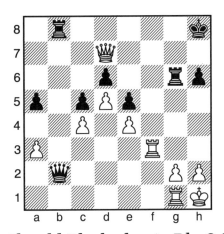

Should Black play 1...Rbg8 ?

1...Rbg8 seems to create a lot of pressure on the g-file. White might play 2.g3 and the attack is stalled.

Instead, Black has 1...Qxg2+! with mate to follow after 2.Rxg2 Rb1+. In wide-open games, every move counts. Know your checkmate patterns.

Diagram 93

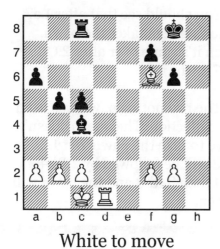

White to move

No deflections or pawn promotions here. Think about 1.Rh1. Black has 18 possible moves, but none of them will stop 2.Rh8#.

Diagram 94

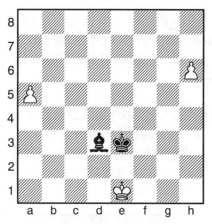

Should White play 1.h7, or 1.a6 ?

It really matters. If you play 1.h7 first, then Black plays 1...Bxh7. Now when White plays 2.a6, Black can retreat the bishop to e4 and stop the pawn from queening. However, after 1.a6 Bxa6, White plays 2.h7 and the pawn can't be stopped. Simple but important.

Diagram 95

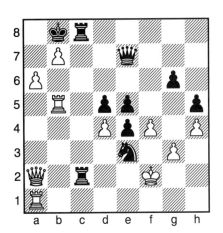

It is a wild-looking position.

However, after 1.Kxe3 R8c3# wins the game for Black. You had a win, and turned it into a loss in one move. After 1.Qxc2 Rxc2+, White will take the knight and then a6-a7+ followed by a8Q is unstoppable. If 1...Nxc2, then 2.a7+ Kc7 and 3.bxc8Q+. It's over.

Should White play 1.Kxe3 ?

Diagram 96

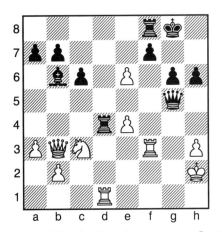

Another good visualization problem. Don't play "hope chess." Don't think 1....Rxd1 and if 2.Nxd1 then 3...Qg1 is checkmate. White can play 2.Qxd1 instead and you have nothing. But 1...Rd2+ deflects the rook. If 2.Rxd2 then 2...Qg1#, while if 2.Kh1 then 2...Qg2#. Deflections are very powerful!

Should Black play 1...Rxd1 ?

Chapter 6

Games to Learn From

This chapter contains ten games. You will learn a lot from the games if you are willing to play through them a few times and develop questions about each game.

Before playing the game on a chessboard, first look at the chess diagrams following each one. For each game, there is a sequencing question. You need to get a visual picture of how the game progresses from beginning to end. It is really important to know which diagram doesn't belong.

Next, play through the game for the first time and get a feel for the flow of the game. On the second or third time, go through a little bit more slowly and put the sequencing questions in order. Ask yourself with each game, "Why did this person win the game?"

When you do the sequencing, you might notice that some of the diagrams are from positions that happen after someone resigned. Try to visualize what happened.

Game 1

Vishy Anand vs. Veselin Topalov
World Championship (Game 4), 2010

1.d4 Nf6 2.c4 e6 3.Nf3 d5 4.g3 dxc4 5.Bg2 Bb4+ 6.Bd2 a5 7.Qc2 Bxd2+ 8.Qxd2 c6 9.a4 b5 10.Na3 Bd7 11.Ne5 Nd5 12.e4 Nb4 13.0-0 0-0 14.Rfd1 Be8 15.d5 Qd6 16.Ng4 Qc5 17.Ne3 N8a6 18.dxc6 bxa4 19.Naxc4 Bxc6 20.Rac1 h6 21.Nd6 Qa7 22.Ng4 Rad8 23.Nxh6+ gxh6 24.Qxh6 f6 25.e5 Bxg2 26.exf6 Rxd6 27.Rxd6 Be4 28.Rxe6 Nd3 29.Rc2 Qh7 30.f7+ Qxf7 31.Rxe4 Qf5 32.Re7, **Black resigns**

Play through the game once. Look at how the players develop their pieces. White's move 23 is important; think about how White continues the attack.

Which phrase best summarizes the game?
a. White's pawns open up the center and then he attacks the king.
b. Black attacks White's king, but White defends well and wins.

140

c. White attacks the kingside while Black's pieces are on the queenside.

d. Black's poor opening play (moves 1 to 14) allows White a decisive advantage.

Put these diagrams in the order in which they happened (one of them does not belong):

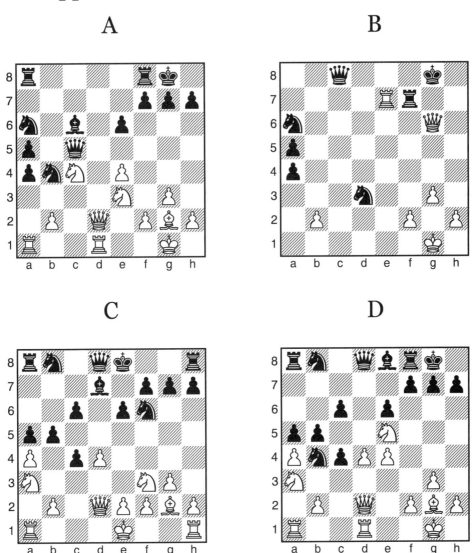

A   B

C   D

E   F

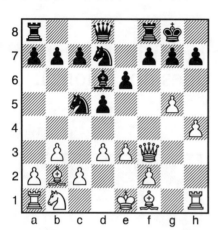   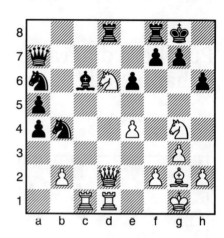

1. ___ 2. ___ 3. ___ 4. ___ 5. ___

What advice would you give Black for the next game?

_____

_____

_____

Game 2

Jan Timman vs. Anatoly Karpov
Montreal 1979

1.c4 Nf6 2.Nc3 e5 3.Nf3 Nc6 4.e3 Be7 5.d4 exd4 6.Nxd4 0-0 7.Nxc6 bxc6 8.Be2 d5 9.0-0 Bd6 10.b3 Qe7 11.Bb2 dxc4 12.bxc4 Rb8 13.Qc1 Ng4 14.g3 Re8 15.Nd1 Nxh2 16.c5 Nxf1 17.cxd6 Nxg3 18.fxg3 Qxd6 19.Kf2 Qh6 20.Bd4 Qh2+ 21.Ke1 Qxg3+ 22.Kd2 Qg2 23.Nb2 Ba6 24.Nd3 Bxd3 25.Kxd3 Rbd8 26.Bf1 Qe4+ 27.Kc3 c5 28.Bxc5 Qc6 29.Kb3 Rb8+ 30.Ka3 Re5 31.Bb4 Qb6, **White resigns**

Play through the game and look at Black's move 15...Nxh2. Why do you think he made that move?

a. He thought he saw a checkmate happening soon.

b. A knight taking a pawn is almost always a good move.

c. Black was worried about White's attack, so he counterattacked.

d. He saw a 4- or 5-move plan which would give him an advantage.

Black's move 17...Ng3 looks like it loses his queen. What's wrong with White playing 18.fxg3 ?

_____

_____

_____

Put these diagrams in the order in which they happened (one of them does not belong):

A   B

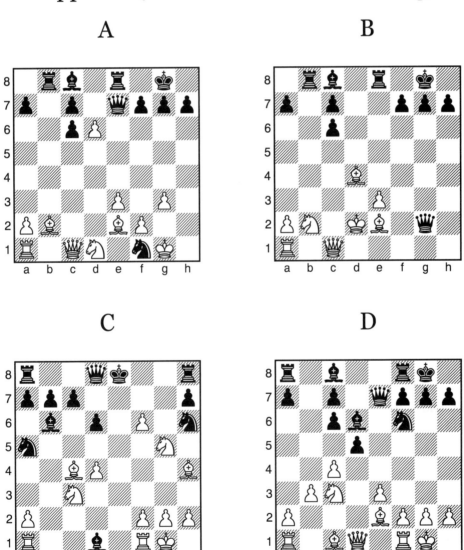

C   D

E   F

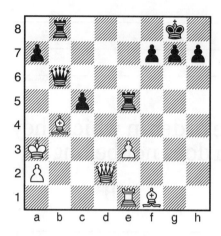 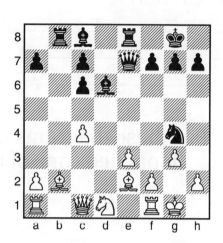

1. ___ 2. ___ 3. ___ 4. ___ 5. ___

Two bishops are worth 6 points and are normally better than a rook. Why are White's bishops ineffective in this game?

_____

_____

_____

Game 3

Ljubomir Ljubojevic vs. Garry Kasparov
Niksic 1983

1.e4 c5 2.Nf3 e6 3.d3 Nc6 4.g3 d5 5.Nbd2 g6 6.Bg2 Bg7 7.0-0 Nge7 8.Re1 b6 9.h4 h6 10.c3 a5 11.a4 Ra7 12.Nb3 d4 13.cxd4 cxd4 14.Bd2 e5 15.Nc1 Be6 16.Re2 0-0 17.Be1 f5 18.Nd2 f4 19.f3 fxg3 20.Bxg3 g5 21.hxg5 Ng6 22.gxh6 Bxh6 23.Nf1 Rg7 24.Rf2 Be3 25.b3 Nf4, **White resigns**

Play through the game. On move 11, Black played ...Ra8-a7. What do you think Black was thinking when he made this move?

a. "I am going to put my rook where it can move across the board as quickly as possible."

b. "The rook on a7 will help the a-pawn move forward."

c. "If Black gets to play ...dxe4 and White plays dxe4, then the rook can move to d7."

d. "I'm not sure what to do and moving my rook to a7 can't lose immediately."

Black gave away the pawns in front of his king. Why?

_____

_____

_____

Place these diagrams in the order in which they happened (one of them does not belong):

A

B

C

D

E

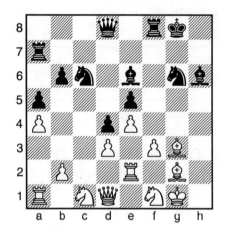

F

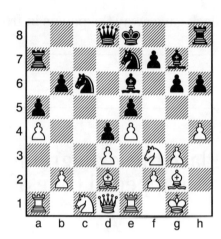

1. ___ 2. ___ 3. ___ 4. ___ 5. ___

Which white piece never was developed?

_____

How can an undeveloped piece hurt your chances?

_____

_____

_____

Game 4

Mikhail Tal vs. Georgi Tringov
Amsterdam 1964

1.e4 g6 2.d4 Bg7 3.Nc3 d6 4.Nf3 c6 5.Bg5 Qb6 6.Qd2 Qxb2 7.Rb1 Qa3 8.Bc4 Qa5 9.0-0 e6 10.Rfe1 a6 11.Bf4 e5 12.dxe5 dxe5 13.Qd6 Qxc3 14.Red1 Nd7 15.Bxf7+ Kxf7 16.Ng5+ Ke8 17.Qe6+, **Black resigns**

Play through the game. What would be a good summary of this game?
a. White got lucky.
b. Too many pawn and queen moves in the opening, and you can lose quickly.
c. Black missed 13...exf4 and if he had made that move, he would have won the game.
d. Both sides had chances, but White was able to play a better endgame and won.

Which of these moves caused Black the most damage: 6...Qxb2, 9....e6, 12...dxe5 ? Why?

_____

_____

_____

Put these diagrams in the order in which they happened (one of them does not belong):

A

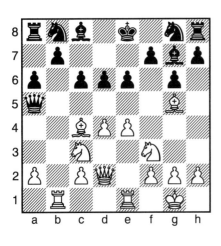

B

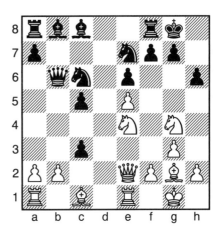

C

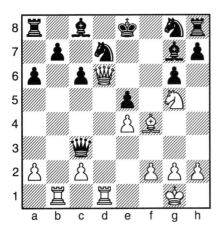

D

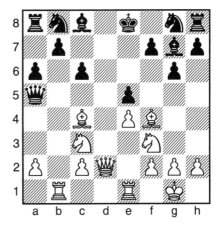

Chapter 6

E

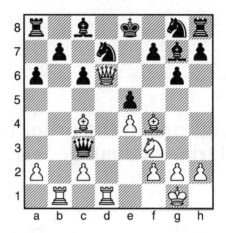

1. ___ 2. ___ 3. ___ 4. ___

Mikhail Tal is considered by most to be one of the greatest attacking players in chess history. Which move was his best attacking move in this game? Why do you think so?

_____

_____

_____

Game 5

Bobby Fischer vs. Reuben Fine
New York 1963

1.e4 e5 2.Nf3 Nc6 3.Bc4 Bc5 4.b4 Bxb4 5.c3 Ba5 6.d4 exd4 7.0-0 dxc3 8.Qb3 Qe7 9.Nxc3 Nf6 10.Nd5 Nxd5 11.exd5 Ne5 12.Nxe5 Qxe5 13.Bb2 Qg5 14.h4 Qxh4 15.Bxg7 Rg8 16.Rfe1 Kd8 17.Qg3, **Black resigns**

Play through the game. Start to make guesses about what the next move might be. How are this game and Game 4 similar? More than one answer may be correct.

    a. In both games, Black makes too many pawn moves.

    b. Black's king was stuck in the center.

    c. In both games, White was ahead after 9 moves if you counted points.

    d. Black's pieces were not developed in either game.

Go back and look at White's move 13.Bb2. What important ideas does that move accomplish?

_____

_____

_____

Put these diagrams in the order in which they happened (as always, one doesn't belong):

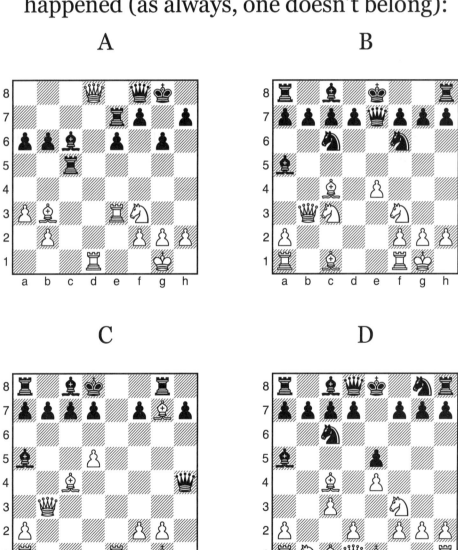

A

B

C

D

Chapter 6

E

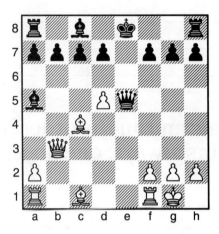

1. ___ 2. ___ 3. ___ 4. ___

In the first five games, all the winners were world champions at some point. If you could ask a world chess champion any question, what would it be?

_____

_____

_____

Game 6

Emanuel Schiffers vs. Nolde
1872

1.e4 e5 2.Nf3 Nc6 3.Bc4 Bc5 4.b4 Bxb4 5.c3 Bc5 6.0-0 d6 7.d4 exd4 8.cxd4 Bb6 9.Nc3 Na5 10.Bg5 f6 11.Bh4 Nh6 12.e5 g5 13.Nxg5 Bg4 14.exf6 Bxd1 15.Re1+ Kd7 16.Be6+ Kc6 17.d5+ Kc5 18.Nge4+ Kc4 19.Rxed1 Bd4 20.Rab1 Bxc3 21.Rdc1 Rg8 22.Rxc3+ Kd4 23.Rb4+ Nc4 24.Rbxc4+ Ke5 25.f4+ Kxf4 26.Ng5+ Ke5 27.Nf3#

Look at the first 5 to 7 moves of this game, and go back and look at the opening moves in the last game. White gives up his b-pawn for free on move 4. Why?
    a. White didn't see that the bishop could take the pawn.
    b. White thought that after he played 5.c3 he could take the bishop for free.
    c. White gave up the pawn to get a lead in development.
    d. White saw a checkmate in the next few moves.

Fischer's game was in 1963 and Schiffers's game was played in 1872. Do you think Fischer had studied Schiffers's game? Why or why not?

_____

_____

_____

You know the drill. By the way, one of these diagrams doesn't belong here. (I'll bet you knew that.)

A

B

C

D

E

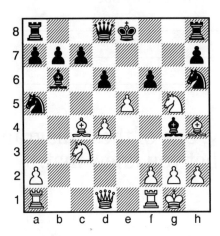

F

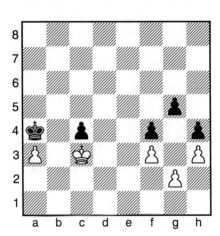

1. ___ 2. ___ 3. ___ 4. ___ 5. ___

On move 14, Schiffers sacrifices his queen. Let's assume that he didn't see the final checkmate position. What did he see in Black's position that told him sacrificing the queen was a good plan?

_____

_____

_____

Game 7

Riazantsev vs. Nevostrujev
Russian Championship 2002

1.d4 Nf6 2.c4 g6 3.Nc3 Bg7 4.Bg5 c5 5.d5 b5 6.cxb5 a6 7.e3 Qa5 8.Qd2 0-0 9.bxa6 e6 10.dxe6 dxe6 11.Ne4 Nxe4 12.Qxa5 Bb2 13.Ne2 Bxa1 14.Bh6 Bxa6 15.Bxf8 Nc6 16.Qc7 Nb4 17.Bh6 Be5 18.Qd7 Nd3+ 19.Kd1 Rb8 20.Nd4 Rb1+ 21.Ke2 Ne1 22.Nb5 Nc3+, **White resigns**

This game is a thing of beauty. Look at it very carefully. Go back and set up the position after Black plays 11...Nxe4. Computers will tell you that White is ahead after he takes Black's queen. Why did Black sacrifice his queen?

a. Black saw a checkmate 11 moves later.

b. Black saw that he could activate all his pieces and attack White's king.

c. Black felt that even though he might be losing after move 11, he would have enormous pressure for a while.

d. Black was trying to trick a superior opponent.

How is this game like Game 6?

_____

_____

_____

Put them in order (one doesn't belong):

A

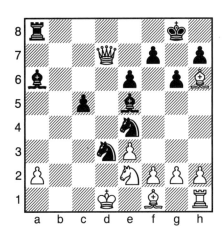

B

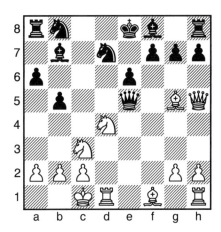

C

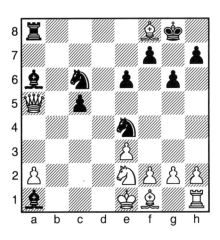

D

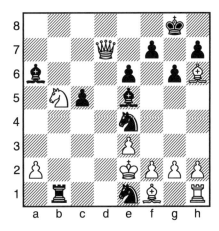

E   F

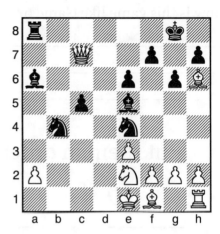

1. ___ 2. ___ 3. ___ 4. ___ 5. ___

Look at Diagram F above. Black just played ...Be5. Why can't White take the bishop?

_____

What big idea helped to cause all the losses in the first 7 games?

_____

_____

_____

Game 8

N. Pegoraro vs. P. Trotto
Arvier Open 2004

1.e4 c5 2.Nf3 d6 3.d4 cxd4 4.Nxd4 Nf6 5.Nc3 a6 6.Bg5 e6 7.f4 b5 8.e5 dxe5 9.fxe5 Qc7 10.Qe2 Nfd7 11.0-0-0 Bb7 12.Qh5 Qxe5 13.Nxe6 g6 14.Nc7+ Qxc7 15.Qe2+ Qe5 16.Qxe5+, **Black resigns**

This is a very short game and White's move 13 is the key move. What do you think White was thinking when he played 13.Nxe6 (more than one answer is possible)?

a. "The position is about even, so I think I will attack."

b. "Black's pieces are not developed."

c. "Black's king is in the center."
d. "All my pieces are developed."

Why do you think White gave up his e-pawn for free on move 12?

_____

_____

_____

If you were Trotto, what would you think after White played 13.Ne6 ?

_____

_____

_____

Sequencing. Just for fun, the diagram which doesn't belong is an important move from a previous game. Which game is it?

A   B

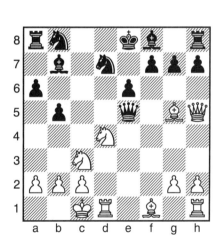

C

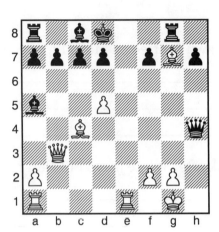

D

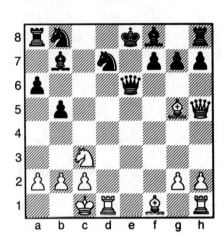

E

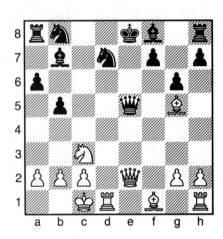

1. ___ 2. ___ 3. ___ 4. ___

Look at Diagram E. If White plays 1.Qxe5+, what are Black's only legal moves? What will happen?

_____

_____

_____

White's rook on h1 never gets developed. Why doesn't that hurt him?

_____

_____

Game 9

Glucksberg vs. Najdorf
Warsaw Olympiad 1929

1.d4 f5 2.c4 Nf6 3.Nc3 e6 4.Nf3 d5 5.e3 c6 6.Bd3 Bd6 7.0-0 0-0 8.Ne2 Nbd7 9.Ng5 Bxh2+ 10.Kh1 Ng4 11.f4 Qe8 12.g3 Qh5 13.Kg2 Bg1 14.Nxg1 Qh2+ 15.Kf3 e5 16.dxe5 Ndxe5+ 17.fxe5 Nxe5+ 18.Kf4 Ng6+ 19.Kf3 f4 20.exf4 Bg4+ 21.Kxg4 Ne5+ 22.fxe5 h5#

This game has a very important idea in it, which we haven't seen much of in the previous games. Go through this game and think, "How is this game different?"
  a. Black attacks the white castled king's position with a bishop sacrifice.
  b. All of White's pieces get developed.
  c. Black uses the center pawns to break open White's king.
  d. White has checkmate possibilities before eventually losing.

After White plays 15.Kf3, Black should sense that White is in big trouble. How should he know that?

_____

_____

_____

How is the final move unique?

_____

_____

_____

Chapter 6

Sequencing (one doesn't belong, but you knew that)

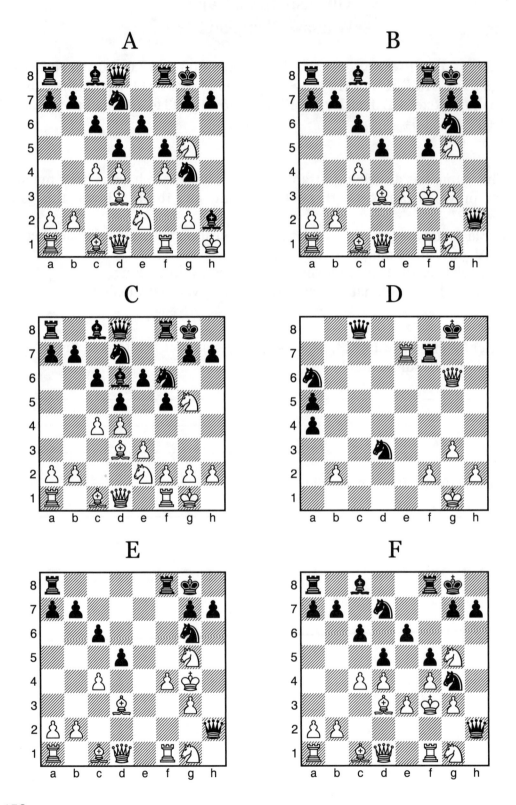

A

B

C

D

E

F

1. ___ 2. ___ 3. ___ 4. ___ 5. ___

In this game, Black played 11...Qe8. In Game 7, Black played 19...Rb8. In Game 3, Black played 11...Ra7. How are those moves similar?

_____

_____

In your own games, how can moves like that make you a better player?

_____

_____

_____

Game 10
Mikhail Tal vs. Lajos Portisch
World Championship Candidates' Match (Game 2), 1965

1.e4 c6 2.Nc3 d5 3.Nf3 dxe4 4.Nxe4 Bg4 5.h3 Bxf3 6.Qxf3 Nd7 7.d4 Ngf6 8.Bd3 Nxe4 9.Qxe4 e6 10.0-0 Be7 11.c3 Nf6 12.Qh4 Nd5 13.Qg4 Bf6 14.Re1 Qb6 15.c4 Nb4 16.Rxe6+ fxe6 17.Qxe6+ Kf8 18.Bf4 Rd8 19.c5 Nxd3 20.cxb6 Nxf4 21.Qg4 Nd5 22.bxa7 Ke7 23.b4 Ra8 24.Re1+ Kd6 25.b5 Rxa7 26.Re6+ Kc7 27.Rxf6, **Black resigns**

A chapter on attacking the king should have two games by the great attacking master, Mikhail Tal, in it. White's move 16 is not a surprise: he is sacrificing a rook. Also his bishop on d3 is hanging (could be taken for free).

What was probably the main factor in Tal's playing 16.Rxe6+ ?
a. He had an internal sense that it was just the right move.
b. He knew he could keep Black's king in the center.
c. He had played moves like these many times before and been successful.
d. He was never afraid to take a calculated risk.

At the end of the game, it would be a little unclear why Black resigned. Why did he resign after 27.Rxf6 ?

_____

_____

_____

Sequencing. Which game does the "this one does not belong" come from? Guess without looking back to the games.

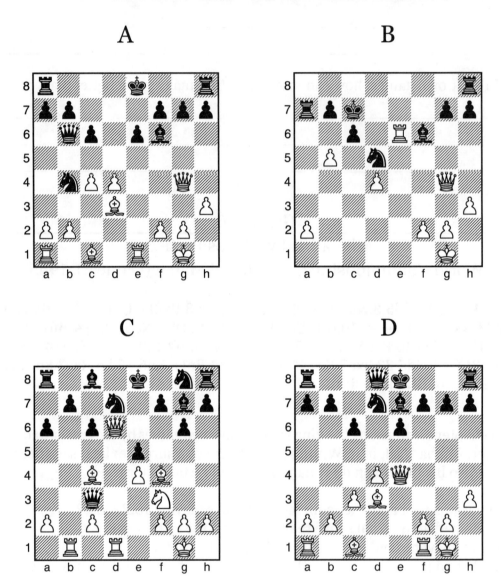

A

B

C

D

E

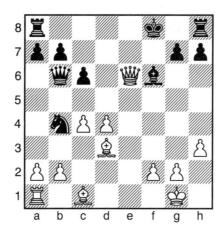

1. ___ 2. ___ 3. ___ 4. ___

How are Diagrams C and E similar?

_____

_____

_____

What ideas appear in most of these games?

1. _____

2. _____

3. _____

4. _____

Chapter 6

Answers

Game 1, Anand vs. Topalov

1. C. Black's pieces get stuck on the queenside while the king gets attacked.

Sequencing   1. C   2. D   3. A   4. F   5. B

Advice: make sure your king has enough protection.

Game 2, Timman vs. Karpov

1. D

Black's move 17: after White plays 18.dxe7, Black plays 18...Nxe2+ and then 19...Nxc1. He ends up an exchange ahead.

Sequencing   1. D   2. F   3. A   4. B   5. E

"Two bishops..." White's king was never safe enough for him to get the bishops to work together.

Game 3, Ljubojevic vs. Kasparov

1. A

"Black gave away...?" Black was attacking the king and the pawns were in the way.

Sequencing   1. B   2. F   3. D   4. E   5. A

"Which white piece...?" White never moved his queen once.

"How can...?" When pieces are not developed, they have very little impact on the game.

Game 4, Tal vs. Tringov

1. B

"Which of ....?" 6...Qxb2 was saying to Tal, "Come and get me!" And Tal did.

Sequencing   1. A   2. D   3. E   4. C

"Tal is ....?" 13.Qd6 might have come as a surprise to his opponent because the knight on c3 is hanging. There were many sharp moves in the game.

Game 5, Fischer vs. Fine

1. B

When you see a king in the center and you are ahead in development... *attack!!*

"Go back....?" 13.Bb2 develops a piece and attacks the queen at the same time. This gains time for White's attack to develop.

Sequencing   1. D   2. B   3. E   4. C

Game 6, Schiffers vs. Nolde

1. C

"Fischer's game...?" All great players study and learn from past players. My guess is that Fischer had seen this game and many more like it, and saw the attack through to the end.

Sequencing   1. B   2. E   3. D   4. A   5. C

"On move 14...?" I think Schiffers saw the ability to drive his opponent's king to the center and maintain the initiative. When you put pressure on people, sometimes they don't make the best moves.

Game 7, Riazantsev vs. Nevostrujev

1. B + C   When all your pieces are developed and your opponent's pieces aren't, it is time to attack.

"How is this...?" Both involve queen sacrifices and a king hunt.

Sequencing   1. E   2. C   3. F   4. A   5. D

Chapter 6

"Look at ....?" If 18.Qxe5, then 18...Nd3+ forks the king and queen.

"What big idea...?" Almost every game has had one person getting a lead in development. All kings were exposed to a direct attack with one side sacrificing pieces.

Game 8, Pegoraro vs. Trotto

1. B, C, and D

"Why do...?" To open lines of attack against the king.

"If you....?" I'm in big trouble!

Sequencing   1. A   2. B   3. D   4. E

"Look at...?" 1.Qxe5+ Be7 and then 2.Qxe7#, or 1.Qxe5+ Nxe5 2.Rd8#. Make sure to calculate all possibilities.

"White's rook...?" White's rook and bishop are never developed, but both of Black's rooks, a knight, and a bishop were never developed. Also, Black's king was stuck in the center.

Game 9, Glucksberg vs. Najdorf

1. C. With his moves 15...e5 and 17...f4, Black rips open the king with center pawns. In a couple of other games, the center pawns had some effect, but in this game the pressure from those pawn sacrifices was dramatic.

"After White...?" Look at all the pieces which White hasn't developed. White was counting on keeping the center closed so that he could organize his defenses, but it never happened.

"How is....?" Checkmate with a pawn.

Sequencing   1. C   2. A   3. F   4. B   5. E

"Black's move 11...?" Each of those moves shows how to plan ahead to get your pieces most involved in the game. 11...Qe8 allowed the queen to go to h5. 19...Rb8 allowed the rook to get to b1. 11...Ra7 allowed the rook to slide over to g7. Think about involving all your pieces in the game and figure out the best way of getting them to places.

"In your own game...?" Know where you pieces need to be, and get them there as efficiently as possible.

Game 10, Tal vs. Portisch

1. A, B, C, and D

"At the end....?" There is a combination. After 27.Rxf6 gxf6, there is 28.Qg7+ and 29.Qxh8 to follow. It is true that Black has a knight and rook for the queen, but White has passed pawns and Black's rook and knight don't work well together. If you are playing in a beginners' tournament and you are Black... *keep playing!!* If you are facing Tal, go ahead and resign.

Sequencing   1. A   2. D   3. E   4. B

"How are...?" The queen is aggressively placed and keeps the king in the center.

"What are....?"

1. Develop your pieces.

2. When you have a lead in development, attack!

3. Most of the time, your opponent's king is very weak when in the center of the board.

4. Be willing to sacrifice material to keep the initiative.

Chapter 7

Endgame Tactics and Smashing the Kingside

When children who are starting to learn chess get to the end of the game, they tend to move very quickly. Students tend to get lost without the queen, and I have seen many endgames where children simply have their hands hovering over the board ready to grab a piece and move it.

We have seen some problems that involve queening a pawn, and now it's time to look at some specific endgame tactics. One word which is used is the German word *"Zugzwang." Zugzwang* means that every move your opponent can make loses very quickly. Here are two examples:

Zugzwang 1　　　*Zugzwang 2*

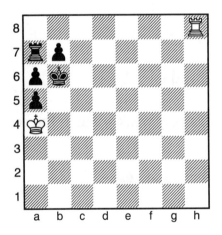 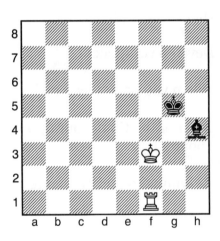

In the first diagram, think about what happens after 1.Rc8. Black has to make a move and the only move is 1...Ra8. Then White plays 2.Rxa8.

White forced Black to make a losing move. In the second diagram, White plays 1.Rh1. We can see that every bishop move loses, and there is only one king move which protects the bishop, 1...Kh5. However, after 2.Kf4, Black's king must move away from the bishop and lose the game.

The idea of looking at your opponent's pieces and forcing them into bad squares is really, really important in endgames. Here are two slightly more complicated examples:

Zugzwang 3

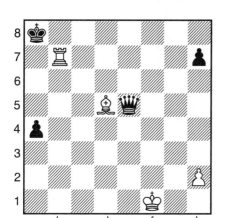

Zugzwang 4

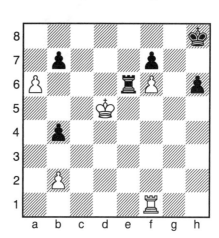

In example 3, White will trap Black's queen. How? White plays 1.Bf3 first. Now look at every square the queen can move to. What about 1...Qa1+ ? Then 2.Rb1+ (discovered check) wins the queen. Try 1...Qh8. But then 2.Rxh7+ wins the queen. Curiously, the queen can safely move 1...Qh5 as there is a trick: if White plays 2.Bxh5, then 2...Kxb7 and if Black marches the king to the h8 corner, the game will be a draw as White's light-squared bishop can't force the king out of the dark square h8. What should White do? 2.Rf7+ moves the rook away from the king and protects the bishop. The queen is lost on the next move.

The first move in Diagram 4 is 1.axb7. That seems reasonable enough. You win a pawn and it might queen. Black has to play 1...Rb6 to stop the pawn from queening. White then plays 2.Ra1 which is logical. The threat is 3.Ra8+ and then the pawn will queen. Now Black has to take the pawn. White plays 3.Ra8+ and Black replies 3...Kh7. Now comes White's devastating move. What is it? 4.Kc6. It attacks the rook and the rook has no safe moves. Check it out for yourself. On any of the 7 squares the rook can move to, one of White's chessmen will take it. It is trapping a piece, but it is also forcing Black to make a losing move.

The other idea in this problem set is smashing the king's castled position (the king usually castles on the kingside). There are 6 squares around the king which can be attacked. Here are the squares (marked with an "x"):

Chapter 7

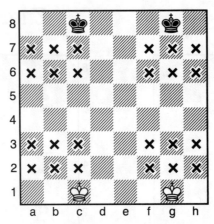

If White's king is castled kingside, then the target squares are f2, g2, h2, f3, g3, and h3. If Black's king is castled queenside, then the squares which can be targets are c7, b7, a7, c6, b6, and a6. Look at the squares around your opponent's king.

Here are some examples:

Smash 1

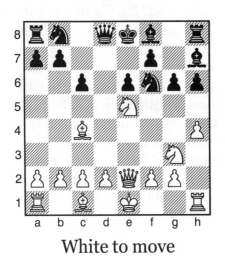

White to move

Smash 2

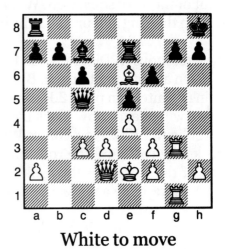

White to move

168

Endgame Tactics and Smashing the Kingside

In Smash 1, White has a lead in development and Black's king is stuck in the center. Black's weakest square is one of those 6 squares. What is the correct move? Think about 1.Nxf7... It does sort of fork the queen and rook. That is not the main thing it does, because Black can play 1...Kxf7. Look at White's queen and bishop after the pawn on f7 has been taken. There is a lot of power aimed at the black king. After Black plays 1...Kxf7, White will play 2.Qxe6+. Black's only move is 2...Kg7 and then 3.Qf7# ends the game.

What about Smash 2? White's rooks are doubled on the open file and his bishop is controlling g8. Those are good things, but what move takes advantage of those things? 1.Qh6! does. Why? If 1...gxh6, then 2.Rg8+ Rxg8 3.Rxg8#. White is also threatening 2.Qxh7+ Kxh7 3.Rh3#. What is Black to do? Black has no useful checks and so 1...g6 seems like the best move. After 2.Rxg6, Black can play 2...Ree8 to stop 3.Rg8+, but then White plays 3.Qg7# instead.

There are a couple of classic bishop smashes to be aware of. Here is an example of both:

Smash 3

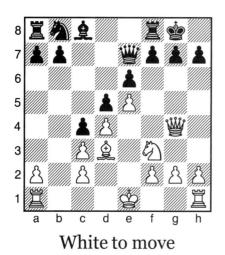

White to move

Smash 4

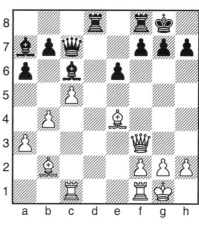

White to move

In Smash 3, White has to make a choice of what to do with the bishop. 1.Bxh7+! is the beginning of the end for Black. If 1...Kxh7, then 2.Qh5+ Kg8 and now 3.Ng5 will force Black to give up his queen to stop checkmate. The white queen was in a great place in this example, but one thing is to try this type of "Greek Gift" problem when the queen is on d1. There are many times when Bxh7+ works and there are times when it doesn't. In the age of computers, there is a good way to practice it: play chess online and look for positions where you think Bxh7+ might work. Just try it and do your best. When the

Chapter 7

game is done, go back and see if it was the right choice. The computer will tell you right away. With so many variations possible, you are trying to develop an instinct for when it's good and when it isn't.

Smash 4 is from Miles–Browne, Lucerne Olympiad 1982. White has to decide what to do with the bishop on e4. This is a wonderful illustration.

1.Bxh7+! Kxh7 2.Qh5+ Kg8 3.Bxg7 Kxg7 4.Qg5+ Kh8 5.Qf6+ Kg8 6.Rc4 and the threat of Rg4# is unstoppable.

Will you successfully checkmate your opponent the first time you try it? Maybe, or maybe not. The most important idea is to learn through trial and error, study, practice some more, and eventually master it.

This chapter is about tactics in the endgame and a specific tactical idea in the middlegame. Learn to develop an instinct for when these ideas are happening in your game, and you will win many games. There will be some tough losses along the way, games where you are winning and then lose. Learn from your mistakes, forget the hurt, and move on.

Being a great chessplayer takes time and practice. For the following set of problems, if it says, "White to move. Win or lose?", you must figure out if White is winning or losing. If it says, "Black to move. Win or lose?", you must figure out if Black is winning or losing. Unless it says "Draw," all other problems are wins for the player to move. Good luck!

Diagram 97

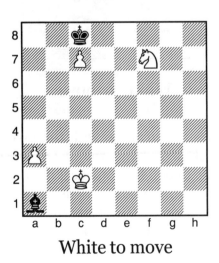

White to move

Diagram 98

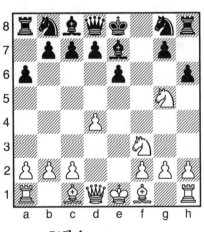

White to move

Diagram 99

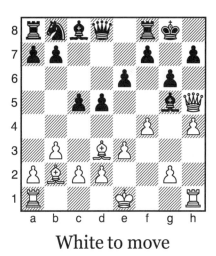

White to move

Diagram 100

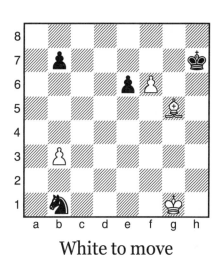

White to move

Diagram 101

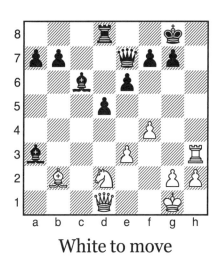

White to move

Diagram 102

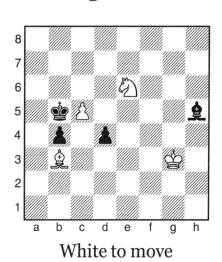

White to move

Diagram 103

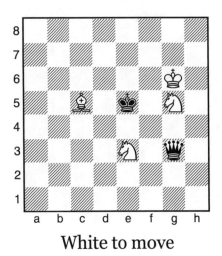

White to move

Diagram 104

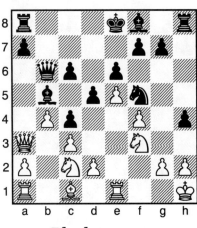

Black to move

Diagram 105

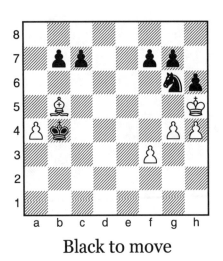

Black to move

Diagram 106

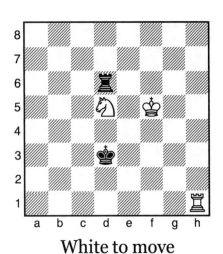

White to move

Diagram 107

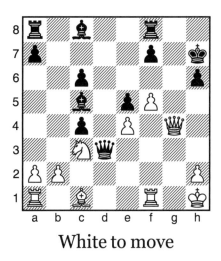

White to move

Diagram 108

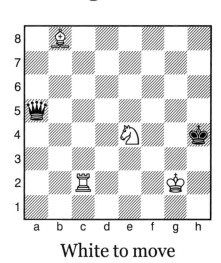

White to move

Diagram 109

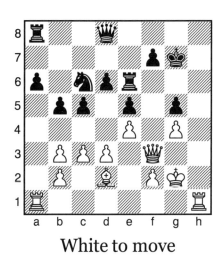

White to move

Diagram 110

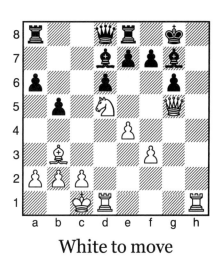

White to move

Diagram 111

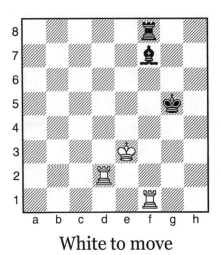

White to move

Diagram 112

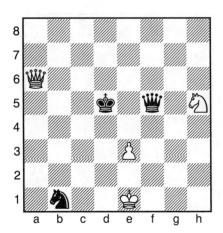

Black to move. Win or lose?

Diagram 113

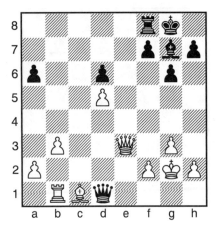

Black to move. Win or lose?

Diagram 114

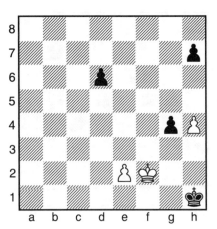

White to move and draw

Diagram 115

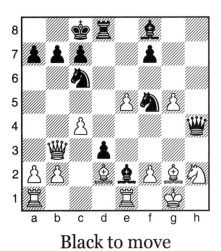

Black to move

Diagram 116

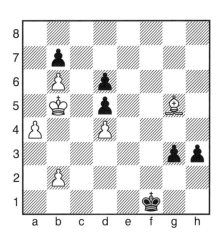

White to move and draw

Diagram 117

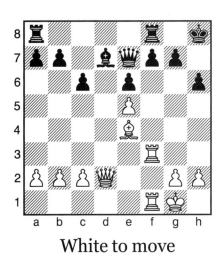

White to move

Diagram 118

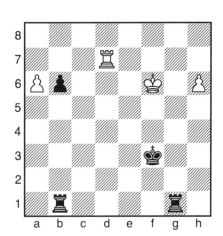

White to move. Win or lose?

Diagram 119

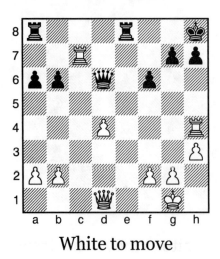

White to move

Diagram 120

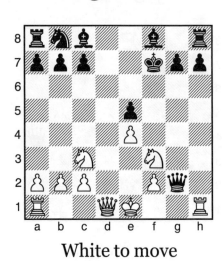

White to move

Diagram 121

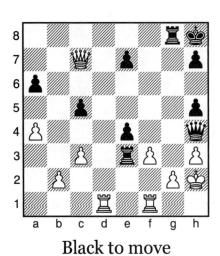

Black to move

Diagram 122

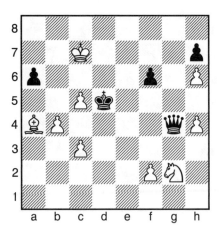

Black to move. Win or lose?

Diagram 123

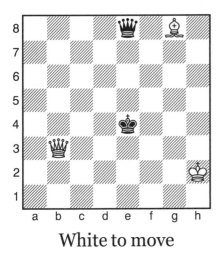

White to move

Diagram 124

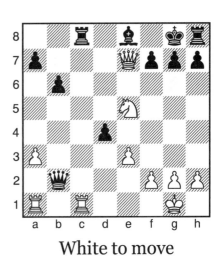

White to move

Diagram 125

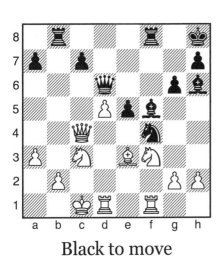

Black to move

Diagram 126

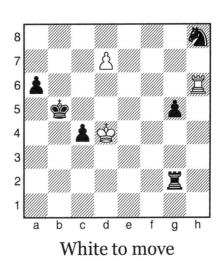

White to move

Diagram 127

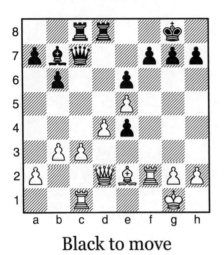

Black to move

Diagram 128

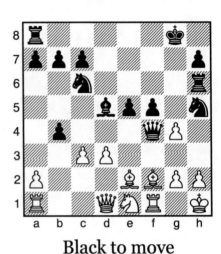

Black to move

Diagram 129

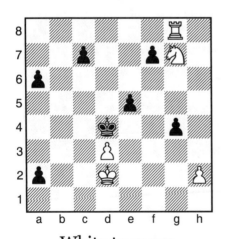

White to move.
Can White stop the a2-pawn?

Diagram 130

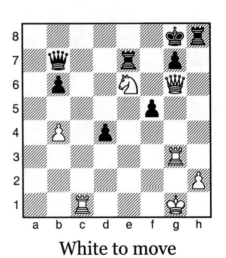

White to move

Diagram 131

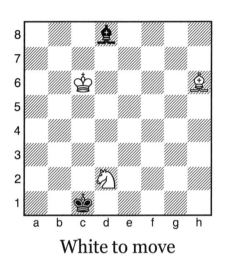

White to move

Diagram 132

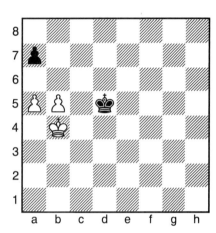

White to move. 1.a6 or 1.b6 ?

Diagram 133

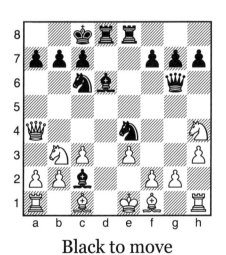

Black to move

Diagram 134

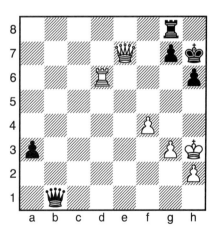

White to move. Win or lose?

Diagram 135

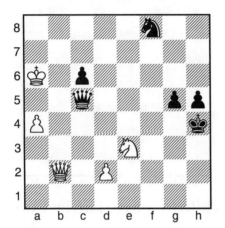

Black to move. Win or lose?

Diagram 136

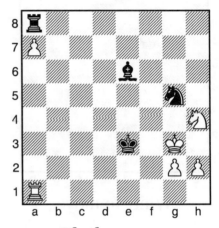

Black to move

Answers

Diagram 97

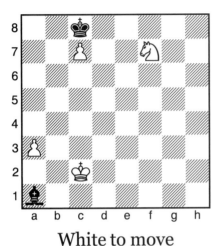

White to move

A really important idea is to be able to calculate your opponent's moves. Let's say you looked at 1.Kb1. Could you see the result of every possible bishop move? What about 1...Bc3 ? Is it safe there? White can play 2.Nd6+ and the king has to take the pawn, or else it will queen. Then White can play 3.Nb5+ forking the king and bishop. The same thing happens after 1...Bd4. What about 1...Bf6 or 1...Bg7 ? The knight plays 2.Nd6+ and then goes to e8, forking the king and bishop. After 1.Kb1, no matter where the bishop goes, it will be taken immediately or forked eventually.

Diagram 98

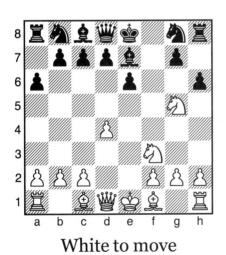

White to move

1.Nf7!. Why? The king has to take and then White will play 2.Ne5+. All of Black's options lose: If 2...Kf6 then 3.Qf3#. If 2...Ke8 then 3.Qh5+ g6 4.Qxg6+ Kf8 and 5.Qf7#. If 2...Kf8, then 3.Ng6+, the king moves, and 4.Nxh8 wins material, plus the coming attack will be overwhelming.

Diagram 99

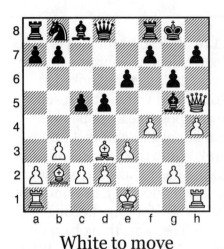

White to move

1.Qxh7+ Kxh7 2.hxg5+ (discovered check) 2...Kg8 and 3.Rh8#.

Two important ideas: The bishop on b2 dominates, and the h-file is opened up by the queen sacrifice.

Diagram 100

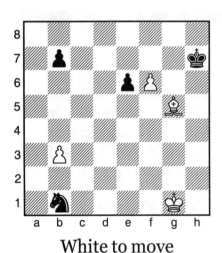

White to move

This one is a little tricky because you need to see how weak Black's knight is. "Knights on the rim are grim." How do you take advantage of that? Moving your pawn to f7 forces Black to play ...Kg7. White plays 2.Be7 and Black is forced to play 2...Kxf7 to stop the pawn. Now White's bishop goes to b4. The knight is trapped and all that needs to happen now is for White's king to march over and take it.

Diagram 101

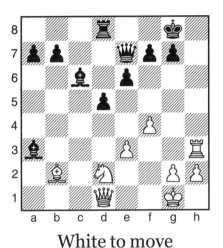

White to move

Black is helpless after 1.Bxg7. Why? We will start with what happens after 1...Kxg7: White plays 2.Qg4+ and if 2...Kf6, then 3.Qg5#. After 2...Kf8, there is 3.Rh8#. What if the king doesn't take the bishop? 2.Qg4 will be crushing, so maybe Black tries 1...f5. There are many wins here, but 2.Be5 threatens 3.Rh8+ and with the queen coming to h5 at some point, it will be over soon.

Diagram 102

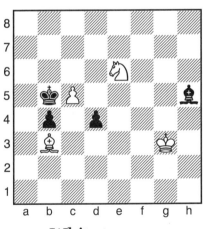

White to move

This is like Problems 97 and 100. You need to develop an ability to visualize where your opponent's pieces can go and what happens. Right now, if White were to play Nf4, Black's bishop would have a safe square with 1...Be8. What can change that?

1.c6 forces Black's king to take the pawn and now 2.Nf4. What's the difference? If Black now moves 2...Be8, then 3.Ba4+ skewers the king and wins the bishop.

Diagram 103

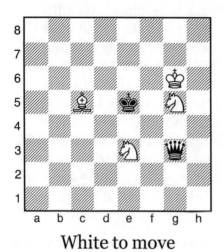

White to move

Look carefully at Black's queen. How may moves can it make? What happens after each move? On nine of the possible moves, the queen is taken immediately or falls victim to a knight fork. The queen can "safely" move to f4. Using this knowledge, what should White do? 1.Ba7 takes away ...Qf4 because then 2.Bb8+ will skewer the king and queen.

You may not know how to checkmate with a knight and bishop vs. king, but it is a win.

Diagram 104

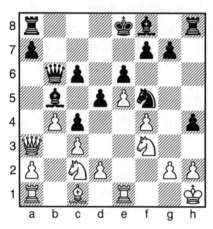

Black to move

This problem is a little bit like Problem 99. Can you see how the h-file will open up? Do you notice the queen on b6? What does it do? The first move is 1...Ng3+. White has to play 2.hxg3. Then Black plays 2...hxg3+ and the h-file comes open. Why can't the king move to g1? Because of the queen on b6. White is forced to play 3.Nh2 and then loses to 3...Rxh2# as the rook is protected by the pawn.

Diagram 105

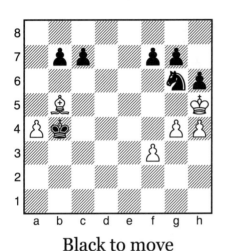

Black to move

1...Nf4#, game over.

Diagram 106

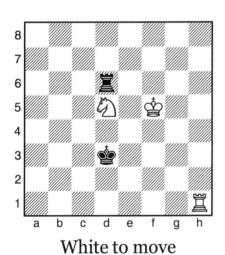

White to move

When you see the position two moves from now, you will think, "That's obvious." The key is to be able to visualize it before it happens. White first plays 1.Ke5. The rook has only two safe moves. Moves like 1...Rg6 are met with the knight fork 2.Nf4+. So Black plays 1...Rd8. Now after 2.Rd1+ the king has only three squares to move to. With 2...Kc2 or 2...Kc4, White plays 3.Ne3+, while on 2...Ke2 White can play 3.Nc3+. Black loses the rook.

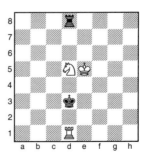

Diagram 107

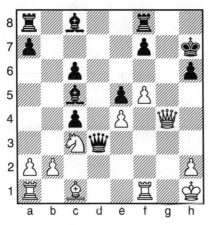

White to move

Look at 1.Bxh6. The first question is, "What if Black plays 1...Kxh6 ?" 2.Rf3 threatening the queen and 3.Rh3+ should win. What if the king doesn't take and plays 1...Rg8 ? What should White do then? (White's king is open, too.) 2.Qh4 threatens 3.Bf8# and Black can give up many pieces to stop it but would then have a losing position.

Diagram 108

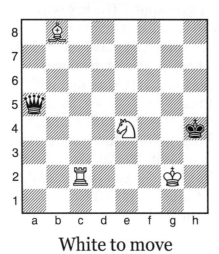

White to move

You should probably know by now that Black's queen will get trapped. How? Start with 1.Bg3+. 1...Kg4 is the only move because 1...Kh5 will be met with 2.Rc5+ and the queen is lost. White plays 2.Rc5 to threaten the queen and then 3.Rg5#. So Black plays the tricky 2...Qd2+. 3.Nxd2 would be stalemate. 3.Nf2+ and the queen has to play 3...Qxf2+. Game over.

Diagram 109

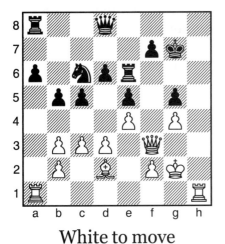

White to move

Notice how White's rooks are connected, and the back rank is clear, and the h-file is open. 1.Rh7+ and the king must take or else 2.Qxf7+ will be mate. After 1...Kxh7 2.Qxf7+, the king can move anywhere. The rook on a1 slides over to h1 and it's checkmate (3.Rh1#).

Diagram 110

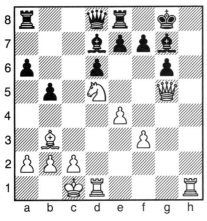

White to move

1.Qxg6!!. What if 1...fxg6 ? Then 2.Ne7++ (double check) 2... Kf8 (the only move) and 3.Nxg6#. And if the pawn doesn't take the queen? Then 2.Qh7+ and 3.Rdg1 will be crushing. Rooks like open files.

Diagram 111

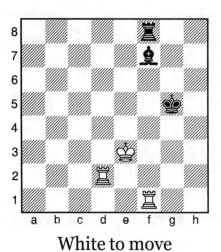

White to move

This problem involves *Zug-zwang*. First, White plays 1.Rg2+ forcing the king to the edge of the board. After 1...Kh6, White plays 2.Rf6+ (if Black had played 1...Kh5, then 2.Rh2#).

Black plays 2...Kh7. In this position (see inset), what should White do? 3.Kf2. All of Black's moves will lose. Think through each one.

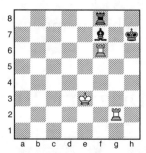

Diagram 112

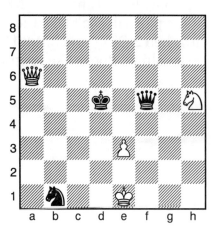

Black to move. Win or lose?

White is threatening 1.Qa5+. The king will have to move to either e4 when there is 2.Ng3+, or to e6 when 2.Ng7+ follows. What can Black do? Look at every queen move. There are 19 of them. All of them fail immediately to forks or captures, except for 1...Qe5. Now after 2.Nf6+ the king has only 2...Kc5. Can you picture it in your head? Here 3.Nd7+ forks the king and queen. Even with the move, Black is losing. This is *Zugzwang*.

Diagram 113

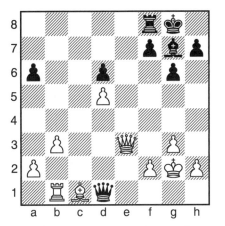

White is ahead a pawn. The king is safe and with two pawns on the queenside, a passed pawn could be created. Is Black winning or losing? 1...Qc2 traps the rook. Black should win then.

Black to move. Win or lose?

Diagram 114

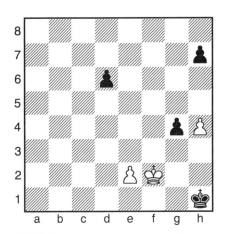

It seems that if Black gets to play ...Kh2 the g-pawn will queen. The only move is 1.Kg3, and then Black plays 1...h5 to protect the pawn. What happens after that? White plays 2.e4 and now Black has to play 2...Kg1. Now White can play 3.e5 because 3...dxe5 is... stalemate! Stalemates happen in the strangest ways.

White to move and draw

Diagram 115

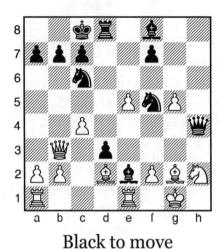

Black to move

1...Qxf2+! then 2.Kxf2 Bc5+ 3.Be3 and now 3...Bxe3#. The knight on f5 and the bishops cover all the important squares.

Diagram 116

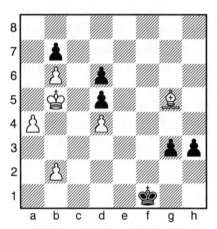

White to move and draw

How does White stop the pawns? How is this a draw? Watch what happens: 1.Bd2. Black can make any move. 2.Ba5. Why that move? Black can make any move. White plays 3.b4 and, no matter what happens, White will have no legal moves. Stalemate. You might think, "Can Black queen a pawn and check the king?" Try it!

Diagram 117

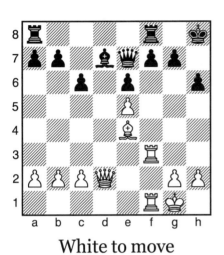

White to move

1.Rf6!!. If 1...gxf6, then 2.Qh6+ Kg8 and 3.Qh7#. What about something like 1...g6? Then 2.Qxh6 and White can slowly go R1f3 and then Rh3, with checkmate soon. Black's queen can play 1...Qc5+ but after 2.Kh1, Black's queen will need to return to e7, otherwise White can play Bxg6 and it will be over.

Diagram 118

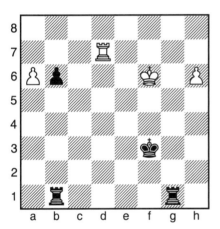

White to move. Win or lose?

White starts with 1.h7. Black must play 1...Rh1 to stop the pawn. Then White plays 2.a7. Black must play 2...Ra1 to stop the pawn. Then White plays 3.Rd1!. If Black tries 3...Raxd1, then 4.a8Q+, or if 3...Rhxd1 then 4.h8Q. A pawn will queen no matter what.

Diagram 119

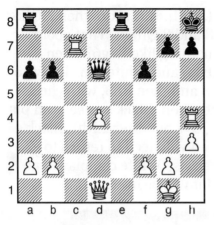

White to move

1.Rxh7+!. Black must play
1...Kxh7 and then 2.Qh5+ Kg8
3.Qf7+ K-any and 4.Qxg7#.

Notice how all of White's pieces
work together to attack on the
seventh rank.

Diagram 120

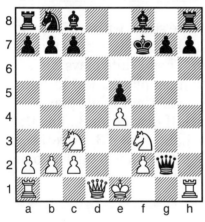

White to move

Black's queen has been grabbing pawns on White's kingside.
How does White take advantage
of that? 1.Rg1. The queen should
just take the rook, but Black could
try 1...Qh3. Do you see what happens next? 2.Ng5+ and the queen
is lost.

Diagram 121

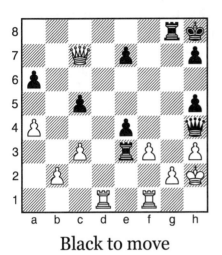

Black to move

Black's pieces seem to have surrounded White's king. How do you break through? 1...Rg2+!. After 2.Kxg2, Black can play 2... Re2+ and White is helpless (3.Rf2 Qxf2+ and mate next move, or 3.Kh1 Qh3+ 4.Qh2 Qxh2#, or 3.Kg1 Qg5+ with mate to follow).

Black was able to exploit weaknesses on White's second rank.

Diagram 122

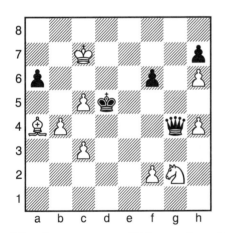

Black to move. Win or lose?

You have seen enough of these problems to start thinking, "Where can Black's queen move to?" (Ne3+ is threatened.) The queen has no safe moves. If 1... Qxg2, then 2.Bc6+ skewers the king and queen. What about 1... Ke5 ? Then 2.f4+ Ke4 3.Bc2+ forces the king back to d5 and Ne3+ wins the queen. If first 1... Ke4, then 2.f3+ Kxf3 3.Bd1+ skewers the king and queen. It is a symphony of skewers and forks.

Diagram 123

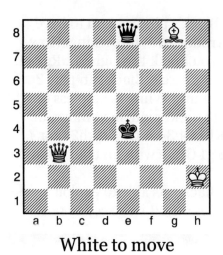

White to move

Study this one carefully: 1.Bh7+. If 1...Ke5, then 2.Qe3+ wins. So, 1...Kd4. After 2.Qb4+ Kd5 we get to the position in the inset below. 3.Bg8+ leads to three different skewers the black king cannot escape: 3...Qxg8 4.Qb3+; 3...Kc6 4.Qa4+; or 3...Ke5 4.Qe1+ skewers and wins. Be very careful in queen endings.

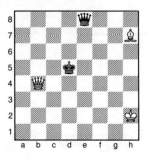

Diagram 124

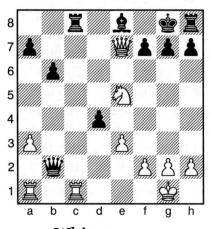

White to move

All moves are forced here and so 1.Qxf7+ Bxf7 2.Rxc8+ Be8 and 3.Rxe8#. The knight on e5 cuts off the king's escape; that happens in many problems like this one.

Diagram 125

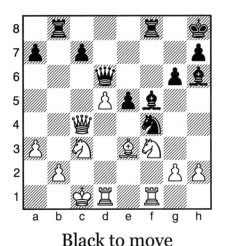

Black to move

This is a great problem. The main idea of it involves deflection. Think about 1...Qb6. Why that move? In a strange way, it threatens both the bishop on e3 and ...Qb2#. Can't White just play 2.Bxb6??? No: 2...Ne2# with double check and there are no flight squares.

Diagram 126

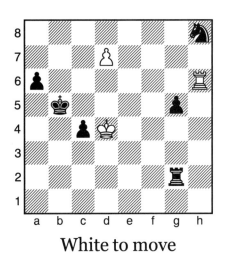

White to move

How does White win this? If 1.d8Q is tried, then 1...Rd2+ skewers the king and queen. But 1.Rb6+!. If 1...Kxb6 then 2.d8Q+ (it's check!) and the knight is lost. There are two king moves: 1...Ka4 and then 2.d8Q, and now if 2...Rd2+ then 3.Kxc4 with the threat of mate. If 1...Ka5, then 2.Rb2 and after 2...Rxb2 White plays 3.d8Q+ and wins the knight.

Diagram 127

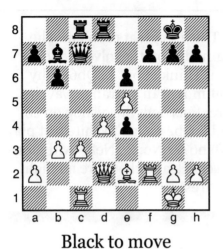

Black to move

There doesn't appear to be much here. However, 1...Qxe5 wins a pawn: 2.dxe5 Rxd2 and Black has a good game. Sometimes there are no giant tactics. The key to this problem is Black's rook on d8 and White's queen across from it. What is between them? The pawn.

This works because White's queen is unprotected.

Diagram 128

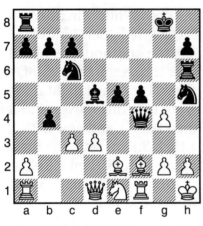

Black to move

Black's pieces are aggressively placed, but where is the break-through? 1...Qxh2+!. White has to play 2.Kxh2 and then Black replies 2...Ng3+!. If White now plays 3.Kxg3, then there is 3...f4#, or 3.Kg1 Rh1#.

You will not learn to see these in games unless you practice them.

Diagram 129

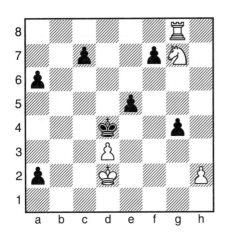

White to move.
Can White stop the a2-pawn?

The answer is yes. The first move is 1.Ne6+. Why? If 1...fxe6, then 2.Rxg4+ and the rook will go to g1 next and stop the pawn. So Black plays 1...Kd5. Now White has the very surprising 2.Nd4!!. If the king takes, then again 3.Rxg4+. Can't Black queen the pawn? 2...a1Q. Hmmm...

Then 3.Rd8+ and the king can only go to c5. Now 4.Nb3+ forks the king and queen. Or if Black captures with the pawn 2...exd4, then 3.Rg5+ Kc6/d6/e6 4.Ra5 stops the a-pawn.

Diagram 130

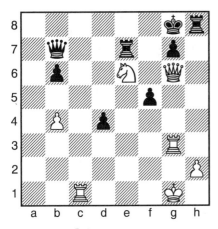

White to move

White is winning, but what is the knockout blow? 1.Rc8+! (deflection). After 1...Qxc8, White plays 2.Qxg7+! Rxg7 3.Rxg7#.

Diagram 131

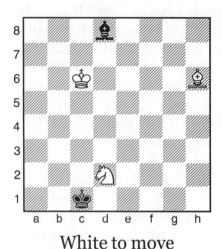

White to move

If you have been reviewing and studying the previous problems, this is an easy one. After 1.Kd7, Black's bishop has no safe moves: If 1...Bh4, then 2.Nf3+; or if 1...Bf6 then 2.Ne4+. On either 1...Bb6 or 1...Ba5, then 2.Nc4+ wins.

Diagram 132

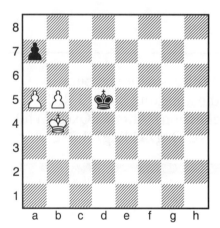

White to move. 1.a6 or 1.b6 ?

The move choice matters, because if 1.b6 then 1...axb6 and if 2.axb6 then 2...Kc6 should draw (keep the opposition). After 1...axb6 White could try 2.a6, but 2...Kc6 keeps the king in the square of the pawn.

After 1.a6, however, White wins. Black plays 1...Kd6 and now 2.b6 by White. If 2...axb6 the a-pawn will queen, while if Black plays 2...Kc6 White can play 3.bxa7 and a pawn will queen.

Diagram 133

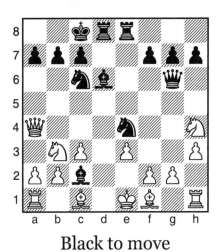

Black to move

This is a tough one. Part of the solution involves visualizing what happens when a piece moves. 1...Qg3!. This threatens 2...Qf2#. Of course White can play 2.fxg3. Then 2...Bxg3+ and White's only move is 3.Ke2. Where is the checkmate? When Black played ...Bxg3+, the rook on d8 suddenly controlled the open file. So now 3...Bd1#.

Diagram 134

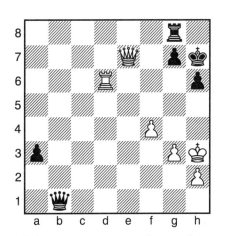

White to move. Win or lose?

Black's pawn on a3 looks dangerous and Black's king seems safe enough. However, 1.Rxh6+! and White wins: 1...Kxh6 2.Qg5+ Kh7 3.Qh5#.

Diagram 135

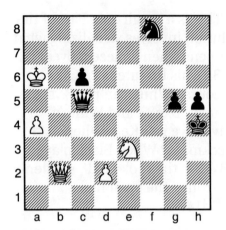

Black to move. Win or lose?

You should have an idea of how to think through this problem. First, you have to know what White's threat is. If it's White's move, 1.d4 attacks the queen and threatens 2.Qh2#. What can Black do? The only real move is 1...g4, making a flight square. Now White plays 2.d4 anyway. Where can the queen go? On 2...Qd6 or 2...Qe7, 3.Nf5+ forks. The only "safe" move is 2...Qg5, and then 3.Qh2#.

Diagram 136

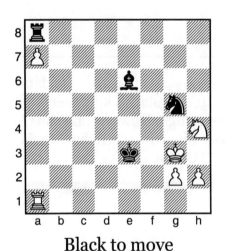

Black to move

White has a pawn on a7 and connected h- and g-pawns. Black has an extra piece. What should happen here? 1...Ne4#.

Now let's move on to Chapter 8.

Chapter 8

Evaluation, Basic Endgames, and Stems

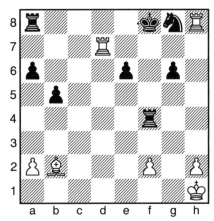

L ast year, I was teaching my beginning students how to evaluate a chess position. This was a position from one of my online games, and I put it on the board:

White to move, how would a computer evaluate the position?

A. Black is one point ahead
B. Black is 2 or more points ahead
C. It's about even
D. White is 1 point ahead
E. White is 2 or more points ahead

Then, I had them discuss the position with a partner and make a decision about what they thought, and I tallied their replies. Roughly 70% of my beginners thought answer "A" was correct. These were students with USCF ratings anywhere from 0 to 500 and who had been playing chess from 1 week to 3 months.

My students had done an excellent job of counting points. Black is 1 point ahead. However, any computer or reasonably strong player will know White is winning, as after 1.Rg7 the game is completely over. The knight will be lost, the rook on a8 will be lost, and there are plenty of checkmates coming.

Chapter 8

The children knew how the pieces moved and some had won trophies at beginners' tournaments. They had solved plenty of one-move checkmates and knew some tactics. Yet, somehow I felt that the ones who had been there a few months should have been able to process this much better and faster. Then it dawned on me that I had not really taught the ideas of "rooks on the seventh (or eighth) rank," "good bishop vs. bad knight," and "important diagonals" very well.

Most books for beginners follow a similar path: "Here is how the queen moves... here is how the knight moves... here is how the rook moves... this is a pin... this is a deflection... this is a one-move checkmate... etc., etc., etc.

Examples tend to be arranged by category and if you study and memorize those categories, you will improve at chess. I agree with that. If you study categorized chess problems, you will get better at chess.

The question is, "Will doing that produce the steepest learning trajectory?" In essence, does studying problems that way allow you to process new and different chess ideas optimally?

You can teach a child a four-move checkmate and various extensions of it, and they will "succeed" in winning some games of chess. They will be happy... for a while. But in the long run that approach becomes detrimental to the learning process. The queen comes out too early and will get kicked around and lost when you face better players. The beginning players who rely on the four-move checkmate simply run out of moves and will give you all their pieces when they can't checkmate you. They will have very little or no interest in learning the endgame. Their joy will turn to sorrow, and either they will have to change how they play or they will quit.

In my chess club, I have had a few students come in who "know" how to play already. They tell you. "I know how to play." At the start of the year, most of my students are beginners, and they can beat the beginners. After a few months, my beginners get better, their store of chess knowledge is bigger, and they start to beat the student who "knew" how to play the game. Intriguingly, I have never had a student who "knew" how to play the game stay in chess once beginners start to beat him or her.

The statistic I have heard is that it takes about 8 times hearing it to learn something and about 28 times to unlearn a bad idea. It is easier for most to quit than to unlearn something.

This places a big premium on learning something right the first time, and in my view there are some problems with how chess is presented to beginners. Here are a few things I find curious about what children *don't* see in chess books:

Evaluation, Basic Endgames, and Stems

1. There are 16 pawns on the board, and pawns – considered "the soul of chess" – are relegated to second-class status. Queening a pawn is important, pawn structures are important, pawns can fork and trap pieces and protect the king. White's a- and b-pawns on the second rank tend to be worth 2 points (there are exceptions). Take those pawns and put them on the sixth rank, and they are an awesome force greater than a rook.

2. The role and interaction of minor pieces. What is a good knight and what is a good bishop? How can you tell? How do major pieces interact with minor pieces?

3. The king, the king, the king. A coward in the opening and middlegame, and a force in the endgame. Kings can fork other pieces, stop the enemy king and pieces from approaching pawns, and chase down enemy pawns with re-markable dexterity.

4. The endgame. I am not talking about whether someone can checkmate with a rook and king vs. a king. Ideas like *Zugzwang* get very little attention, if any at all, and yet a basic understanding of that idea is central to chess thinking. That is, "If I make my move, what can my opponent do?" With an understanding of *Zugzwang*, you know your opponent will lose.

I can see where authors of beginners' chess books have a problem. They have a lot of ideas and they have about 100 to 150 pages to fill with problems.

In the book you are holding in your hands, what you will see is an attempt to create a complex schema, initially, so that students can process higher levels of chess information quicker, with a higher level of success over time.

There is a downside to this and it can best explained by my friend, Tom Crain, who comes to my chess club and helps out. After watching students try-ing to learn many complex ideas at once and then watching them play chess, he pointed out, "They haven't seemed to learn anything." A child learning a new set of complex ideas will not be successful at first.

Last year, after six weeks of practice, I took 8 students to quads for beginners. We lost 22 out of 23 games. (That was 1 more win than I thought we would get...)

After nine months, two of my students were rated over 1000 (a boy and a girl). I had an 8-year-old girl rated over 800. You can check those ratings after nine months against other boys and girls their age. I am very happy with their progress.

Chapter 8

A sufficiently complex schema will eventually become prior knowledge that a child activates when more-challenging information comes in. Whatever concepts you can effectively embed in your chess schema at the start will greatly expedite learning later and throughout the process.

On the next several pages, there is an integration of ideas that are more complicated than just "Queen moves this way... rook moves that way... knight fork... deflection... one-move checkmate... blah, blah, blah." My goal is for students to memorize the answers in order, memorize them when they are mixed up, apply them to similar problems, and use them in games.

Don't get me wrong, there will be one-move checkmates alongside knight forks and other ideas, but there will be very little of the "Here are 50 pins, solve them" variety of exercise.

Why? Two reasons. First, when solving that many problems of the exact same type, the brain develops over-reliance on a pattern. The brain doesn't look for knight forks or blockades when it's looking for something it knows is a pin. A little bit of that is OK, but too much of that creates a cognitive regression where the brain narrows its focus and is not developing the most optimal thought process.

In teaching, I don't say, "Today, we are learning the 'long E' sound. Everybody say the word 'read.' Now we are done with that, let's move on." Students need to see things *multiple times* and *in a variety of contexts*. They need to know initially when the word "read" is read as in, "I am going to read the book today" (long E sound) vs., "I read the book yesterday" (short E sound).

It is true that teaching that way causes more initial confusion. However, by exposing them to the possibilities early on, children will be much better cognitively equipped to handle the increasingly complex demands of reading later.

If there is a broad, far-reaching idea for chess in all these problems, it is this: "Look at the position and develop a habit of looking, not only at how your pieces move, but also at how your opponent's pieces move."

I am for solving problems and for solving lots of them. I like seeing children learning math facts very quickly. I am for the creation of a strong system by which information moves from short-term memory to long-term memory as fast and efficiently as possible. I am for a really, really big store of instantaneously accessible information in rote memory.

However, the initial schema that needs to be created so that children learn chess best must have in it all the ideas that chess is about. That is a challenge.

Secondly, I personally have never had an opponent look at me and say, "I can only use knight forks, so that's all you need to look for." Chess analysis is a spiral of thought whose foundation lies in a series of patterns that can be retrieved *(Perception and Memory in Chess,* A. de Groot & F. Gobet, Netherlands 1996).

To that end, the patterns learned initially should be integrated, and preferably in simple examples.

Some may say there is an incongruity there: the foundations of chess learning should be diverse and integrated, and yet the knowledge of math facts comes before applying it to greater things.

The answer to that is simple. When my students learn chess, they have zero prior knowledge. What they learn on the very first day, the very first week, or the first month will have an impact on them for their entire chess career. In chess, they will have to sit down and solve many chess problems and commit them to memory. However, the initial schema is vitally important.

Third-graders learning a multiplication fact are a different case, because they have been learning math for a while. (Albeit maybe not that successfully if they don't know simple math facts.) They have seen a number line, shapes, word problems, and some addition and subtraction.

In school, the most important year of learning takes place at preschool. (Some would argue that it's what takes place in the years before preschool, but as an educator I can't change that.) The pacing and types of information and how a child learns to process that information will have a profound effect on all subsequent years in school. By the third grade, there is a pretty well-formed schema involving numbers. Adding math facts to rote memory makes the schema stronger and faster.

Having a child who knows nothing about chess solve 100 one-move checkmates will produce some learning. Creating an initial schema that contains the fundamentals of how the chess pieces interact will not only make those 100 problems more meaningful, but it will also greatly decrease the number of one-move checkmates that a child needs to learn.

Let's think our way through this problem:

Chapter 8

Evaluation 1

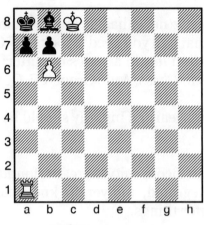

White to move

It is a strange-looking position. White has 16 possible moves. One of those moves will win immediately. We should look at captures and checks, but none of those moves seem very productive (after 1.bxa7, Black plays 1...Bxa7 and it should be a draw). What we need to start doing is asking the following question: "If I make this particular move, what will/can my opponent do?" If White makes any of the moves Ra2, Ra3, Ra4, or Ra5, then Black will play 1...a6. If there is a king move, the bishop moves, or if the rook slides across between b1 and h1, then Black can play 1...axb6 and while Black's position is cramped, there is not much White can do to take advantage of it.

If you have been counting, that leaves one move: 1.Ra6. That seems like a silly move. Black can play 1...bxa6. Ah, but then there is 2.b7#. What else can Black do? Black can move the bishop. After any bishop move, White can play 2.Rxa7#. We have seen positions like this before: 1.Ra6 puts Black in *Zugzwang* (every possible move loses).

To figure out the best move, you needed to look at your opponent's possible moves.

Let's evaluate these positions:

Evaluation 2

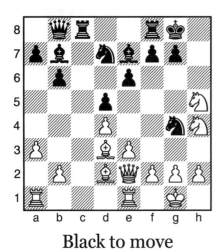

Black to move

Evaluation 3

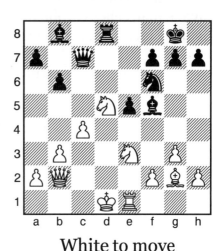

White to move

If you are teaching beginners, these positions will reveal some weaknesses. I will tend to create multiple-choice questions like this for the first problem:

In this position (see Evaluation 2):

a. It is about even
b. White has a slight edge because most of his/her pieces are attacking Black's king
c. Black's rook on the open c-file means Black is slightly better.
d. White is winning
e. Black is winning

You would be amazed at how many students will choose a, b, c, or d. If I have given students a series of two-move checkmates and then give them this problem, they will all get it right and I might think, "These students know the idea." I would be wrong. If they know the idea when you give them a clue but don't know it when there isn't a visual or auditory cue, then they don't know the idea. Of course, 1...Qxh2+ 2.Kf1 Qh1# is the answer.

The next problem (Evaluation 3) is similar. If I ask, "Which piece can White take for free?", they will all get it right. but if I ask, "What's the best move?", many beginners will try 1.Nxc7 and have to be told, "You can't do that because the knight is pinned to the king." 1.Nxf5 wins a piece.

Chapter 8

The idea is to create a thought process that starts with simple moves and spirals outward to think of more complex ideas. All grandmasters do that, but they have so many chess problems in long-term memory that they get through all the simple ideas amazingly fast, almost instantaneously.

Let's try another position. This idea is very important for beginners. When should I trade queens?

Evaluation 4

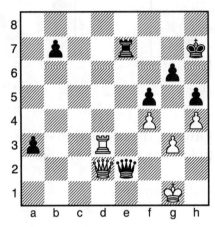

Black to move. Should Black play 1...Qxd2 ?

The first thought should be, "Do I have a checkmate or can I capture a piece for free?"

Those ideas are not possible here. So, should Black play 1...Qxd2 ? What is the thought process behind it? When you are losing, you want to keep your queen on the board as long as possible because it gives you the best chance to turn the game around. If you are clearly winning, then you don't want your opponent to have their queen.

So the question is, "Does Black have a decisive win if the queens are traded?" If Black protects the a- and b-pawns, pushes the pawns forward, and activates the king, Black is completely winning. Set up the position with a partner and see what happens. As long as you are careful, Black should win every single time.

Now we get to a problem which is a little bit more of a challenge:

Evaluation 5

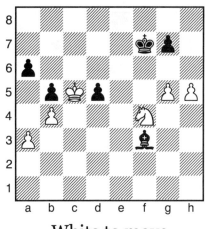

White to move

If I put this diagram on a demonstration board and say to students, "Tell me something you see in this position," I will get many intriguing responses. "Black is winning because the bishop is better than the knight and Black has a passed pawn," or "It's even."

Of course, after White plays 1.h6 the position is completely hopeless for Black. If students didn't see that, what is it that they missed? First, the black king will be tied to the g- and h-files (an outside passed pawn). Second, the pawn on d5 will be taken quickly, and – most importantly – the very active white king and knight will go over and take the a- and b-pawns and then queen White's own a- and b-pawns.

Going over this and playing through it until you have mastered the ideas will create an imprint in your brain, and that imprint will give you confidence when positions like this happen.

Another problem that has a similar idea to the previous one:

Chapter 8

Evaluation 6

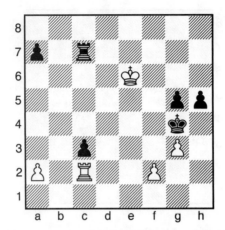

Black to move. What is Black's plan?

On the surface, White's king could be called active and Black's c-pawn is stopped. This would seem very easy, but I have seen students try **1...Rc6+** (just because there is a check doesn't mean it's the best move) **and then move the rook over to the a-file and give up the c-pawn to take the a-pawn. Planless moves turn winning positions into draws and losses.**

The idea that is just crushing is creating the outside passed pawn by moving **1...h4** and then placing the black king on f3. The "active" white king has zero effect on the game. Black has the active king, and the outside passed pawn is decisive because White will have to sacrifice the rook to stop the h-pawn.

Here is another important idea:

Evaluation 7

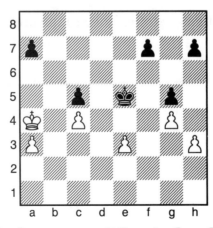

Black to move. What is the plan?

White has a very clear plan. He has just played 1.Ka4 and will take Black's a-pawn and queen his own a-pawn. How many moves will that take?

I count 9 moves. Black could play 1...Kd6 and 2...Kc7, but I have a bad feeling about that.

Black plays 1...f5. Why? When White moved 1.Ka4, the king ended up far away from the kingside. The main line would go something like this: (after 1...f5) 2.gxf5 h5 3.Ka5 (there is no time for the king to go back – if 3.Kb3, then 3...g4 4.hxg4 hxg4 5.Kc3 g3 6.Kd2 g2 7.Ke2 g1Q) 3...g4 4.hxg4 hxg4 5.Ka6 g3 6.Kxa7 g2 7.a4 g1Q. There should be plenty of time for the king and queen to go stop White's pawns, but you should play through it until you master it.

What is the lesson in both of the last two problems? In both cases, the white king seemed "active" but had left the part of the board where it was most needed.

Evaluation 8

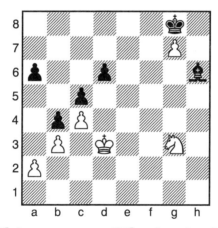

White to move. Who is winning?

I know everyone reading this book is smart. ☺ Smart people think this way: "I have seen something like this before, and what did I learn from it?" This is like Evaluation 5. What would be the important idea? "Useful king activity." So after 1.Ke4 Bxg7 (if 1...Kxg7, then 2.Nf5+ K-moves and 3.Nxg7. Black's king is caught on the other side of the board, and White's king will take all the pawns and queen his own pawns.) Therefore 1...Bxg7 2.Kd5 followed by 3.Nf5 and White will start taking all of Black's pawns, though you should play through it to make sure you see how to do it.

Evaluation 9

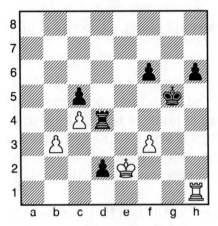

Black to move. Should Black play 1...d1Q ?

Because you are smart, you will know you have seen something like this before. You would like your pawn to queen in a way where it couldn't be taken. Is there a risk in trading off rooks and giving up your d-pawn? So what happens after 1...d1Q+ 2.Rxd1 Rxd1 3.Kxd1? What advantage does Black have? The plan is very simple: 3...Kf4 and push the h-pawn. White's king must try to stop it: 3...Kf4 4.Ke2 h5 5.Kf2 h4 6.Kg2 h3+ 7.Kxh3 and now 7...Kxf3 and Black can race back across the board and gobble up the b-pawn and maybe the c-pawn, queening one of the two remaining black pawns.

That might take 20 moves, but if you have seen the plan and practiced the plan you will be confident in your ultimate success.

Evaluation 10

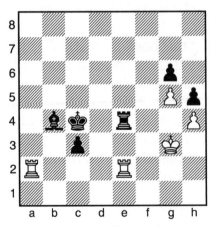

Black to move. Should Black play 1...Rxe2 ?

Evaluation, Basic Endgames, and Stems

You are starting to see a pattern. Many of these decisions in the end of the game come from understanding the strength of your king. A strong king is a powerful weapon. 1...Rxe2 2.Rxe2 and then Black plays 2...Kd3. White's rook is under attack, and Black can safely play ...c3-c2 next. One line could go like this: 1...Rxe2 2.Rxe2 Kd3 3.Re8 c2 4.Rc8 Kd2 5.Rd8+ (what else is there?) 5...Ke1 6.Re8+ Kd1 7.Rd8+ Bd2. No more checks, and the pawn will queen.

We started the process of evaluating positions with some very simple problems. There were a one-move checkmate and a free piece. All good chessplayers scan the board on every move to make sure they haven't missed something simple.

Imagine that someone were to ask you, "How many moves do you see ahead?" If you can understand the elements of a position, you can answer them this way: "Sometimes all I need to see is one move ahead, but in certain positions I can see 20+ moves ahead."

The next part of this chapter deals with basic endgame knowledge. Some ideas come up repeatedly and are worth simply memorizing right away.

Here is one example:

Basic endgame idea 1

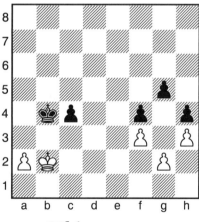

White to move

If you paid attention to the first part of this chapter, the idea to this is very straightforward. White plays 1.a3+. Two responses are possible. If Black plays 1...Ka4, then play goes like this: 2.Kc3 Kxa3 3.Kxc4 Kb2 4.Kd4 Kc2 5.Ke4 Kd2 6.Kf5 Ke2 7.Kxg5 Kf2 8.Kxf4 Kxg2 9.Kg4 and White has protected the h-pawn, while the f-pawn can queen. The king wins the race to the other side of the board. Or Black can play 1...Kc5 instead and then 2.Kc3, K-any 3.a4 and whenever Black's king takes the a-pawn, White will gobble up the c-pawn and win the race to the other side of the board. The outside passed pawn doesn't always win, but it is a big advantage.

Basic endgame idea 2

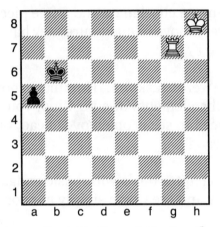

White to move. Is 1.Rg5 or 1.Rg6+ the best move?

This idea behind this one is easy, but if you have never seen the problem you might miss it. White plays 1.Rg5 (1.Rg6+ merely draws). After 1.Rg5, Black's king cannot help the pawn. If Black were to simply play mindless king moves, White's king could walk down the h-file to h2 and then across the board to the a-file and simply pick up the pawn.

After 1.Rg5 a4 2.Kh7 a3 3.Rg3 a2, now 4.Ra3 wins the pawn and the game. If you move Black's king and pawn forward one square from the starting position, the game is a draw. Notice how 1.Rg6+ pushes the king forward one square. The check makes the king a better piece, while 1.Rg5 restricts the king.

Basic endgame idea 3

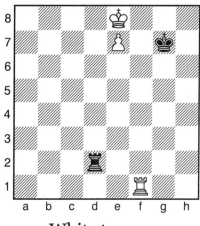

White to move

Every book on chess should have this ending in it, as it has a big idea. Many rook endings come down to a position like this, and if you know what to do, you win. The pattern is about checking Black's king so that it is two files away from the pawn, so 1.Rg1+. Black could try 1...Kf6 but now 2.Kf8 and the pawn queens. After 1.Rg1+, Black's king moves to the h-file (1...Kh8/h7/h6) 2.Rg4 any 3.Kf7 Rf2+ 4.Ke6 Re2+ 5.Kf6 Rf2+ 6.Ke5 Re2+ 7.Re4 and the pawn queens. This does not work on the a- and h-files, but it is very important to know how to do this.

Basic endgame idea 4

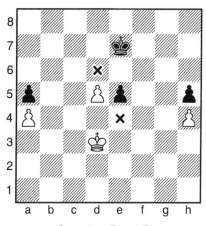

What is the idea?

We have seen this idea before, but somehow in king-and-pawn endings, people can forget very basic things. The idea is, "Whoever moves to the square marked with an "X" will lose." If White moves 1.Ke4, then Black plays 1...Kd6 and suddenly White has to give up the d-pawn. If White plays 1.Ke3 and Black plays 1...Kd6, then White plays 2.Ke4 and Black must lose the e-pawn.

Basic endgame idea 5   Basic endgame idea 5a

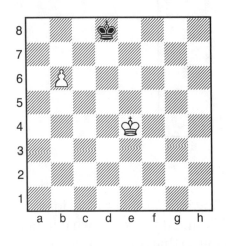
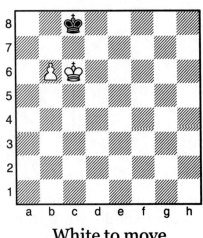

White to move

White knows that if the position gets to 5a and it's Black's move, then White wins, while if it is White's move it is a draw. The plan is pretty easy: **1.Kd5 Kd7 2.Kc5** and now Black has only bad choices. If **2...Kc8 3.Kc6** and White wins. However, if **2...Kd8 3.Kd6 Kc8 4.Kc6** and White still wins. This has been mentioned before, but it is an idea called "the opposition." The big idea is to make it your opponent's move.

Here are two more problems which will help with the idea of the opposition:

Basic endgame idea 6   Basic endgame idea 7

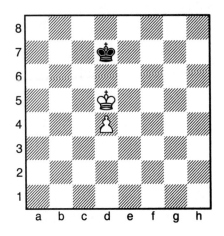

Evaluation, Basic Endgames, and Stems

There doesn't appear to be a big difference between these problems, but looks are deceiving. In Basic endgame 6, it does not matter whose move it is: White wins. We can try that out. Let's say Black moves first: 1...Kc8 2.Ke7 and White will march the d-pawn down the board safely. Or 1...Ke8 2.Kc7 with the same result.

If it is White's move: 1.Ke6 (or 1.Kc6) and the black king plays 1...Ke8 (or 1...Kc8 and 2.Ke7 wins). Now 2.d6 and suddenly it is Black's move and after 2...Kd8 3.d7 Kc7 4.Ke7 the pawn will queen.

How is Basic endgame 7 different? If it is Black's move, White wins: 1...Kc7 2.Ke6 Kd8 3.Kd6 Kc8 (or 3...Ke8) and 4.d5 Kd8, and we have reached Diagram 6, with White winning.

But if White has to move in Diagram 7, it should be a draw: 1.Ke5 Ke7 2.d5 Kd7 3.Kd4 Kd6 4.Ke4 Kd7 5.Ke5 Ke7 6.d6 Kd7 7.Kd5. Now we are at Black's most important move. 7...Kd8 (7...Kc8 and 7...Ke8 both lose because of either 8.Kc6 or 8.Ke6, getting the opposition and winning). After 7...Kd8, White can only hope that Black makes a mistake when 8.Ke6 or 8.Kc6 is tried. As long as every time White plays Ke8 or Kc8 Black replies ...Ke6 or ...Kc6 respectively, then it is a draw. White has nothing better than to eventually push the pawn to d7 and then, after ...Kd8, White must abandon the pawn or else play Kd6 with stalemate.

That all seems long and complicated, and you might think, "How can I master that?"

Get an opponent, a clock, and a board and pieces. Set up Diagram 7 and put one minute on the clock. First, make it White to move and see how often Black can draw. Make sure, when White's pawn is on d6 and White's king goes to e6 or c6, that Black's king mirrors it by moving to e8 or c8. On all other moves, Black's king can just play ...Kd7 and ...Kd8. If White moves to e6 or c6, Black follows. What happens if White moves to Kc5 and the black king is on d8? Should Black then move over to c8? *No!!!!!!!!!!* In that case, White will play Kc6 and it will be Black's move, and so Black will lose.

Take turns and go back and forth, trying to hold the draw. This is one you must know with absolute certainty.

Basic endgame idea 8

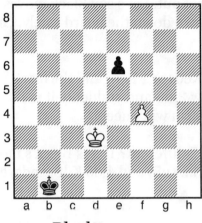

Black to move

Can Black save the pawn? There are really two choices, 1...Kb2 or 1...Kc1. One move draws and the other one loses. There have been enough problems where you should be able to figure this one out: 1...Kc1 2.Ke4 Kd2 3.Ke5 Ke3 and, after 4.Kxe6 Kxf4, it's a draw.

Basic endgame idea 9

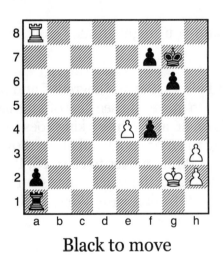

Black to move

Basic endgame idea 9a

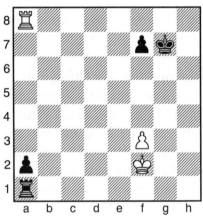

Black to move

To solve Basic endgame 9, let's look at 9a. 1...Rh1 creates two threats. First, if White doesn't take the a-pawn, Black will queen it. So White plays 2.Rxa2, but then 2...Rh2+ skewers the king and rook.

Evaluation, Basic Endgames, and Stems

Back to Diagram 9. What can Black do? 1...f3+ and White can't do anything. For example, 2.Kxf3 Rf1+ and the pawn will queen (and also protect the rook on f1). White could try 2.Kf2, but then there's 2...Rh1 and we are more or less back at Diagram 9a. Black's rook is not in a good position, but White's king was in a worse place. There was no way to escape the checks.

Basic endgame idea 10

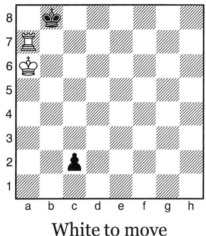

White to move

While White has the move, how can he stop the pawn?? 1.Rb7+ Kc8 and now what? 2.Rb5!! and if 2...c1Q, then 3.Rc5+ Qxc5 is stalemate!.

In almost every problem in this chapter, the position of the king relative to the other pieces was really important. There are many more basic endgame problems. What needs to happen now is for you to see how some of these basic endgame ideas can get used in more complex endgames. In education terminology, there is a base of prior knowledge, and we are going to connect it to practical examples. I call those examples "stems," and I am sure there are other terms for it.

As we look at the stems, the goal is to figure out what basic ideas will be involved. There is some evaluation and some of the problems may look like some of the first problems in this chapter, and that's because they are. In most of these positions, the plan is clear-cut.

Chapter 8

Stem 1

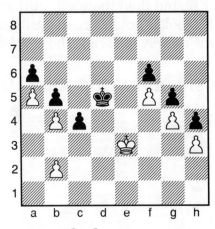

Black to move

This is simple: 1...Ke5 and White's king is forced to give way. On either 2.Kf2 or 2.Kf3, Black can play 2...Kd4 3.Ke2 c3 4.b3 (4.bxc3+ Kxc3 and the king will take the b- and a-pawns and then queen his own b- and a-pawns) 4...c2 5.Kd2 c1Q+ 6.Kxc1 Kc3, and all of White's queenside pawns fall. If 1...Ke5 2.Ke2 Ke4 3.Kd2 Kf3, and Black will grab all the kingside pawns. 1...Ke5 2.Kd2 Kd4 3.Kc2 Ke3 again grabs all the kingside pawns.

So 1...Ke5 gets the opposition and drives the white king backwards, and Black will end up taking White's pawns. If we imagine that White's king started out on d4 and Black's king on d6, then White's king would be able to swing between Kd4 and Ke4 and no one could make progress.

Stem 2

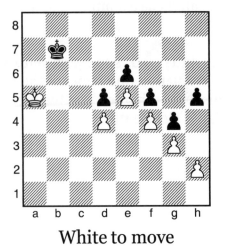

White to move

Just as in the last example, the kings' position and whose move it is means a lot. If it is Black's move, 1...Ka7 2.Kb5 Kb7 3.Ka5 Ka7 4.Kb5 Kb7. If White tries to get tricky and maybe plays 4.Kb4, then Black can reply 4...Kb6 or 4...Kb8 (but not 4...Kb7, because then White plays 5.Kb5 and gets the opposition).

White to move, play goes 1.Kb5 Kc7 2.Kc5 Kd7 3.Kb6 Ke7 4.Kc6 followed by 5.Kd6, and Black's e-pawn will fall, followed by the d-pawn and White will queen.

With the opposition, White's king penetrates and wins.

Stem 3

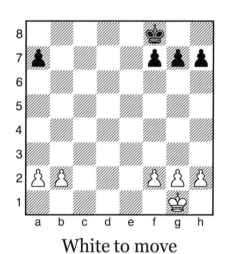

White to move

The win is there, and it should be easy. I show it on a demonstration board and have students practice the idea against each other without a clock. Again, these are absolute beginners who know how the pieces move, know some tactics, and have been to one or two beginners' tournaments.

Then, after they have practiced it against each other once as White and once as Black, they use a clock and set it for 3 minutes. The goal for White is to checkmate the king. Then as a coach, you watch train wreck after train wreck. You see students win as Black and see students stalemate someone in K+Q vs. K endgames. It is amazing some of the things that can go wrong.

Do the students know to centralize the king? Yes. Do they know how to use the diversion of creating an outside passed pawn by using the a- and b-pawns? Yes. Can they checkmate with the K+Q vs. K? Yes! Can they do it all at once, right away? *No!*

However, with practice they all eventually get it, and there is somewhere in their brains a form of what an endgame is, and there is connectivity within that form.

Chapter 8

With tactics and checkmates, that connectivity is generated by embedding simple material within slightly more complex material. With endgames, that connectivity is generated by showing students the form of how endgames go from the beginning of the endgame to the end – the absolute end.

Stem 4

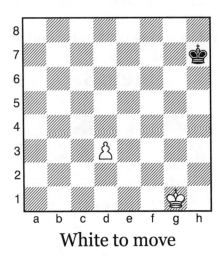

White to move

If you are a student trying to learn chess, what I would like you to do is think about this: "Where will the pieces be in four moves?" Make a diagram and write down some reasons why you think so. What is the plan?

This problem contains a number of really good ideas. The king should be in front of a pawn, and kings move diagonally and forward at the same time. The opposition comes into play here. Is the pawn able to simply queen? (Is the black king in the square of the pawn?) Many beginners will push the pawn and hope it queens... and sometimes it will!

Stem 4a

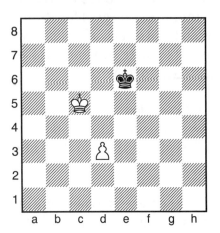

Stem 4b

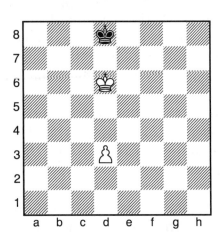

If, in your mind, you can picture the position getting from Diagram 4 to 4a and then from 4a to 4b, you have put all the right ideas together. Once you can get the white king to d6 and with a couple spare pawn moves, it's over. There are some different possibilities in there, but the first part is very important: get the king in front of the pawn. Push the pawn first, and it should be a draw.

From there you get to this:

Stem 4c

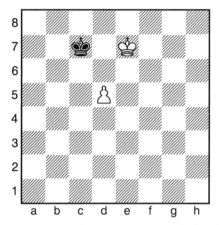

Now it's pushing the pawn , getting a queen, and checkmating your opponent.

Now for another idea:

Stem 5

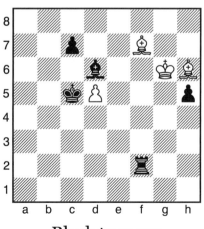

Black to move

Chapter 8

Black is winning, but with two bishops and a pawn on d5 this could take a while. What should Black do? After 1...Rxf7 2.Kxf7 Kxd5, the whole board has changed. White's king will be behind both black pawns. Black's king and bishop can escort their pawns. What will happen? Eventually, White will sacrifice his bishop to stop one of the pawns and the other pawn will queen. If you count only points, you have given up a 5-point rook for a bishop and a pawn (4 points). However, White has 0 chance to save the game. Try it with a partner and see how hopeless White's position is after 1...Rxf7.

Stem 6

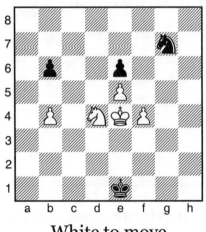

White to move

White has several ways to win this, but there is one really fast way, and the idea behind it is important. Part of Black's problem is that his king is completely out of play. What should White do to take advantage of that?

1.Nxe6 is devastating. The idea is that connected pass pawns are a force. After Black plays 1...Nxe6, White can play 2.f5 and the king and two pawns will completely dominate the knight. Play through it yourself and try to stop the king and two pawns. By itself, the knight has no chance.

There are millions of chess problems, but in this chapter we learned to evaluate key ideas, memorize basic facts, and put those facts to use in more challenging problems. You will encounter all these ideas many times in your games of chess.

Chapter 9

The Active King

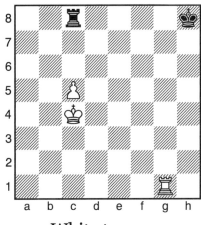

White to move

The king is a mysterious piece. At the beginning of the game, the goal is king safety. If you bring your king out to the middle of the board too soon, you will be checkmated. There comes a point, though, when the king becomes a powerhouse on the chessboard.

What would you do in the above example? Many new students might think, "1.Rh1+" and check the king around for a few moves to see what happens. Maybe Black will walk into a skewer and you can win the rook. More likely, that idea will move Black's king toward the pawn, and you will end up with a draw.

One idea is that White's rook is keeping the black king under lock and key. *Don't let the king out!* Checking Black's king toward the pawn is a bad idea.

White's king is active. 1.Kb5 Rb8+ 2.Kc6 Rc8+ 3.Kb6 Rb8+ 4.Kc7. The pawn will move forward next, and the king and pawn defeat the rook. White's active king dominated the board, while Black's king was stuck.

The next few games are battles where active kings win the day. Pay careful attention to the how and when of making a king active.

Chapter 9

Game 1

Eduard Gufeld vs. Lubomir Kavalek
Marianske Lazne 1962

1.e4 e5 2.Nf3 Nc6 3.Bb5 Bc5 4.c3 f5 5.d4 fxe4 6.Ng5 Bb6 7.d5 e3 8.Ne4 Qh4 9.Qf3 Nf6 10.Nxf6 gxf6 11.dxc6 exf2+ 12.Kd1 dxc6 13.Be2 Be6 14.Qh5 Qxh5 15.Bxh5 Ke7 16.b3 Bd5 17.Ba3 Ke6 18.Bg4+ f5 19.Bh3 Rhg8 20.Nd2 Bxg2 21.Bxg2 Rxg2 22.Rf1 Rd8 23.Ke2 Rxd2+ 24.Kxd2 e4 25.Bf8 f4 26.b4 Rg5 27.Bc5:

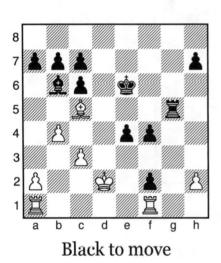

Black to move

A strange game so far. It will get a little stranger. Black can take White's bishop two different ways. Black plays 27...Rxc5. Why? The important square is e3 and if 27...Bxc5 28.bxc5 Rxc5, Black's pawns will have a hard time moving forward. If Black were to ever play ...f4-f3, White could respond Ke3 and the pawns would be blockaded. Black's plan is to use the king and bishop to keep White's pieces away.

27...Rxc5 28.bxc5 Bxc5 29.Rab1 f3 30.Rb4:

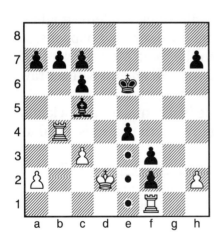

Look at the three dots. They form a wall. What happens if Black plays 30...Bxb4 ? Then 31.cxb4 and White's king gets to e3 and should win. The control of e3 is too important. What is Black's next move? 30...Kf5. It is headed to f4, where it can control e3 and then push the pawns forward. This simple king activation decides the game.

30...Kf5 31.Rd4 Bxd4 32.cxd4:

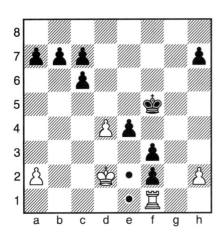

If it were White to move, White would play Ke3 and win. Black had thought this through and knew he would play ...Kf4 first and then control e3. From there, the pawns march forward. White can sacrifice his rook, but Black will have many extra pawns and win.

This king activation involved simply moving two squares to the correct place, where it dominated the board.

32...Kf4, **White resigns**

Game 2

Carl Schlechter vs. Arthur Kaufmann
Vienna 1916

1.d4 d5 2.c4 e6 3.Nc3 c6 4.Nf3 Nd7 5.e4 dxe4 6.Nxe4 Ngf6 7.Bd3 b6 8.0-0 Bb7 9.Qe2 Be7 10.Bf4 Nxe4 11.Bxe4 Nf6 12.Bc2 0-0 13.Rad1 Qc8 14.Bg5 Re8 15.Ne5 c5 16.Bxf6 Bxf6 17.Bxh7+ Kf8 18.Be4 cxd4 19.f4 Bxe4 20.Qxe4 Rd8 21.Rd3 Qc7 22.g4 g6 23.g5 Bg7 24.Rfd1 Rac8 25.Rxd4 Qc5 26.Kg2 Rxd4 27.Rxd4 Bxe5 28.Qxe5 Qxe5 29.fxe5 Ke7:

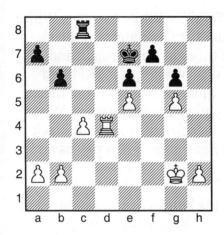

White is a pawn ahead. Rook-and-pawn endings can be very drawish. As you play through the rest of this, think of the first example of the chapter. White wants to activate his king, while keeping Black's king away.

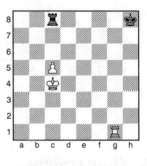

30.Kf3 Rh8 31.h4 Rc8 32.Ke4 Rc5 33.b4 Rc8 34.Kd3 Rc7 35.Kc3 Rc8 36.Kb3 Rc7 37.Ka4 Rc8 38.Kb5 Ke8 39.Ka6 Rc7:

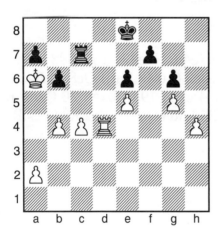

White's king has moved all the way across the board and Black's king – well, Black's king has been trapped on the kingside. The game isn't over yet, because White has to make a plan. That plan is to create a passed pawn.

The king will still have a few more moves to make as it coordinates with the pawns.

40.a4 Ke7 41.a5 bxa5 42.Kxa5 Rc6 43.c5 Rc7 44.Ka6 Ke8 45.Kb5 Rc8 46.c6 Rc7:

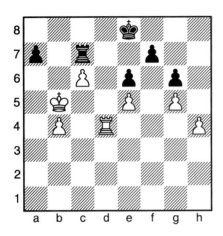

White now has a passed pawn and Black's king... is still stuck on the kingside. The question is, "Is White's rook doing anything?" The answer is, "Yes, it is keeping Black's king away." That is very important.

This is because White has a very smart rook and that rook knows, "My king and advanced pawn can beat Black's rook."

White's rook remembers the first diagram.

47.Kc5 Rc8 48.b5 Rc7:

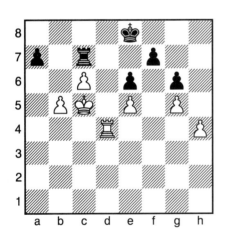

After 49.b6 axb6 50.Kxb6, what will this position resemble? A much easier version of the original diagram, because the pawn is one more square forward. White's rook's job was to shut Black's king out.

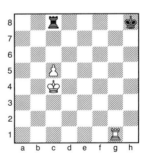

49.b6, Black resigns

Chapter 9

Game 3

Ruslan Ponomariov vs. Alexander Morozevich
Tal Memorial 2006

1.e4 c5 2.Nf3 d6 3.d4 cxd4 4.Nxd4 Nf6 5.Nc3 a6 6.Be3 e6 7.g4 d5 8.g5 Ne4 9.Nxe4 dxe4 10.Qg4 Nd7 11.0-0-0 Qa5 12.Nb3 Qf5 13.Qg3 Be7 14.h4 Qf3 15.Qh2 Qf5 16.Bg2 0-0 17.Qc7 Bd8 18.Qc4 Bb6 19.Bxe4 Bxe3+ 20.fxe3 Qe5 21.Qd4 Rb8 22.h5 b6 23.h6 g6 24.Nd2 b5 25.Nf3 Qxd4 26.exd4 Rb6 27.Rhf1 b4 28.Rde1 a5 29.Ne5 Nxe5 30.dxe5 Rb5 31.Bd3 Rc5 32.Rf4 Bb7 33.Rc4 Rfc8 34.Rxc5 Rxc5 35.Kd2 Rd5 36.Re4 Kf8 37.c4 Rc5 38.Re3 Ke7 39.b3 Kd8 40.Be4 Bc8 41.Bf3 Kc7:

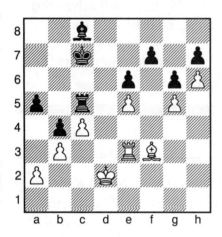

Material is "even," but White's pawns are stronger. Black's kingside pawns are all on light squares. With bishops of the same color, White's bishop can attack the pawns. Black's bishop cannot attack White's kingside pawns.

The bigger question is, "How does White make progress?"

42.Kd3 Kb6 43.Ke4 Rc7 44.Rd3 Rd7 45.Rd6+ Kc5:

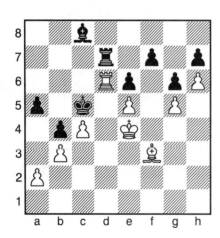

It is decision time for White. What about 46.Rxd7 ? Black will play 46...Bxd7, and then what can White do? White doesn't seem to be getting in.

White plays 46.Kf4. Why? Think of every possible move for Black: The king can't move. If the bishop moves, White plays Rxd7, and if the rook moves, White will play Rd8 and win the h7-pawn. Black has to trade rooks. Why is that so bad? Let's see.

46.Kf4 Rxd6 47.exd6 Kxd6:

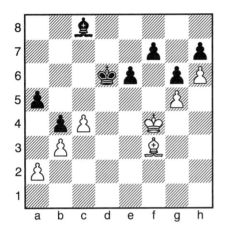

White saw this a few moves ago. White really wants to get his king to e5 and then go after Black's kingside pawns. How does he get in? 48.c5+. For one pawn, White's king gains entrance to the kingside. Is it worth it?

48.c5+ Kxc5 49.Ke5 Ba6 50.Kf6 Kd6 51.Be4 Be2 52.Kxf7 Bg4:

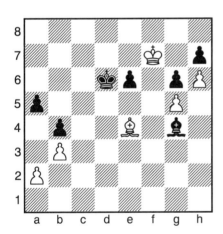

The king has now penetrated the kingside. There is nothing Black's bishop can do to White's kingside pawns. Good tactics come from good strategy, and because White's king is so strong, and the bishop is well placed, there is a promotion tactic: 53.Bxg6 and now it is over. Black can try 53...hxg6, but 54.h7 and h8Q will be unstoppable.

Sometimes you give up material to gain entry for the king. The king is a weapon.

53.Bxg6, **Black resigns**

Chapter 9

Game 4

Michelet vs. Kieseritzky
Paris 1845

1.e4 e5 2.f4 exf4 3.Nf3 g5 4.Bc4 g4 5.Ne5 Qh4+ 6.Kf1 f3 7.d4 Nf6 8.Nc3 Bg7 9.g3 Qh3+ 10.Kf2 d6 11.Nxf7 Rf8 12.Ng5 Qg2+ 13.Ke3 Bh6+ 14.Kd3 Nc6 15.a3 Bxg5 16.Bxg5 Ne4 17.Qe1 Bf5+ 18.Ne4 f2 19.Qe3 Kd7 20.Bd5 Rae8 21.Raf1 Bxe4 22.Bxe4 Rf3:

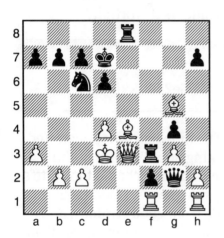

There are many strange things here. For one, White's bishop on e4 is pinned. Black has a pawn on the second rank. White's queen is pinned to the king.

White does have to play 23.Qxf3, but there is something White saw that I am not sure Black saw: Black's queen will get trapped and that allows White's king to move slowly up the board. Black will be trying to free his queen.

23.Qxf3 gxf3 24.Bf5+ Re6:

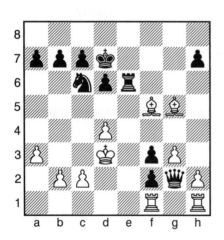

White's king hasn't moved again, but it will soon. In two moves, the whole game has changed. Black's rook is pinned and the queen has no moves.

Should White play 25.Bxe6+ ? *No!!* 25.d5 attacks the pinned piece. Watch that pawn carefully.

25.d5 Ne5+ 26.Ke4 h5 27.dxe6+ Ke8 28.Bf6:

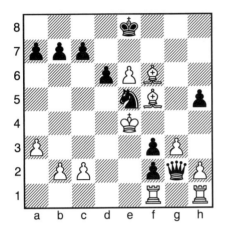

Black is trying to free the queen by rushing the h-pawn down the board to break things open.

White's king is moving closer and closer to the goal. Where does the king want to be?

28...h4 29.Bxe5 dxe5 30. Kxe5 hxg3:

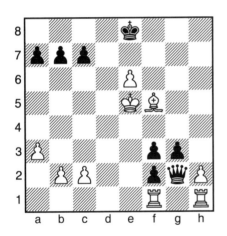

Black's queen will be free next move, and so is White panicking?

The king slides over to f6 and the e-pawn will queen. There is a checkmate, too. See if you can find it.

Go back and look at the first diagram. As pieces were traded off, the king became stronger and stronger.

31.Kf6, **Black resigns**

Chapter 9

Game 5

Nigel Short vs. Jan Timman
Tilburg 1991

1.e4 Nf6 2.e5 Nd5 3.d4 d6 4.Nf3 g6 5.Bc4 Nb6 6.Bb3 Bg7 7.Qe2 Nc6 8.0-0 0-0 9.h3 a5 10.a4 dxe5 11.dxe5 Nd4 12.Nxd4 Qxd4 13.Re1 e6 14.Nd2 Nd5 15.Nf3 Qc5 16.Qe4 Qb4 17.Bc4 Nb6 18.b3 Nxc4 19.bxc4 Re8 20.Rd1 Qc5 21.Qh4 b6 22.Be3 Qc6 23.Bh6 Bh8 24.Rd8 Bb7 25.Rad1 Bg7 26.R8d7 Rf8 27.Bxg7 Kxg7 28.R1d4 Rae8 29.Qf6+ Kg8 30.h4 h5:

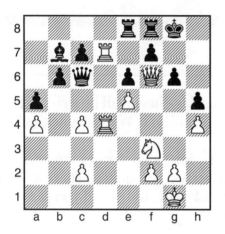

White controls the d-file and has a well- placed queen. There does not appear to be a break-through anywhere. White's knight cannot move or he will be checkmated, and so he needs another piece to join in. Watch...

31.Kh2 Rc8 32.Kg3 Rce8:

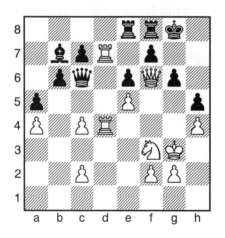

Where is the king headed? You would think, with all the pieces Black has, that this couldn't be a safe journey, but in the last two moves Black's army has not accomplished anything.

The king can operate with complctc safety.

33.Kf4 Bc8:

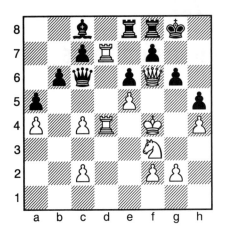

This is just one move later, but since the first diagram, the king has simply marched up the board. It is headed to h6 and from there, Qg7 will be checkmate.

Does this mean that you should rush your king out into danger every game? No. When your pieces are on good squares and you control diagonals and files, you have a chance of involving your king. It took 31 moves of preparation for this to happen.

34.Kg5, **Black resigns**

Chapter 10

Some Ideas from Grandmaster Games

There are many ways to get better at chess, and two of the most important are playing through your own games and learning from your mistakes, and playing through grandmaster games. There are plenty of game collections out there. Sitting down and looking through Bobby Fischer's best games, Capablanca's best games, or Carlsen's best games will give you an idea about what their games look like, the strategies they use, and what mistakes look like at grandmaster level.

This chapter will not have 100 games or attempt to cover all the ideas. There will be 12 games. They will come in pairs. First will be games about castling on opposite sides; White will win a game and then Black will use a counter-strategy to win the game. With the two games involving queenside pawn majorities, Black wins the first game. Then, White will win in both games involving isolated queen pawns (IQP). There will be four games where the knight-vs.-bishop concept is explored, and last are two games about seeing the entire board.

There are many players who will have a vastly greater understanding of these games, but my job is to make sure that, as much as possible, the most basic ideas are explained. Detailed analysis of long series of moves is not what's important here. If you can look at the games and start to see the patterns and look at the broad strategies, you will be headed in the right direction.

In this book, there is no mention of a specific opening. In most of the games in Chapter 6, one side completely misplayed the opening and fell behind in development. That will not be the case in this set of games. If you look carefully at the first 10 moves, most of the games will be fairly even. Look at how the best players create balance in the openings.

These are games that are worth playing through a couple of times and really thinking about why certain moves are made. One thing you can do as you play through a game is to try to think about where the first bad move was. Check out your idea on a computer. On the computer, the bad moves are given in red type. So see how good your instincts are in finding good and bad moves.

Castling on Opposite Sides

Anatoly Karpov vs. Veselin Topalov
Wijk aan Zee 1998 (Blitz)

1.Nf3 f5 2.d4 Nf6 3.Bg5 e6 4.Nbd2 Be7 5.Bxf6 Bxf6 6.e4 0-0 7.Bd3 g6 8.Qe2 Bg7 9.c3 Nc6 10.0-0-0 d5 11.e5 b6 12.h4 h6 13.Rdg1 Ne7 14.g4 f4 15.h5 g5 16.Nxg5 hxg5 17.h6 Bh8 18.Nf3 c5 19.Nxg5 cxd4 20.Bh7#

Visweswaran vs. Ward
2001 Politiken Cup

1.e4 c5 2.Nf3 d6 3.d4 cxd4 4.Nxd4 Nf6 5.Nc3 g6 6.Be3 Bg7 7.f3 Nc6 8.Qd2 0-0 9.0-0-0 Bd7 10.Kb1 Rc8 11.g4 Ne5 12.h4 h5 13.g5 Ne8 14.Nd5 Nc7 15.Nf4 b5 16.b3 a5 17.Be2 b4 18.Nd3 Nxd3 19.Bxd3 d5 20.Qe2 e5 21.Nb5 dxe4 22.Bc4 exf3 23.Qf2 Nxb5 24.Bxb5 Bxb5 25.Rxd8 Rfxd8 26.Bb6 Re8 27.Bxa5 e4 28.Bb6 Re6 29.Be3 Rec6 30.Rd1 Be2 31.Rc1 Be5 32.Bd4 Bf4 33.Be3 Bxe3 34.Qxe3 Bd3, **White resigns**

The first thing to do is to look at both games after a few moves in the opening:

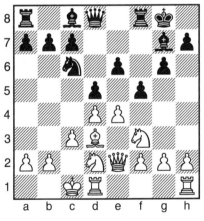

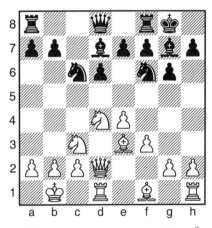

Karpov vs. Topalov   Visweswaran vs. Ward

These positions are slightly different, but they have a common theme: White has castled on the queenside and Black on the kingside.

There is only one plan for White. The g- and h-pawns will get pushed and will crack open the black king. White may sacrifice pieces, because it's a race to get at the opposing king. White's rooks will typically be placed on g1 and h1.

Chapter 10

Black will be trying to attack White's king with either pawns or pieces, and getting rooks to the c-file can be important. Sometimes Black will sacrifice pieces, too. It's like a swordfight, and you must be unafraid to play and also have a short memory for losses. Learn from mistakes and move on.

Let's look at things a few moves later:

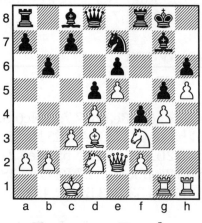

Karpov vs. Topalov

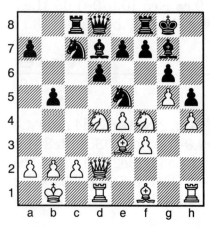

Visweswaran vs. Ward

The g- and h-pawns appear to be blocked in both games. If White doesn't break through, Black usually will.

What does Karpov do?

He sacrifices his knight with 16.Nxg5. Black has to take. Then he brings his other knight into the fray (Nd2-f3-g5). Notice that as Black's g- and h-pawns disappear, White's rooks look very strong.

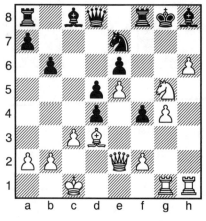

Karpov vs. Topalov

Some Ideas from Grandmaster Games

What's the final move? ... Do you see it? I'm not telling.

The other game lasted a few moves longer and White was unable to break through on the kingside. This gave Black the chance to line up all his forces and break through.

We will see a diagram after 25 moves and then on the last move of the game.

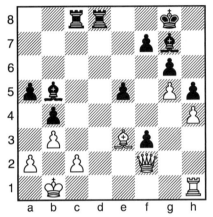

Visweswaran vs. Ward
(After move 25)

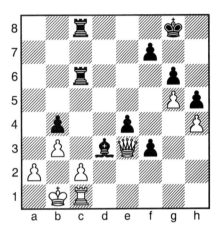

Visweswaran vs. Ward
(After 34...Bd3)

Black sacrificed his queen for a rook and a bishop plus a pair of connected passed pawns in the center. He looked for the best pressure point (c2) and lined up his pieces to attack it. Look at White's h- and g-pawns: they ended up blocking White's pieces. Why did White resign after 34...Bd3? Because of 35.cxd3 Rxc1+ 36.Qxc1 Rxc1+ 37.Kxc1 f2 and Black's f-pawn will queen.

Queenside Pawn Majorities

Frank J. Marshall vs. José Raúl Capablanca
New York 1909

1.d4 d5 2.c4 e6 3.Nc3 c5 4.cxd5 exd5 5.Nf3 Nc6 6.g3 Be6 7.Bg2 Be7 8.0-0 Nf6 9.Bg5 Ne4 10.Bxe7 Qxe7 11.Ne5 Nxd4 12.Nxe4 dxe4 13.e3 Nxf3+ 14.Nxf3 exf3 15.Qxf3 0-0 16.Rfc1 Rab8 17.Qe4 Qc7 18.Rc3 b5 19.a3 c4 20.Bf3 Rfd8 21.Rd1 Rxd1+ 22.Bxd1 Rd8 23.Bf3 g6 24.Qc6 Qe5 25.Qe4 Qxe4 26.Bxe4 Rd1+ 27.Kg2 a5 28.Rc2 b4 29.axb4 axb4 30.Bf3 Rb1 31.Be2 b3 32.Rd2 Rc1 33.Bd1 c3 34.bxc3 b2 35.Rxb2 Rd1 36.Rc2 Bf5 37.Rb2 Rc1 38.Rb3 Be4+ 39.Kh3 Rc2

239

40.f4 h5 41.g4 hxg4+ 42.Kxg4 Rh2 43.Rb4 f5 44.Kg3 Re2 45.Rc4 Re3 46.Kh4 Kg7 47.Rc7 Kf6 48.Rd7 Bg2 49.Rd6 Kg7, **White resigns**

Alexander Alekhine vs. Max Euwe
World Championship Match (Game 1) 1935

1.d4 d5 2.c4 c6 3.Nf3 Nf6 4.Nc3 dxc4 5.a4 Bf5 6.Ne5 Nbd7 7.Nxc4 Qc7 8.g3 e5 9.dxe5 Nxe5 10.Bf4 Nfd7 11.Bg2 Be6 12.Nxe5 Nxe5 13.0-0 Be7 14.Qc2 Rd8 15.Rfd1 0-0 16.Nb5 Rxd1+ 17.Rxd1 Qa5 18.Nd4 Bc8 19.b4 Qc7 20.b5 c5 21.Nf5 f6 22.Ne3 Be6 23.Bd5 Bxd5 24.Rxd5 Qa5 25.Nf5 Qe1+ 26.Kg2 Bd8 27.Bxe5 fxe5 28.Rd7 Bf6 29.Nh6+ Kh8 30.Qxc5, **Black resigns**

You might wonder, "Were these players from 1909 or 1935 any good?" or, "How would they do today?"

Today, we have very strong computers to guide our analysis. In getting ready for this book, I ran the games through a computer to see if there were giant errors. In the first game, Capablanca played smoothly from beginning to end. I could not find a significant error he made. In general, the mistakes Marshall made were fairly small. What Capablanca did was to slowly accumulate small advantages. He transitioned from the opening to the middlegame, and then from the middlegame to the endgame, seemingly without effort.

I think if Capablanca played today, he would be one of the top players in the world and maybe world champion. His games are studied by all the top players.

This game revolves around an idea, "How do you handle a 3-on-2 queenside pawn majority?" Here are diagrams from the openings.

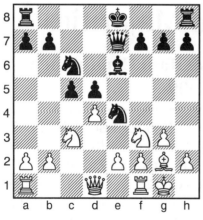

Marshall vs. Capablanca

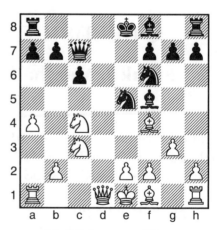

Alekhine vs. Euwe

Some Ideas from Grandmaster Games

One thing worth knowing is that the Marshall–Capablanca game was played 26 years before Alekhine–Euwe. You might wonder, "Had Alekhine seen that game?" I don't know for a fact, but I am guessing Alekhine and Euwe knew most if not all of Marshall's and Capablanca's games. Great players study other great players' games to get better. Alekhine knew how Capablanca had won and was already taking preventive measures to stop Black's pawn majority. Alekhine knew that if Black had all day, his three queenside pawns would come down and eventually create a passed pawn and give Black winning chances.

Let's see the games a few moves further on:

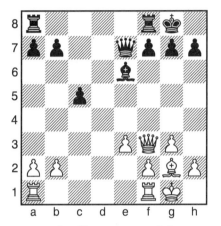

Marshall vs. Capablanca

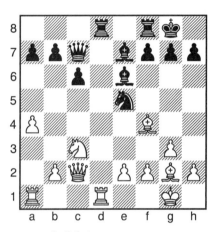

Alekhine vs. Euwe

The strategy is set for both games. In the Capablanca game, Black's pieces are ideally placed to start pushing the queenside pawns forward. In the Alekhine game, White will start something called a "minority attack." That is when two pawns break apart three pawns and leave them unable to have an effect.

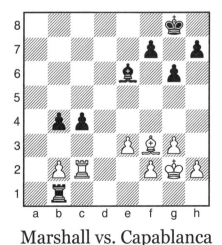

Marshall vs. Capablanca

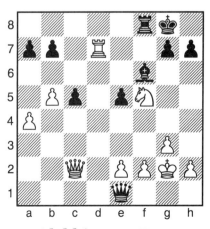

Alekhine vs. Euwe

You can start to see a real difference. Capablanca's pawns have safely moved forward and are supported by the bishop. His rook is causing problems behind White's pawn.

Alekhine has completely stopped Black's pawns and has a rook on the seventh rank. Black's queen looks dangerous, but it needs another piece to really make something happen.

Now we look at the final positions:

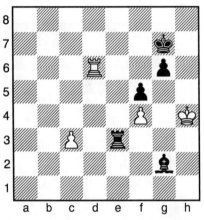

Marshall vs. Capablanca

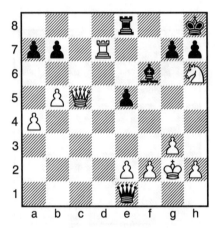

Alekhine vs. Euwe

In Capablanca's game, he was able to force White to give up his bishop to stop a pawn from queening. Just because you are a piece ahead, doesn't mean you win or that your opponent will quit.

For beginners, Capablanca did something very important. He never let the c-pawn come close to queening. The surest way to lose a won game is to ignore your opponent's pawns. Look at Black's moves 36 and 37. White's rook and pawn get stuck, and Black simply uses small advantages. There are no big tactics, just smooth, precise play.

The question is, "Why does Marshall resign at this point?"

He is going to be checkmated, and he knows it. See if you can find it.

In the Alekhine game, it is White to play. What is the winning move? With White's final move, 30.Qc5, he had attacked the rook, and for the sake of thinking about White's next move, I put Black's rook on e8. It could have just as easily been placed on b8 or a8. What will White do?

The idea is Qc4!. If Black plays ...gxh6, then White plays Qf7 and checkmate is unstoppable. On any other move by Black, White will play Qg8+ then ...Rxg8 and Nf7# ("smothered mate").Two awesome games by two of the greatest players of all time.

What are some lessons we can learn from these games?

1. Study the games of great players from all time periods.
2. When both kings are castled kingside and there is a 3-on-2 pawn majority on the queenside, that side is where much of the strategy will be.
3. Rooks on the seventh/second rank are dangerous.
4. Connected pawns become more dangerous the further they move ahead.
5. Some chess games end quickly, but top-level players are willing to sit and think, looking for small advantages. Chess requires patience. Games can last 5 or 6 hours.

Isolated Queen Pawns

In many openings, either White or Black will end up with an isolated queen pawn (or d-pawn). How do you know if the isolated queen pawn is a good or bad thing? It can be a good thing if the pawn is free to move forward. The pawn moving forward can rip through an opponent's position and cause great damage.

However, if the pawn gets stuck, it will become a target and tie all the pieces to its defense. Sometimes, when the pawn is blockaded, there will be an opportunity for the person blockading the pawn to open up an attack on another part of the board.

Smyslov vs. Karpov
USSR Championship 1971

1.c4 c5 2.Nf3 Nf6 3.Nc3 d5 4.cxd5 Nxd5 5.e3 e6 6.d4 cxd4 7.exd4 Be7 8.Bd3 0-0 9.0-0 Nc6 10.Re1 Nf6 11.a3 b6 12.Bc2 Bb7 13.Qd3 Rc8 14.Bg5 g6 15.Rad1 Nd5 16.Bh6 Re8 17.Ba4 a6 18.Nxd5 Qxd5 19.Qe3 Bf6 20.Bb3 Qh5 21.d5 Nd8 22.d6 Rc5 23.d7 Re7 24.Qf4 Bg7 25.Qb8 Qxh6 26.Qxd8+ Bf8 27.Re3 Bc6 28.Qxf8+ Qxf8 29.d8Q, **Black resigns**

Chapter 10

Botvinnik vs. Zagoriansky
Sverdlovsk 1943

1.Nf3 d5 2.c4 e6 3.b3 Nf6 4.Bb2 Be7 5.e3 0-0 6.Nc3 c5 7.cxd5 Nxd5 8.Nxd5 exd5 9.d4 cxd4 10.Qxd4 Bf6 11.Qd2 Nc6 12.Be2 Be6 13.0-0 Bxb2 14.Qxb2 Qa5 15.Rfd1 Rfd8 16.Rd2 Rd7 17.Rad1 Rad8 18.h3 h6 19.Ne5 Nxe5 20.Qxe5 Qc5 21.Bf3 b6 22.Qb2 Rc8 23.Qe5 Rcd8 24.Rd4 a5 25.g4 Qc6 26.g5 hxg5 27.Qxg5 f6 28.Qg6 Bf7 29.Qg3 f5 30.Qg5 Qe6 31.Kh1 Qe5 32.Rg1 Rf8 33.Qh6 Rb8 34.Rh4 Kf8 35.Qh8+ Bg8 36.Rf4 Rbb7 37.Rg5 Rf7 38.Qh5 Qa1+ 39.Kg2 g6 40.Qxg6 Bh7 41.Qd6+ Rbe7 42.Qd8+, **Black resigns**

We will see that in both games White has an isolated queen pawn. Here are diagrams from the opening:

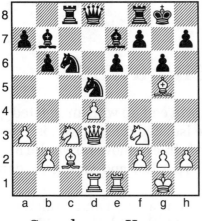

Smyslov vs. Karpov

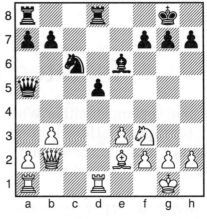

Botvinnik vs. Zagoriansky

Here are both games after 15 moves. In Karpov's game, White's d-pawn is completely stuck. In Botvinnik's game, the square in front of the d-pawn is controlled by four white pieces.

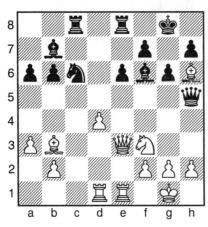

Smyslov vs. Karpov

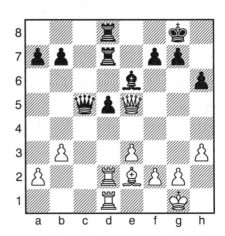

Botvinnik vs. Zagoriansky

Some Ideas from Grandmaster Games

In the Karpov game, Black played 20...Qh5. How did White respond?

He immediately pushed the pawn forward. The question might be, "What if Black plays ...exd5 ?" Then White plays Qxe8+ and Black will get checkmated.

According to the computer, if Black had played 20...Qd8 instead of 20...Qh5, White would have had a slight advantage, while after 20...Qh5 White was at almost +5 points (about a rook's worth). In the final position, Black is only down one piece. There doesn't appear to be a checkmate happening soon. Why does Black resign? There are at least two reasons.

First, chess can be exhausting, and there is mental fatigue when you are playing the top players in the world. It's a mental marathon. There is no particular reason to waste time and effort when you have another game the next day.

Also, there is the quality of opponent you are facing. If Karpov were playing a lesser opponent, he might have kept on playing. Vassily Smyslov was not going to lose that position. He was one of the best players in the world, and there was no reason to drag things out.

I would bet that Karpov never made that particular mistake again. All the top players make mistakes, and sometimes they make bad mistakes, but what makes them the best is that they learn from those mistakes.

There is an old saying, "Fool me once, shame on you. Fool me twice, shame on me."

In the Botvinnik game? Here are things after move 25:

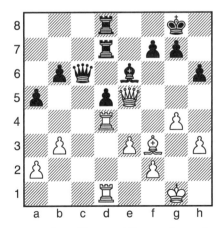

Botvinnik vs. Zagoriansky

How's the d-pawn doing? Not very well. White has four **pieces aimed at the d-pawn** and if Black is not careful, White might play e3-e4 **and get the d-pawn.**

Look at the trades White has made. What color bishop does he have? It's the light-squared one. What does Black have? A light-squared one. To a beginner, that might seem like a good thing. Sadly, the black bishop **acts like a big pawn** and more than anything else it's just getting in the way. **In the diagram above,** you can start to see White's plan.

White has completely locked up the center, and now he **attacks on the kingside.** This is the right strategy, but it must be done *very* carefully! One wrong move, and Black could get right back in the game. However, **White had studied** many games like this and he was a world champion, so he **was able to success-fully reach this position:**

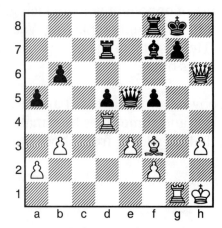

Botvinnik vs. Zagoriansky

White has just played 33.Qh6. The attack that follows is **a great example of** how to win a won game. It all started with blocking the d-pawn. **Even though** all of White's pieces are active and Black's pieces are mostly **passive, the next** nine moves are important to study.

Knights vs. Bishops

When really good players talk about knights, they use words like **"outpost"** or "centralized." A strongly placed knight in the **center of the board can be** worth as much as a rook. In the following two games, **the knight becomes the** dominating piece. While the openings are different, **the side with the knight** uses similar strategies to win the game.

Boleslavsky vs. Lisitsin

USSR Championship 1956

1.e4 c5 2.Nf3 d6 3.d4 cxd4 4.Nxd4 Nf6 5.Nc3 g6 6.Be3 Bg7 7.f3 0-0 8.Qd2 Nc6 9.0-0-0 Nxd4 10.Bxd4 Qa5 11.Kb1 e5 12.Be3 Be6 13.a3 Rfd8 14.Nb5 Qa4 15.c4 Bxc4 16.Nc3 Qb3 17.Bxc4 Qxc4 18.Bg5 Qe6 19.Bxf6 Qxf6 20.Nd5 Qh4 21.Qe2 Bf8 22.Qf1 Rac8 23.g3 Qg5 24.h4 Qh6 25.g4 g5 26.hxg5 Qxg5 27.Rh5 Qg6 28.g5 h6 29.Rxh6 Qxg5 30.Rh5, **Black resigns**

Fischer vs. Gadia

Mar del Plata 1960

1.e4 c5 2.Nf3 d6 3.d4 cxd4 4.Nxd4 Nf6 5.Nc3 a6 6.Bc4 e6 7.Bb3 b5 8.0-0 Bb7 9.f4 Nc6 10.Nxc6 Bxc6 11.f5 e5 12.Qd3 Be7 13.Bg5 Qb6+ 14.Kh1 0-0 15.Bxf6 Bxf6 16.Bd5 Rac8 17.Bxc6 Rxc6 18.Rad1 Rfc8 19.Nd5 Qd8 20.c3 Be7 21.Ra1 f6 22.a4 Rb8 23.Nxe7+, **Black resigns**

There does not appear to be any great similarity after 10 moves:

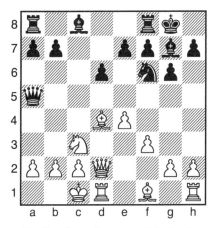

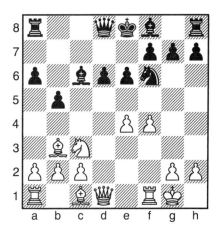

Boleslavsky vs. Lisitsin   Fischer vs. Gadia

Let's check in a few moves later in each game:

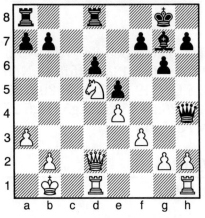

Boleslavsky vs. Lisitsin

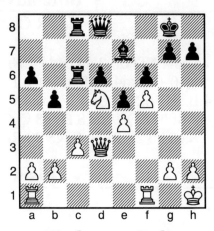

Fischer vs. Gadia

Both players made a plan to trade off minor pieces and create an outpost for their knight. They gave Black a dark-squared bishop and entombed it with its own pawns.

Now the big question: What do the players do to win the game? They have a strategically won game, but there is the matter of actually winning it. Play through to the end and see what happens.

They carry out the exact same plan, only on different sides of the board:

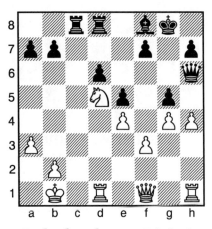

Boleslavsky vs. Lisitsin

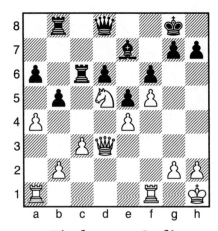

Fischer vs. Gadia

Do you see what they did? They locked up the center with a great knight. Then they pushed pawns on the side opposite from their king. It's been pointed out by players much stronger than me that they both had better moves at different points in the game.

Some Ideas from Grandmaster Games

In the age of computers, there will always be better moves. Fischer's opponent did collapse with 22...Rb8. (White played 23.Nxe7+, and if 23...Qxe7 White would go 24.Qd5+, winning the rook.) Fischer was never in danger of losing. Rd1a1 and then a2-a4 was going to win.

When a grandmaster sees a guaranteed win, they will do it every time. In the world of computers, you might see a move where a player will be ahead by 20 points, and the player chooses a plan which will have them ahead by 5 points. Did they make a mistake? No! They made a choice to win a game in a way they saw.

If they have a choice to make a move that puts them ahead by 20 points, and instead they make a move which has them losing by 5 points... now, *that's* a mistake.

When you look through the games of great players, try to find the patterns they use. If you wanted to be a great runner, would you want to train with a world-class sprinter or 5-kilometer specialist, or would you want to train with a guy who sat on his couch and ate doughnuts all day?

You should see that there are some similarities in the strategies between the Botvinnik–Zagoriansky isolated queen pawn game and these two games: the opponent gets tied to one weakness, and then the winner creates another weakness and wins. This is called the "principle of the two weaknesses." Did I create that term? No, I learned it from reading books about chess.

Do you think Boleslavsky and Fischer had seen Alekhine's games? My guess is that they had many of Alekhine's games in long-term memory (and those of earlier champions like Capablanca and Steinitz).

Look at great games from great players. You don't need to reinvent the wheel, study the people who made the wheel first.

Now we turn our attention to bishops. They like open space. They can target something from clear across the board, and they can work very well with other pieces. In fact, both games have other really important strategic elements in them. These are games where open files get controlled and rooks invade positions, but playing a strong supporting role are the bishops.

Chapter 10

Cheparinov vs. Alekseev
Grand Prix, Elista 2008

1.e4 e5 2.Nf3 Nc6 3.Bb5 a6 4.Ba4 Nf6 5.0-0 Be7 6.Re1 b5 7.Bb3 d6 8.c3 0-0 9.h3 Nb8 10.d4 Nbd7 11.Nbd2 Bb7 12.Bc2 Re8 13.a4 Bf8 14.Bd3 c6 15.b3 Qc7 16.Bb2 g6 17.Qc2 Rac8 18.Bf1 Qb8 19.Rad1 Bg7 20.g3 Ba8 21.axb5 axb5 22.b4 Bf8 23.Qb3 h6 24.dxe5 Nxe5 25.c4 bxc4 26.Nxc4 Nfd7 27.Nfxe5 Nxe5 28.Nxe5 dxe5 29.Rd7 Re7 30.Red1 Rce8 31.Bc4 Kg7 32.Qf3 c5 33.Qxf7+ Rxf7 34.Rxf7+ Kh8 35.Rdd7, **Black resigns**

Polugaevsky vs. Ftacnik
Luzerne 1982

1.Nf3 Nf6 2.c4 c5 3.Nc3 e6 4.g3 b6 5.Bg2 Bb7 6.0-0 Be7 7.d4 cxd4 8.Qxd4 d6 9.Rd1 a6 10.b3 Nbd7 11.e4 Qb8 12.Bb2 0-0 13.Nd2 Rd8 14.a4 Qc7 15.Qe3 Rac8 16.Qe2 Ne5 17.h3 h5 18.f4 Ng6 19.Nf3 d5 20.cxd5 h4 21.Nxh4 Nxh4 22.gxh4 Qxf4 23.dxe6 fxe6 24.e5 Bc5+ 25.Kh1 Nh5 26.Qxh5 Qg3 27.Nd5 Rxd5 28.Rf1 Qxg2+ 29.Kxg2 Rd2+, **White resigns**

Let's see what has happened after 10 moves:

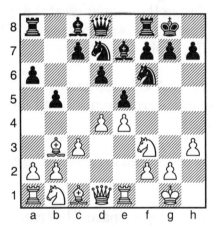
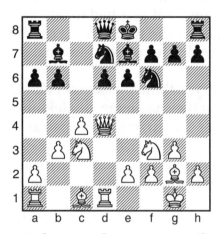

Cheparinov vs. Alekseev   Polugaevsky vs. Ftacnik

There is something we will see in the Cheparinov game. When no pawns are traded, the position is called "closed" because there are no open files. In closed positions, players move their pieces around, and at times it will look like they are undeveloping their pieces. Part of what players are doing is thinking about, "When the chessboard opens up, where should my pieces be?"

Some Ideas from Grandmaster Games

Anticipating the open files and diagonals and important squares is the difference between winning and losing. One of my favorite parts of the Cheparinov game is move 16.Bb2. The bishop is put in a place where it seems to have no future at all, but in the end it, dominates the game.

After move 15:

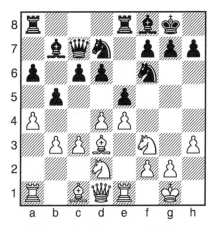

Cheparinov vs. Alekseev

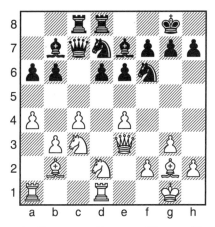

Polugaevsky vs. Ftacnik

No pieces have been traded. In the Polugaevsky game, Black's formation is called a "hedgehog." A hedgehog formation in chess is when you make no aggressive moves and let your opponent move too far forward. Then, at the right moment, you counter-attack.

Chess can be a game of all-out attacking, but many games require patience and planning and looking for weaknesses in your opponent's position.

After 20 moves:

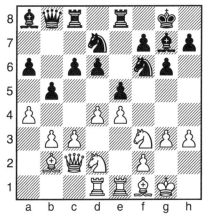

Cheparinov vs. Alekseev

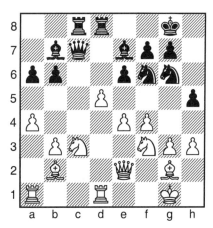

Polugaevsky vs. Ftacnik

Chapter 10

The Cheparinov game is roughly level, but what is happening in Polugaevsky–Ftacnik?

Black does not have any weaknesses. One thing about pushing pawns in front of your king: pawns don't move backwards. The computer has Black at about +1.5 points ahead. After 20...h4, White has real problems.

Now after move 26 in Cheparinov and 25 in Ftacnik:

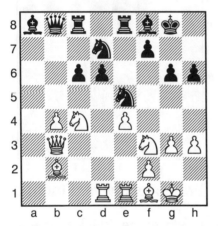

Cheparinov vs. Alekseev

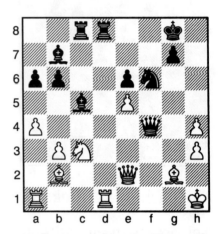

Polugaevsky vs. Ftacnik

Look at the bishop on b2 in the Cheparinov game. It has been sitting patiently on that square and, suddenly, it has a long diagonal. Very soon, White will have an open file for his rooks.

That is planning and strategy.

Polugaevsky–Ftacnik will be over soon. Here is where you need to sit and calculate and make sure. White is threatening Bxb7. (Did you notice that?)

How does Black react to the threat of Bxb7? He allows White to take his knight by moving ...Nf6-h5. The threat is ...Ng3+, forking the king and queen. So White plays Qxh5. Now there is a silent but deadly move: after Black moves ...Qg3, there are three one-move checkmate threats (...Qh3#, ...Qxg2#, and ...Bxg2#).

White's only hope is to block the a8-h1 diagonal with Nd5. Now after ...Rxd5 White doesn't have a good move. If he plays Rxd5, then ...Bxd5 and it's over. So he moves Rf1. What happens when all your pieces are on good squares and the enemy king is open? Great tactics occur. The move ...Qxg2+ is made possible by all the previous moves.

Some Ideas from Grandmaster Games

Grandmaster Ftacnik didn't suddenly look at the board and think, "I can sacrifice my queen now." It was the accumulation of small advantages and White's deciding to take a risk.

Lesson: if your opponent wants to open up his king, let him, and have your pieces in the right place.

Let's look at the end of the Cheparinov game:

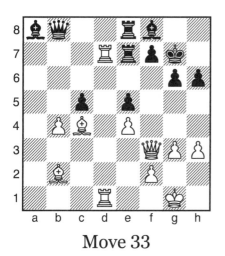 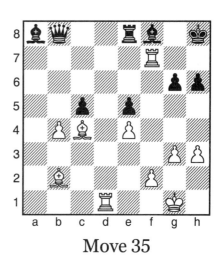

Move 33 Move 35

White sacrifices his queen on f7 and by move 34 you can see the effect. What should White do now? 35.Rdd7. His bishops and rooks completely dominate the game. White threatens Rh7#. Black's only try is 35...Re7, but then White plays 36.Rxe7 Bxe7 37.Rxe7. Again Rh7# is threatened, and the bishop that has sat on b2 for 20 moves now threatens Bxe5+.

Using the Entire Board

In watching students play, there is a time when I know for certain they are about to miss something. It is when they stare at a particular part of the board for a long time and lose sight of pieces outside their area of focus. Suddenly, their opponent's queen, rook, or bishop swoops in and takes something, and the game is over.

Great players use the whole chessboard. These next two games have nothing in common, except that there is action everywhere. It should be noted that the Carlsen game was played blindfolded. All grandmasters can play chess blindfolded because they have the patterns so well remembered. Even so, this would be a great game even if they were looking at the board.

Chapter 10

Loek van Wely vs. Magnus Carlsen
Amber Tournament 2008 (Blindfold)

1.d4 Nf6 2.c4 e6 3.Nc3 Bb4 4.Qc2 d5 5.a3 Bxc3+ 6.Qxc3 c5 7.dxc5 d4 8.Qg3 Nc6 9.b4 e5 10.e4 0-0 11.Bd3 b6 12.Nf3 bxc5 13.b5 Nh5 14.Qg5 Qxg5 15.Bxg5 Na5 16.Rb1 f6 17.Bd2 Nb7 18.h3 g5 19.Ke2 Nd6 20.g4 Ng7 21.a4 Bb7 22.h4 Nxe4 23.hxg5 Nc3+ 24.Bxc3 e4 25.Bxe4 Bxe4 26.Bd2 Rae8, **White resigns**

I have never met Magnus Carlsen, but in looking at this game I think I learned a little bit about him and how he thinks about chess.

Let's look at a diagram from early on in the game.

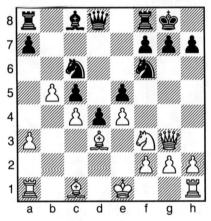

The opening play has been a little different and now Carlsen has a knight attacked by a pawn on one side of the board. What does he do? He plays 13...Nh5, attacking White's queen. He is making his opponent think on all sides of the board.

Watching beginners play, you notice that they sometimes develop tunnel vision. They focus on the 16 squares around the king and don't see pieces on the edge of the board. Look at the second diagram:

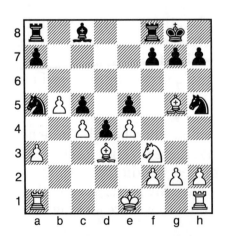

Some Ideas from Grandmaster Games

Look at Black's knights. They are deliberately placed on the edges of the board. He is having fun in this game.

There is a bit of showmanship here, but it's well calculated and interesting to see.

The final pair of diagrams:

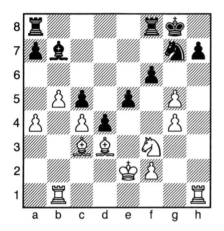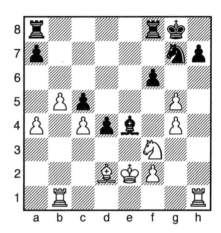

Carlsen's ultimate plan is a central pawn breakthrough. He makes two very well calculated in-between moves. In the diagram on the left, he could simply play 24...dxc3, but the much stronger move is pushing the e-pawn to e4, forking the bishop and knight.

(When I say it's "stronger," I am saying so based on computer calculations.)

The second diagram is even more interesting. The obvious move is 26...Bxb1. In fact, when I created this diagram I thought, "There must be some mistake here, he can just take with the bishop."

What does Black do? He plays 26...Rae8. The computer I use had Black at +2 points after 26...Bxb1. But it had Black ahead +6 after 26...Rae8, for example 27.Rbc1 (getting away from the capture) 27...Bb7+ 28.Kf1 Bxf3, winning a whole piece.

The ability to "see" the board without looking at it and to make deep, accurate calculations is an amazing thing, but most people can develop that skill if they practice.

Each year I read stories to my students. One of those stories is about a character named Tyl Uilenspiegel. He is sort of the Dutch version of Robin Hood. Tyl is very bright, creative, charitable, and a trickster (but not in a mean sense).

Chapter 10

Every now and then, Tyl gets himself in trouble and has to creatively think his way out of it. No matter what happens, it's always fun to see.

If Tyl played chess, his games would look like these.

———————

During the early 1980s and into the '90s, I was going to college and starting a career as a teacher. In the '80s, the world of chess was dominated by the Karpov-Kasparov rivalry. Anatoly Karpov was a great world champion, and I don't think that he gets the credit he deserves in the West. People in the West, for the most part, wanted Kasparov to be the champion. There was plenty of drama and tension, and it was like Muhammad Ali vs. Joe Frazier or any other great rivalry.

My brother is rated about 2200 and understands much about the games that were played in the Karpov-Kasparov matches, but I didn't quite see the genius of Kasparov. I knew he was a great player and a deserving world champion.

As I was looking at games to put in this book, I wanted to include a number of games by world champions.

I ran across the following game (Piket–Kasparov, Tilburg 1989). As much as any game by Garry Kasparov, it showed me how good and how creative he was. This is a game worth playing through several times, because you can miss a lot. I will probably not give it the justice it deserves, but my goal is to make some of the ideas accessible to children who are starting out in chess. I will also use the sequencing format here that was used extensively in Chapter 6.

The opening is not unique. It's been played a few times, starting out quietly and then, all of a sudden – *boom!* – the board just explodes.

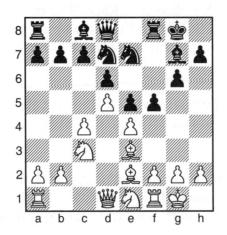

Some Ideas from Grandmaster Games

White's basic plan is to attack on the queenside, while Black will attack on the kingside by pushing pawns and bringing his knights and other pieces into the battle.

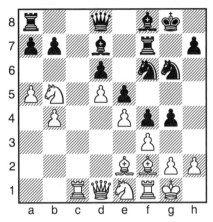

So far, everything is going as planned. White is making progress on the queenside and Black is expanding on the kingside.

The next diagram needs to be looked at carefully, because of the move Black is about to make:

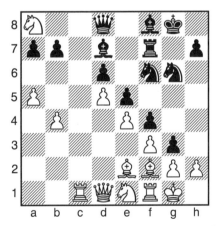

Black could play ...gxf2+, then White's rook would take the pawn. Black would then play ...Qxa8.

Or Black could play ...Qxa8.

He does neither, and plays ...Nf6-h5 instead. My computer has a hard time with that move... for a while.

Chapter 10

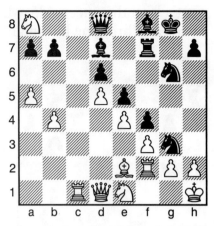

There is a lot going on here, visually. White's knight is over in the corner. He would like to bring it back to safety on c7. He is in check. **What should he do?**

We know he doesn't take the knight, but why? **If White plays hxg3, then Black** plays ...Qh4+. The threat is ...fxg3 attacking the rook and **threatening ...Qh2#.** It's an impossible threat for White to stop. **White has to play Kg1.**

Next diagram:

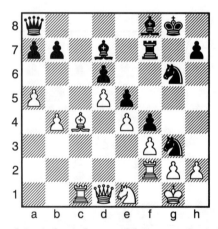

Black has captured White's knight, and his own knight still **can be taken, and** the queen can no longer move to h4. It is unclear how Black **can make progress.** But then he sees a way to exploit the position of White's king and rook.

How can he take advantage of those pieces? One of the **signs that you are** making progress in chess is when you find ways to involve **all your pieces in** the attack.

The problem for Black is that, when the queen took the **knight on a8, it moved** away from being able to attack the kingside.

Some Ideas from Grandmaster Games

What's the right move? Let's look at the situation a couple of moves later:

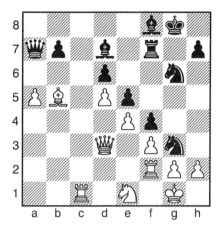

Black has pushed his a-pawn to a6, allowing the queen to get to the a7-g1 diagonal. After ...Qa7, White can no longer take the knight because after 1.hxg3 fxg3 White's rook will be pinned and lost.

What is Black's next move? ...Nh1! Knights don't belong in corners, and yet there it goes. The problem is that White has no useful moves. If Kxh1, then Black plays ...Qxf2 and comes out a piece ahead. If he doesn't take it, the knight will hop back and take the rook and Black will be even further ahead.

Now I am going to take five of the six diagrams and mix them up. (I will add one that doesn't belong.)

A

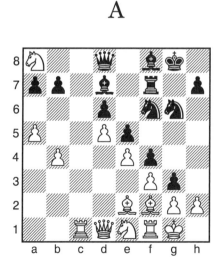

B

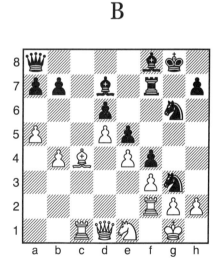

C

D

E

F

1. ___ 2. ___ 3. ___ 4. ___ 5. ___

Which diagram does not come from the Kasparov game?

What was unique about that game?

_____

_____

Describe in your own words these moves made by Black:

21...Nh5 _____

_____

Some Ideas from Grandmaster Games

23...Ng3 _____

_____

25...a6 _____

_____

28...Nh1 _____

_____

Chapter 11

Practice Thinking

The purpose of this chapter is for the student to develop an effective chess thinking process. Each move changes the game, and so sometimes what you need to think about is relocating one of your pieces and other times your opponent gave up something for free.

Chess thinking is based on pattern recognition. At the very beginning of a chess thought are the simple things, like one-move checkmates, pieces for free, simple tactics, and – before you make your own move – checking the board to make sure you are not doing something terrible. If you have quickly covered those things, you have more time to probe deeper.

You can have the deepest chess thoughts in the world, but if you consistently miss one-move checkmates you will lose most of your games. Having the basics mastered and going through a thought process that checks for simple things will make a huge difference to your future success.

My belief is that the best way to learn a chess thinking process is to have to sort through a variety of types of problems. I would strongly encourage you to study each problem and look at the features of the problem. Look at each piece and especially pieces like bishops on open diagonals and rooks on open files. Are there pieces which are not protected, or do many pieces seem to be aimed at the king? Train your brain to look at the entire board. Don't get stuck on any problem for more than five minutes. There are some hard problems and some easy ones right next to each other.

If you give up on a problem and look at the answer, try to understand how the answer works. Set it up on a board and play through it. There are two components of "knowing" something. The first one is that you can say the answer fast. How fast? Imagine that I asked you your name. Be able to solve each problem as fast as you know your name. Secondly, and equally as important, be able to explain the answer to someone. If your little brother or sister asked you, "How does that problem work?", could you tell them about the important squares and features of the position? Is it checkmate? Or is it winning material?

Speed and accuracy are very important, but if all you do is memorize answers without any understanding, you will *not* make real progress.

Practice Thinking

I will give you an example of a problem that gave me trouble. The reason it gave me trouble is important. I had spent a lot of time looking at some problems where queens were getting sacrificed and came to this problem:

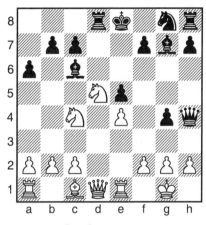

Black to move

My first thought was, "Is this really Black to move?" My brain was focused on queen sacrifices (...Qxh2+ and ...Qxf2+) which are terrible moves. Then I thought , "Maybe it is supposed to be White's move?" It is easy to make mistakes when looking at thousands of problems.

I am stubborn, and broke my own 5-minute rule. I was going to figure out this problem. I did some other things and came back and looked at it... nothing. I went and did a few other things, and still nothing. Finally I thought, "What are the simple things I need to look at and my brain shouted at me, "Look at the knight on c4, it's unprotected!!"

Five seconds later, the answer hit me: 1...Bxd5 2.exd5 g3, threatening a pawn fork with 3...gxf2+ and also ...Qxc4. I was so focused on a hard thing that I completely missed the easy thing. (Instead of 2.exd5, White does have a resource which is a little better. Can you find it?)

Most chess moves are not spectacular. First, we develop our pieces and try to control open files, diagonals, and key squares. In most games, there comes a point where you need to be able to calculate or know that your opponent has missed something. It could be a very simple thing or a very complex thing, but your brain must approach each move with simple things first.

There are enough problems randomly placed here that if you start and look for one-move checkmates and easy captures first, you will be rewarded for your efforts. Then, let your brain look for patterns it remembers from previous problems.

Chapter 11

Let's do a few more examples first:

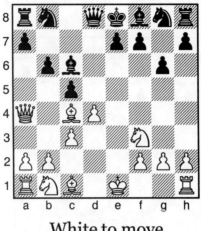

White to move

Black has just played ...Bc6 and White's queen is under attack. If this were your game, what would you think about? Most people start out by grabbing their queen and moving it to b3. It is safe there, and the pawn on f7 is under attack. There is a pattern here that is important. Black is behind in development. It's true that White is not completely developed, but if you thought f7 was weak, you were on the way to the right answer. 1.Ne5! attacks the bishop twice and also threatens Bf7 mate. Black loses.

This next one is a little bit harder, but it has a pattern worth knowing.

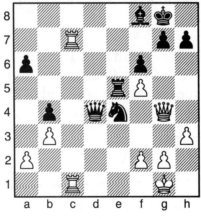

White to move

White has control of the c-file, but Black is threatening either ...Nxf2 or ...Qxf2+. White has pressure on g7, but what should happen? **1.Rxg7+ Bxg7 2.Rc8+ Kf7 3.Qh5+** and now White is threatening **4.Qe8+ Kd6 5.Qd7#.**

Practice Thinking

It would be easy to go wrong here. 1.Rxg7+ Bxg7 2.Rc8+ Kf7 3.Rc7+ Ke8 4.Qxg7?? which does threaten Qg8# but gives Black a free move: 4...Qxf2+ 5.Kh2 Qf4+ 6.Kg1 (6.Kh1 Nf2+ 7.Kg1 Re1#) 6...Qf2+ 7.Kh2 Qf4+, with perpetual check.

When sacrificing material, exact calculations become very important, and when you get to the point where your opponent has a free move, you need to be able to see everything. That will not happen without practice and without mistakes being made along the way.

One other thing is that simply because you have a lot of chess knowledge, doesn't mean you will win all your games.

Every time you go to a chess tournament, there are new challenges. You will find that each new experience will cause growth. Sometimes it will be the losses that cause the most growth. If you have a great thinking process in place, you will be able to understand the losses better and make faster progress.

A couple more examples before the main problem set.

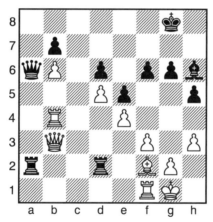

Black to move

Black has successfully brought the rooks to the second rank, the queen is in a good place, and the bishop has a useful diagonal. That does not mean that the win is easy. There are no free pieces or one-move checkmates. For this book, this is about as hard as problems will get.

Before you make the first move, you need to see the entire process in your mind. If somehow you miscalculate, go back and see where the mistakes were. This is a position where combinations happen. 1...Qxf1+ 2.Kxf1 Rxf2+ and if 3.Ke1, then 3...Rg2 (threatening ...Rg1#) 4.Kf1 Raf2+ 5.Ke1 Bd2+ 6.Kd1 Bxb4 7.Qxb4 Rg1+ 8.Qe1 (forced) 8...Rxe1+.

Or 3.Kg1 Rg2+ 4.Kh1 Rac2 (threatening ...Rc1+) and White will have to give up a lot of material.

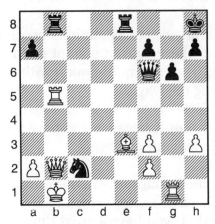

It is Black to move in this position. The question is, "Is 1...Rxb5 a good move?" If you think one move deep, you will say, "No, because of 2.Qxb5." However, 1...Rxb5 is a great move because after 2.Qxb5 Black can play 2...Na3+ forking the king and queen.

The previous problem was a complex calculation involving many moves. This problem was a two-move knight fork. In a game of chess, your opponent is not likely to tell you what is happening. Chess moves are not played "randomly" but you do not get to know whether the next move is going to be a simple one or a big thought.

Practice, starting with all the basic ideas and working your thought process out like a spiral. Double-check and be careful.

The more you work on speed and accuracy with comprehension, the faster you get to the point where it becomes automatic.

Do grandmasters start with the simple moves first? Yes, but the patterns, because of the practice they put in, make the process look simple. You can do the same thing.

The last bit of advice is this. Let's say you solve 30 problems a day. What should you do the next day? First, go back and look at the problems from the day before. Make sure you understand every problem. Then solve some new problems. On the third day, go back and review all the problems you have done and add some more. On the fourth day, do the same thing. You will not be spending much time on the problems from the first day, but quickly think about the ideas. On Day 5 you can stop looking at the first day's problems. You have looked at them for four days and should have them mastered. Follow that pattern.

There is one other thing to know about these 300 problems. You will come across three "problems" which are really endgame stems based on the concept of king activity. They will be called "Active King Study" numbers 1, 2, and 3. These are not one- or two-move problems, but extended ideas about the role of the king in the endgame. Look at them and play through them with a friend. Then look at the answer. Once you have seen the first one, you will have an idea about the second one.

Good luck!

Diagram 137

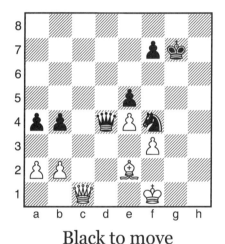

Black to move

Diagram 138

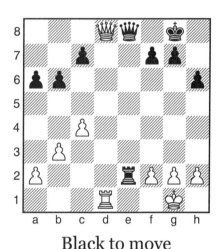

Black to move

Diagram 139

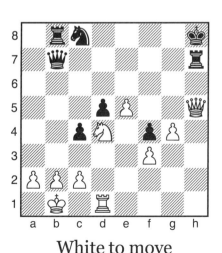

White to move

Diagram 140

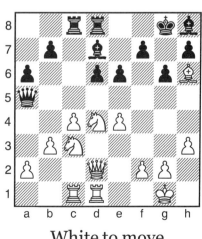

White to move

Chapter 11

Diagram 141

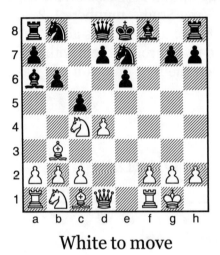

White to move

Diagram 142

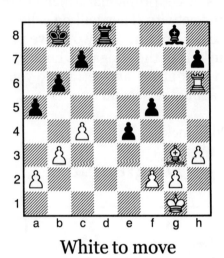

White to move

Diagram 143

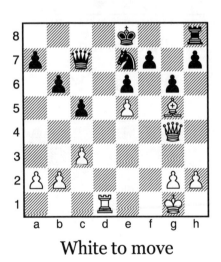

White to move

Diagram 144

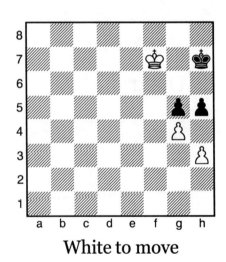

White to move

Diagram 145

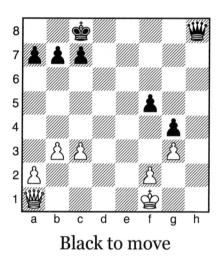

Black to move

Diagram 146

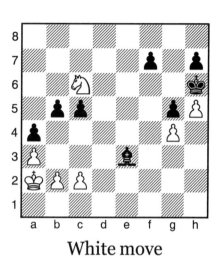

White move

Diagram 147

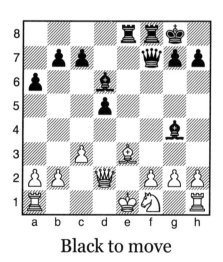

Black to move

Diagram 148

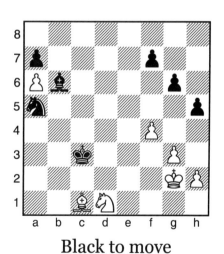

Black to move

Diagram 149

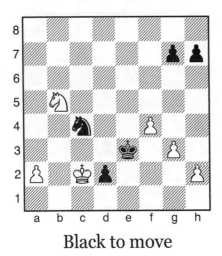

Black to move

Diagram 150

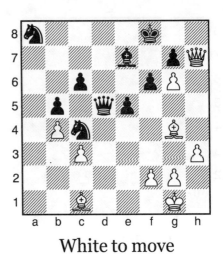

White to move

Diagram 151

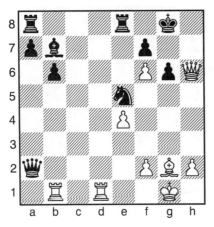

Can Black stop 1.Qg7# ?

Diagram 152

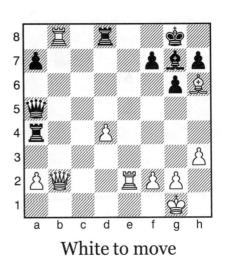

White to move

Diagram 153

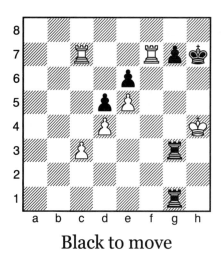

Black to move

Diagram 154

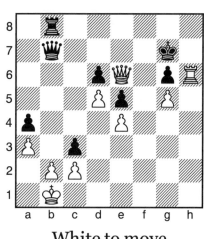

White to move

Diagram 155

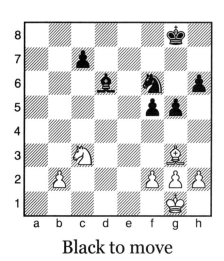

Black to move

Diagram 156

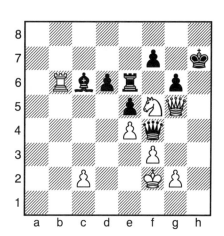

Should White trade queens?

Diagram 157

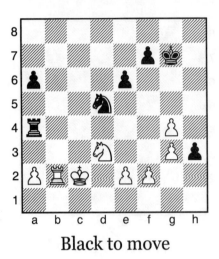

Black to move

Diagram 158

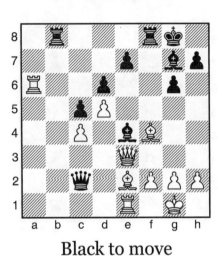

Black to move

Diagram 159

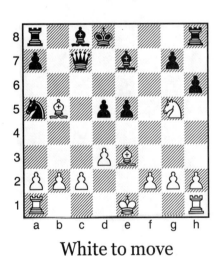

White to move

Diagram 160

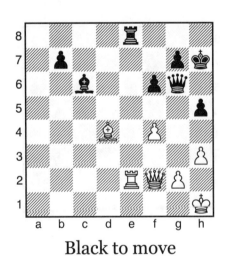

Black to move

Diagram 161

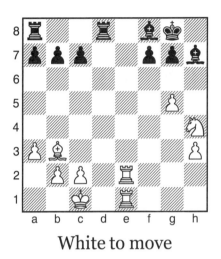

White to move

Diagram 162

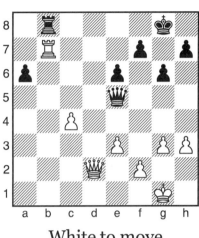

White to move

Diagram 163

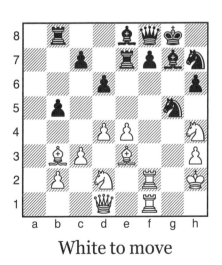

White to move

Diagram 164

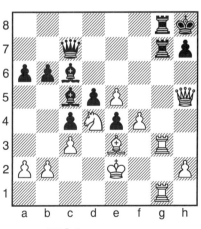

White to move

Diagram 165

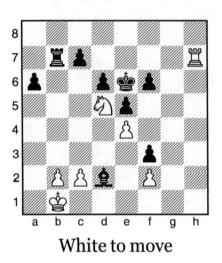

White to move

Diagram 166

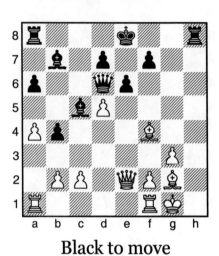

Black to move

Diagram 167

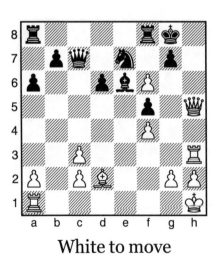

White to move

Diagram 168

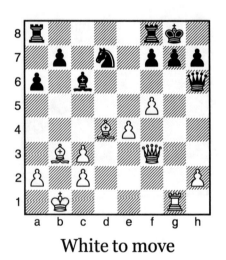

White to move

Diagram 169

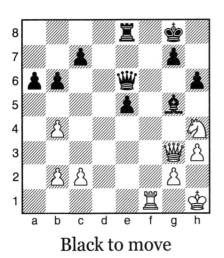

Black to move

Diagram 170

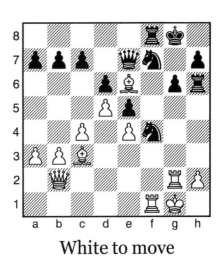

White to move

Diagram 171

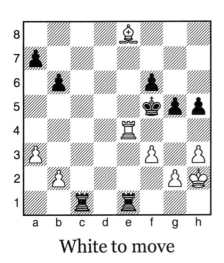

White to move

Diagram 172

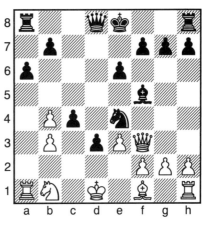

Black to move

Chapter 11

Diagram 173

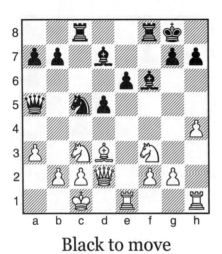

Black to move

Diagram 174

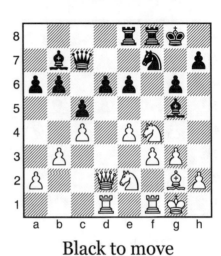

Black to move

Diagram 175

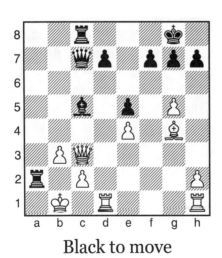

Black to move

Diagram 176

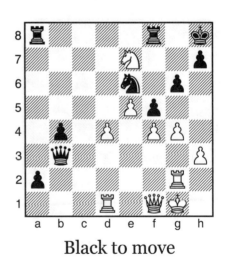

Black to move

Diagram 177

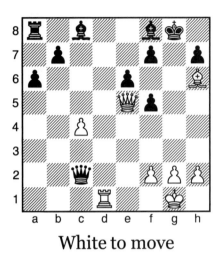

White to move

Diagram 178

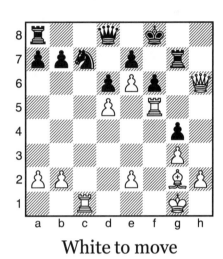

White to move

Diagram 179

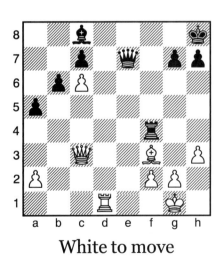

White to move

Diagram 180

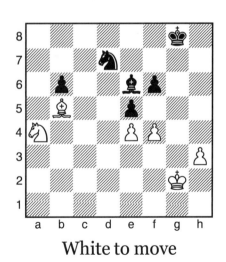

White to move

Diagram 181

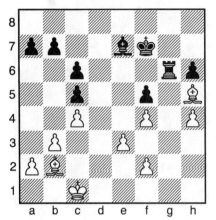

Is 1.Bxg6+ White's best move?

Diagram 182

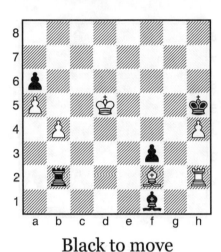

Black to move

Diagram 183

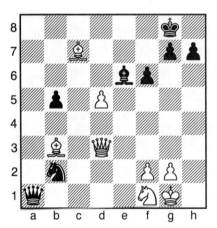

Should White move the queen?

Diagram 184

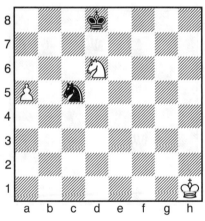

White to move

Diagram 185

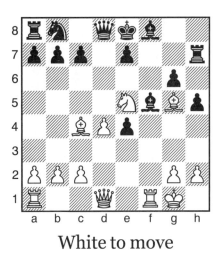

White to move

Diagram 186

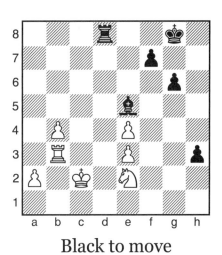

Black to move

Diagram 187

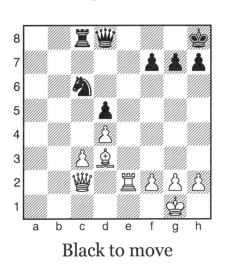

Black to move

Diagram 188

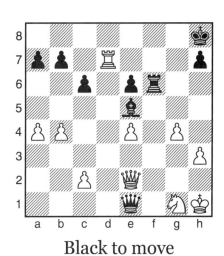

Black to move

Diagram 189

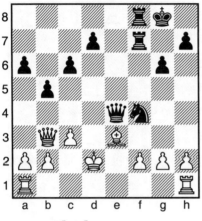

Black to move

Diagram 190

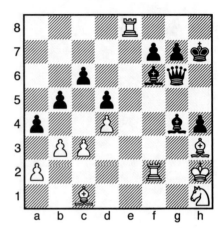

Is 1...Bxh3 Black's best move?

Diagram 191

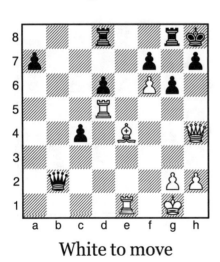

White to move

Diagram 192

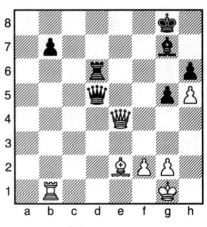

White to move

Diagram 193

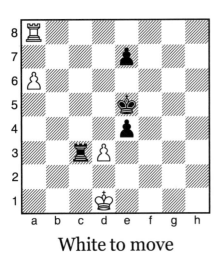

White to move

Diagram 194

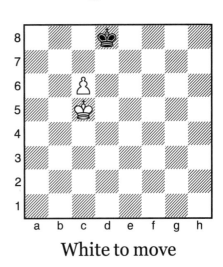

White to move

Diagram 195

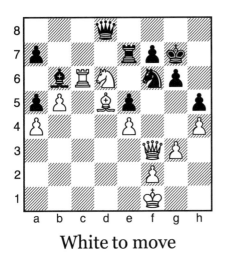

White to move

Diagram 196

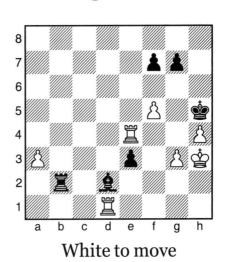

White to move

Diagram 197

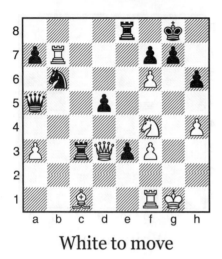

White to move

Diagram 198

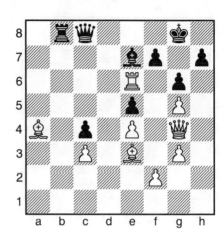

White to move.
Should White resign?

Diagram 199

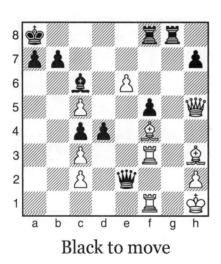

Black to move

Diagram 200

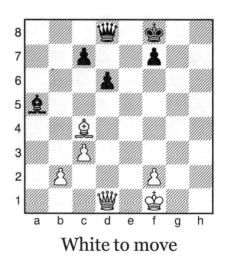

White to move

Diagram 201

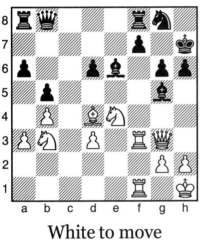

White to move

Diagram 202

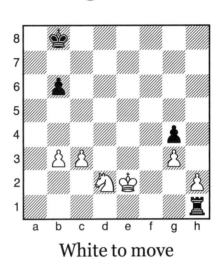

White to move

Diagram 203

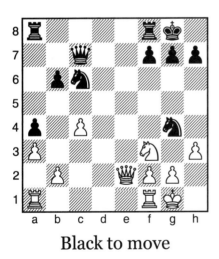

Black to move

Diagram 204

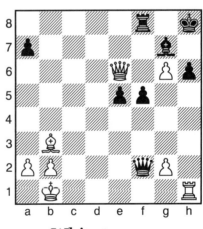

White to move

Diagram 205

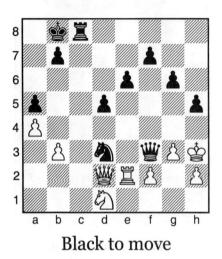

Black to move

Diagram 206

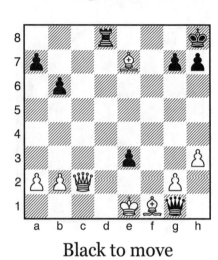

Black to move

Diagram 207

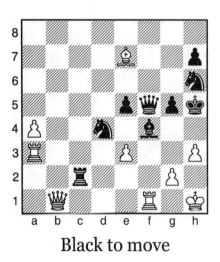

Black to move

Diagram 208

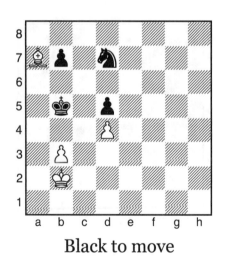

Black to move

Diagram 209

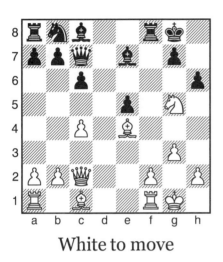

White to move

Diagram 210

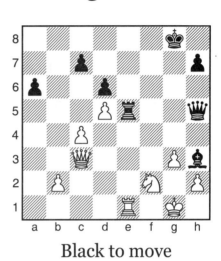

Black to move

Diagram 211

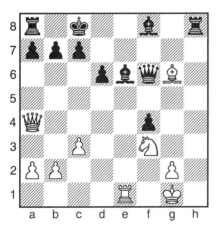

Is 1.Rxe6 White's best move?

Diagram 212

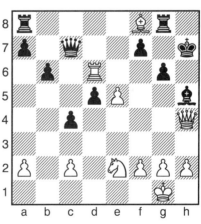

White to move

Diagram 213

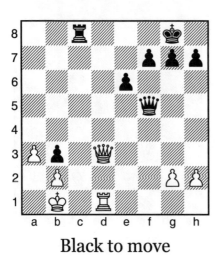

Black to move

Diagram 214

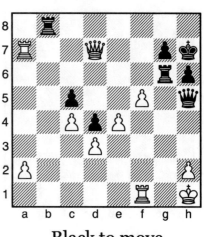

Black to move

Diagram 215

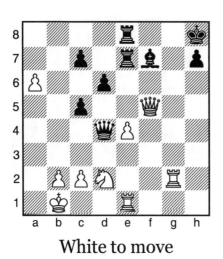

White to move

Diagram 216

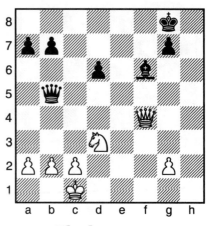

Black to move

Diagram 217

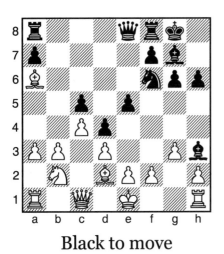

Black to move

Diagram 218

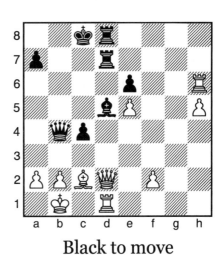

Black to move

Diagram 219

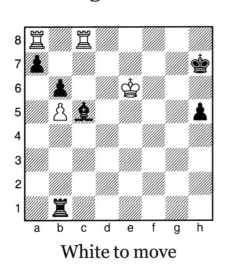

White to move

Diagram 220

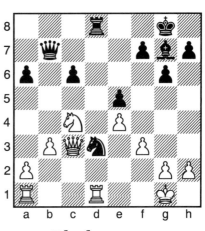

Black to move

Diagram 221

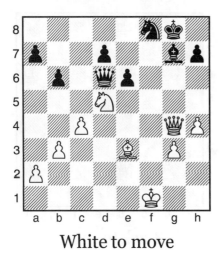

White to move

Diagram 222

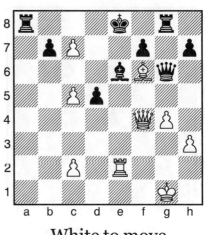

White to move

Diagram 223

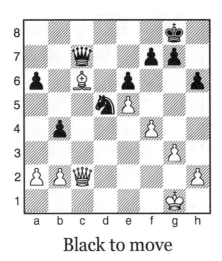

Black to move

Diagram 224

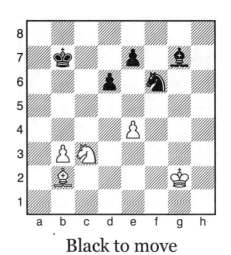

Black to move

Diagram 225

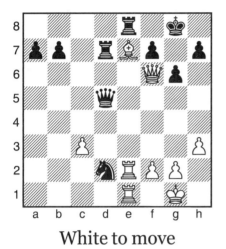

White to move

Diagram 226

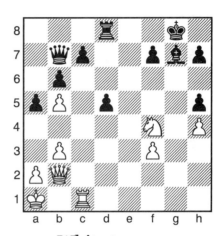

White to move.
Should White resign?

Diagram 227

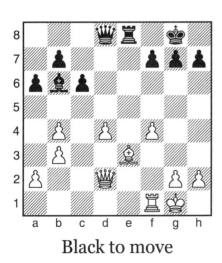

Black to move

Diagram 228

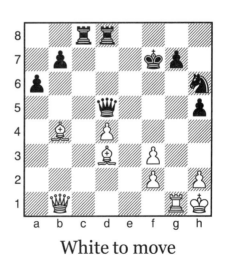

White to move

Diagram 229

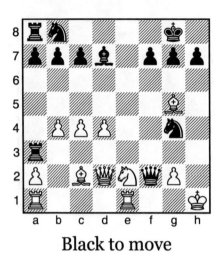

Black to move

Diagram 230

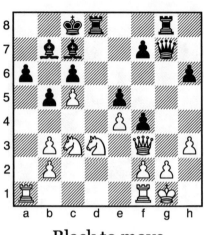

Black to move

Diagram 231

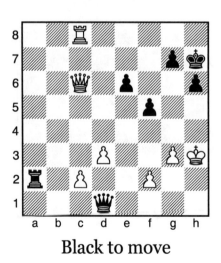

Black to move

Diagram 232

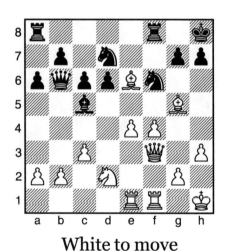

White to move

Diagram 233

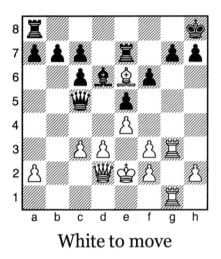

White to move

Diagram 234

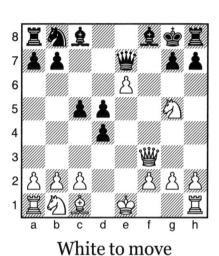

White to move

Diagram 235

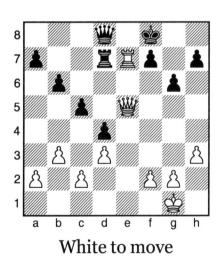

White to move

Diagram 236

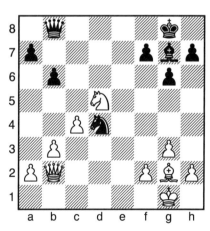

Which is better,
1...Ne2+ or 1...Nf3+ ?

Diagram 237

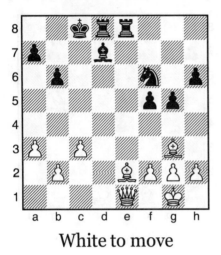

White to move

Diagram 238

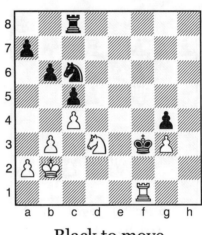

Black to move

Diagram 239

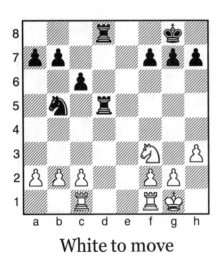

White to move

Diagram 240

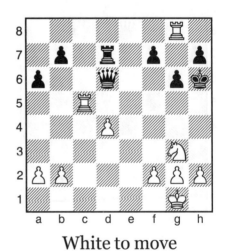

White to move

Diagram 241

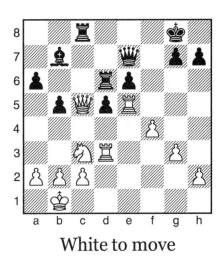

White to move

Diagram 242

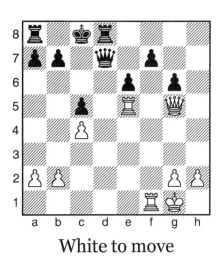

White to move

Diagram 243

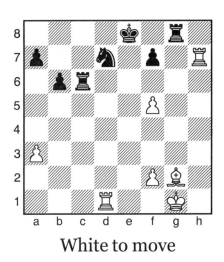

White to move

Diagram 244

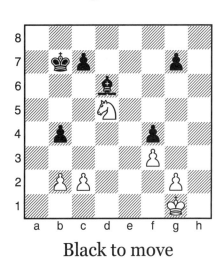

Black to move

Diagram 245

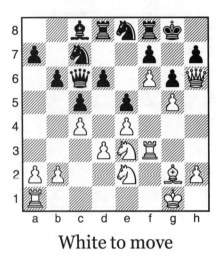

White to move

Diagram 246

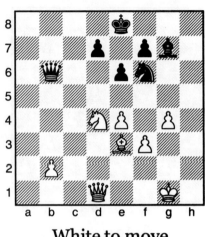

White to move

Diagram 247

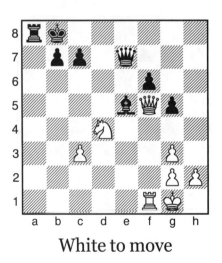

White to move

Diagram 248

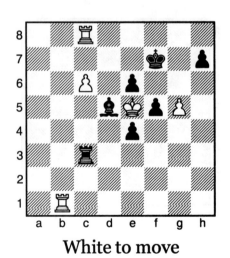

White to move

Diagram 249

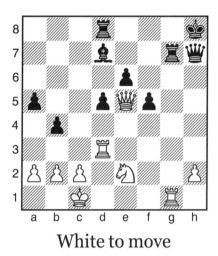

White to move

Diagram 250

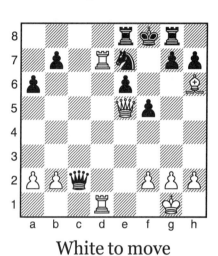

White to move

Diagram 251

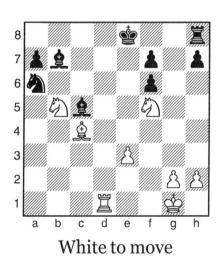

White to move

Diagram 252

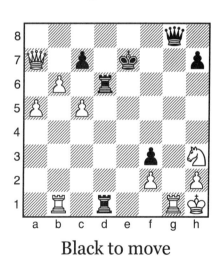

Black to move

Diagram 253

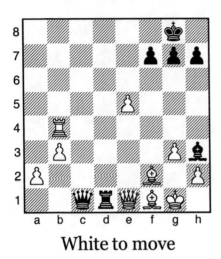

White to move

Diagram 254

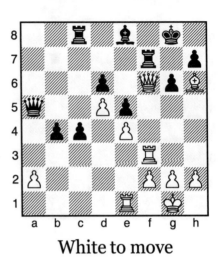

White to move

Diagram 255

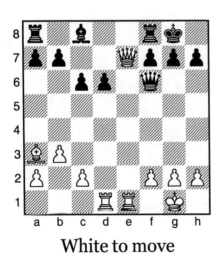

White to move

Diagram 256

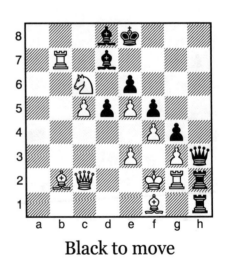

Black to move

Diagram 257

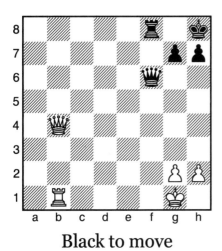

Black to move

Diagram 258

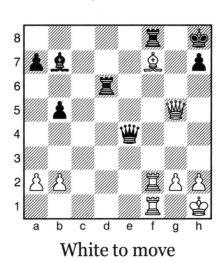

White to move

Diagram 259

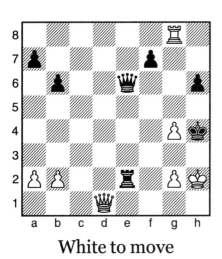

White to move

Diagram 260

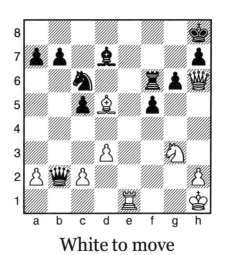

White to move

Diagram 261

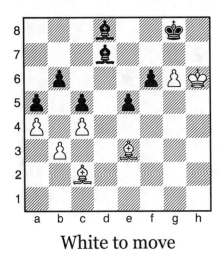

White to move

Diagram 262

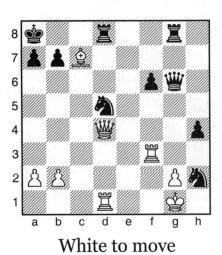

White to move

Diagram 263

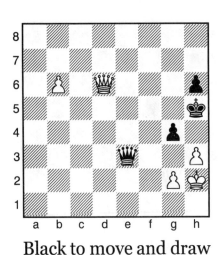

Black to move and draw

Diagram 264

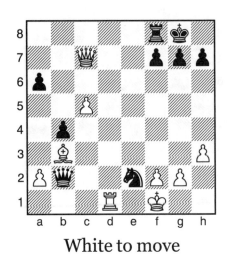

White to move

Diagram 265

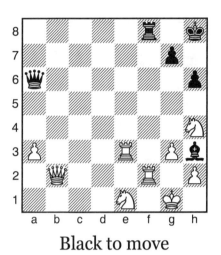

Black to move

Diagram 266

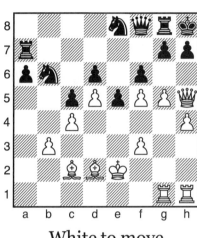

White to move

Diagram 267

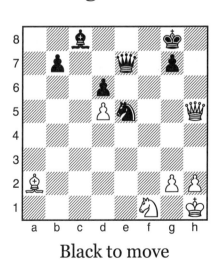

Black to move

Diagram 268

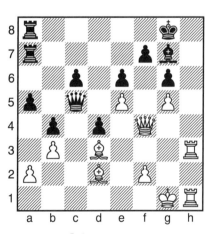

White to move

Diagram 269

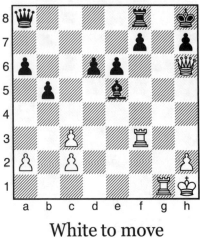

White to move

Diagram 270

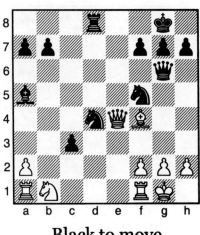

Black to move

Diagram 271

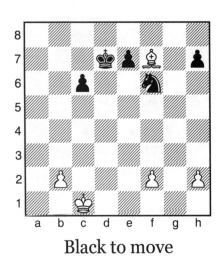

Black to move

Diagram 272

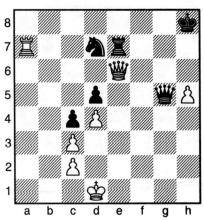

White to move **and draw**

Diagram 273

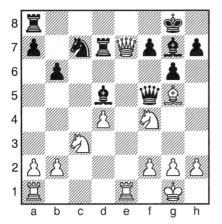

Is 1.Ncxd5 White's best move?

Diagram 274

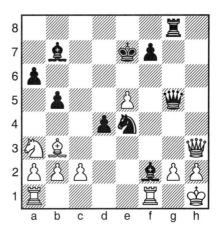

Black to move

Diagram 275

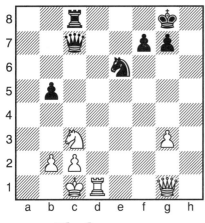

Black to move

Diagram 276

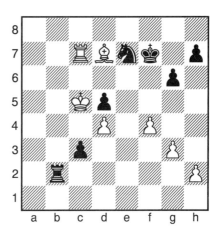

Is 1...Rb7 Black's best move?

Diagram 277

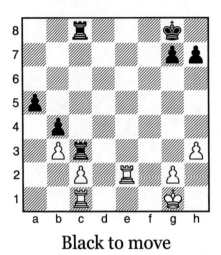

Black to move

Diagram 278

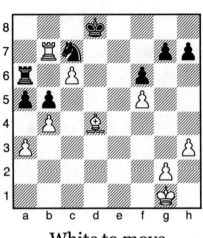

White to move

Diagram 279

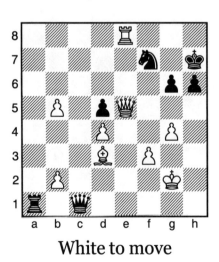

White to move

Diagram 280

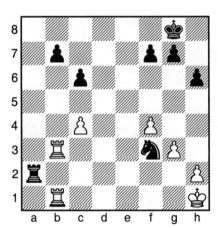

Is 1...Nd2 Black's best move?

Diagram 281

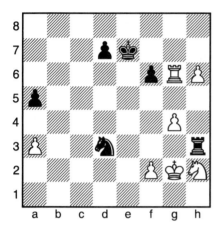

Is 1.Kxh3 White's best move?

Diagram 282

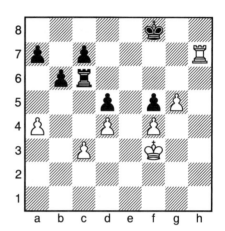

Active King Study 1:
White to move

Diagram 283

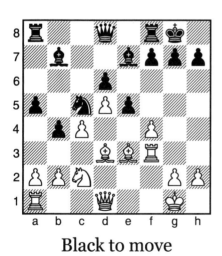

Black to move

Diagram 284

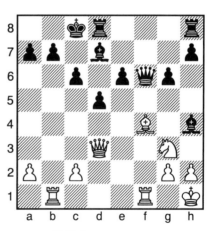

White to move

Diagram 285

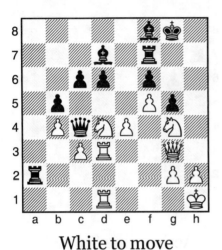

White to move

Diagram 286

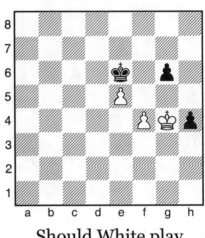

Should White play
1.Kxh4 or 1.Kh3 ?

Diagram 287

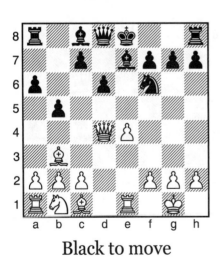

Black to move

Diagram 288

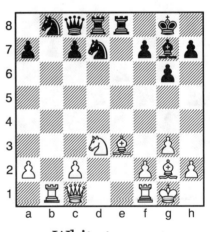

White to move

Diagram 289

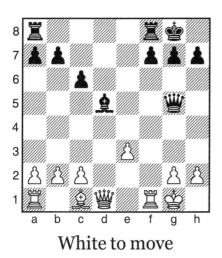

White to move

Diagram 290

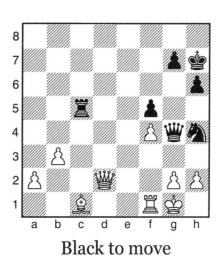

Black to move

Diagram 291

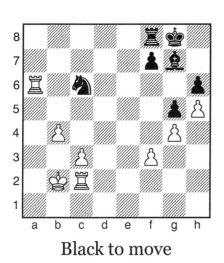

Black to move

Diagram 292

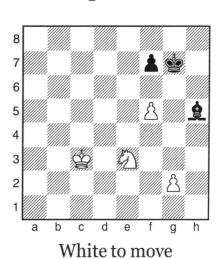

White to move

Chapter 11

Diagram 293

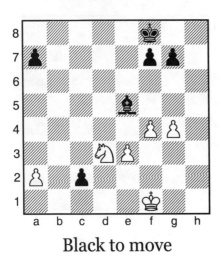

Black to move

Diagram 294

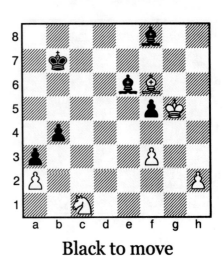

Black to move

Diagram 295

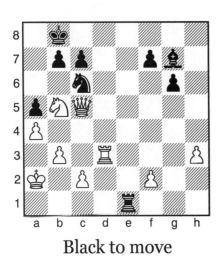

Black to move

Diagram 296

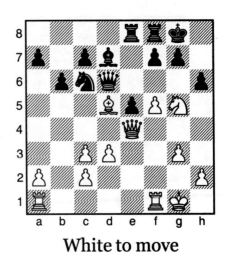

White to move

Diagram 297

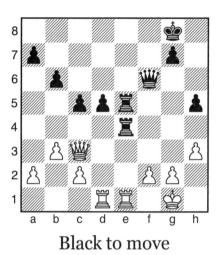

Black to move

Diagram 298

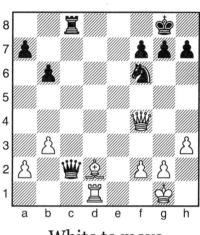

White to move

Diagram 299

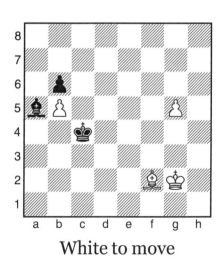

White to move

Diagram 300

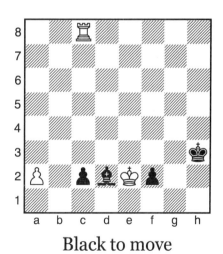

Black to move

Diagram 301

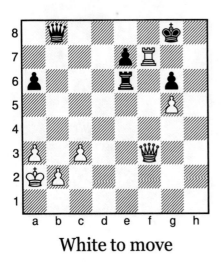

White to move

Diagram 302

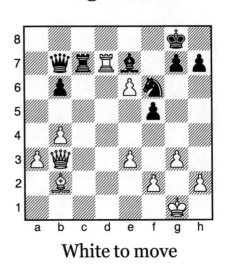

White to move

Diagram 303

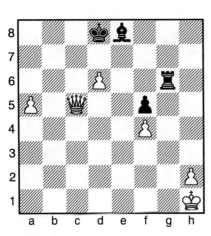

Black to move and draw

Diagram 304

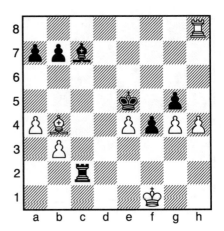

Active King Study 2:
Black to move

Diagram 305

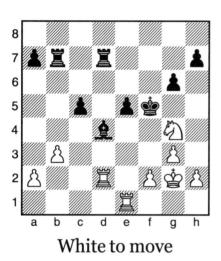

White to move

Diagram 306

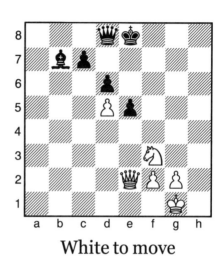

White to move

Diagram 307

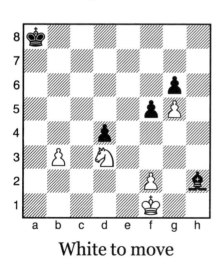

White to move

Diagram 308

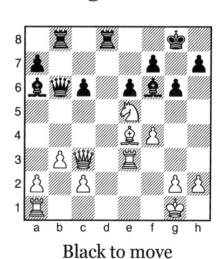

Black to move

Diagram 309

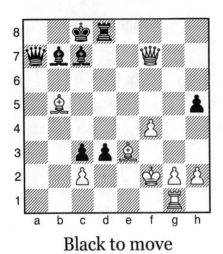

Black to move

Diagram 310

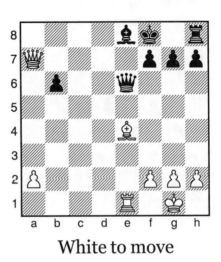

White to move

Diagram 311

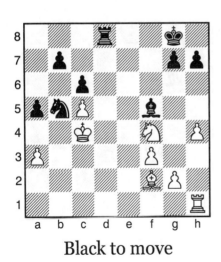

Black to move

Diagram 312

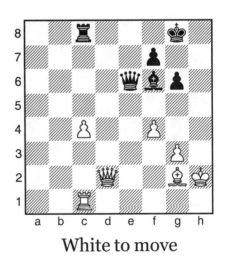

White to move

Diagram 313

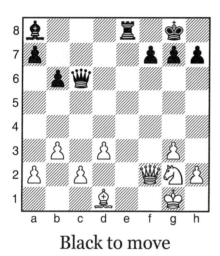

Black to move

Diagram 314

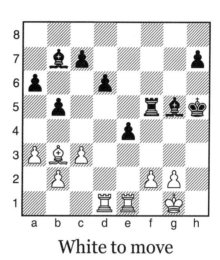

White to move

Diagram 315

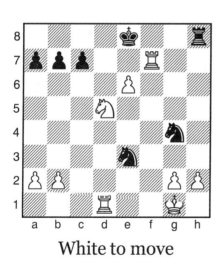

White to move

Diagram 316

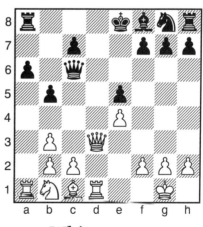

White to move

Diagram 317

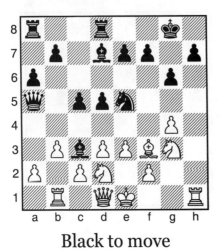

Black to move

Diagram 318

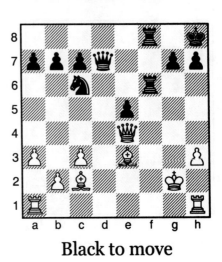

Black to move

Diagram 319

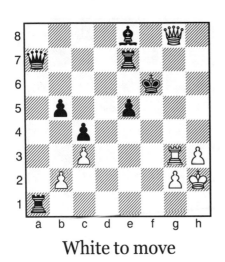

White to move

Diagram 320

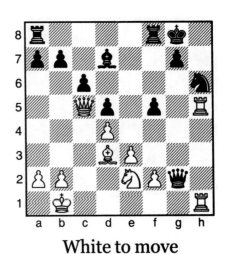

White to move

Diagram 321

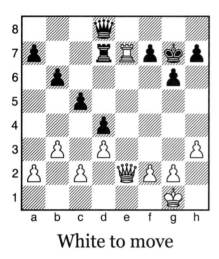

White to move

Diagram 322

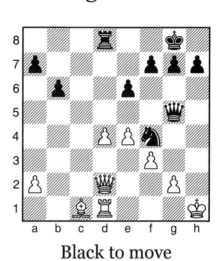

Black to move

Diagram 323

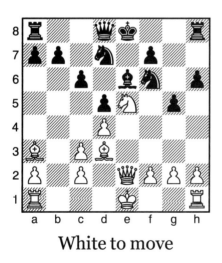

White to move

Diagram 324

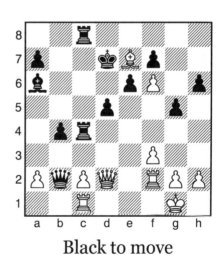

Black to move

Diagram 325

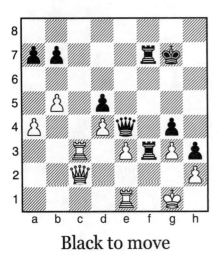

Black to move

Diagram 326

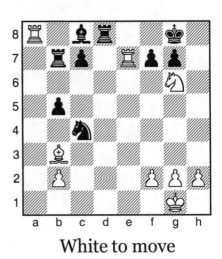

White to move

Diagram 327

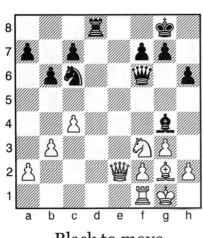

Black to move

Diagram 328

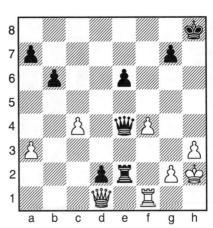

White to move and draw

Diagram 329

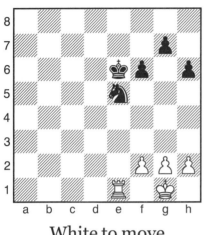

White to move

Diagram 330

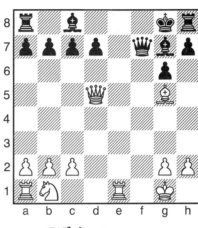

White to move

Diagram 331

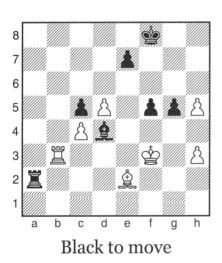

Black to move

Diagram 332

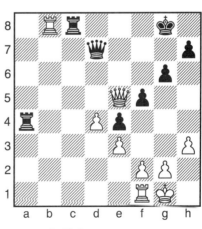

White to move

Diagram 333

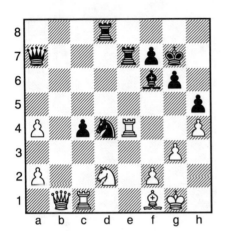

Should Black play 1...Rxe4 ?

Diagram 334

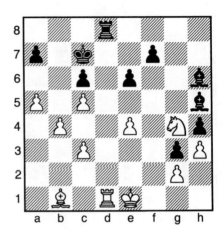

Should Black play 1...Rxd1+ ?

Diagram 335

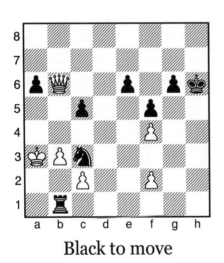

Black to move

Diagram 336

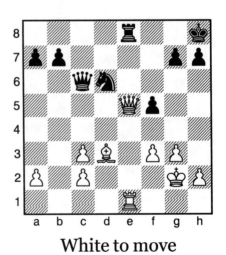

White to move

Diagram 337

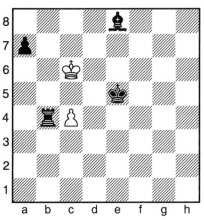

White to move and draw

Diagram 338

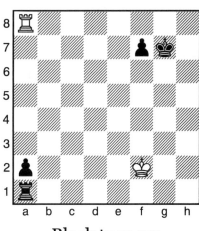

Black to move

Diagram 339

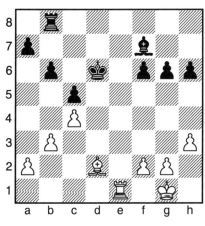

White to move

Diagram 340

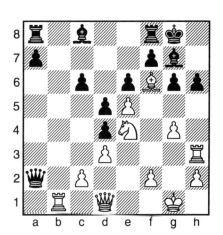

What two threats
does 1.Qc1 make?

Diagram 341

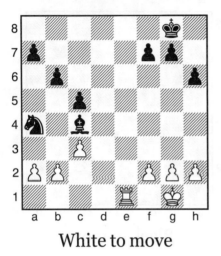

White to move

Diagram 342

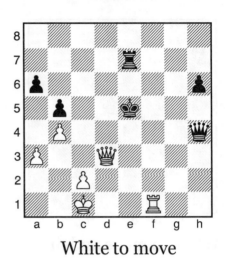

White to move

Diagram 343

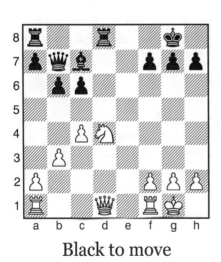

Black to move

Diagram 344

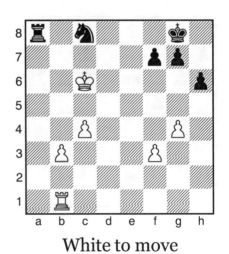

White to move

Diagram 345

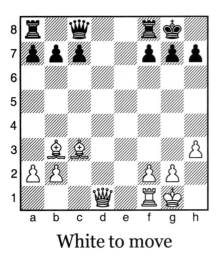

White to move

Diagram 346

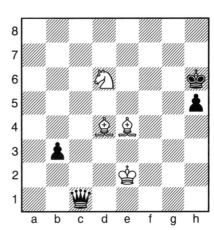

What happens after
Black plays 1...Qc7 ?

Diagram 347

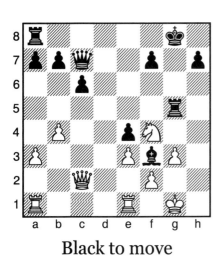

Black to move

Diagram 348

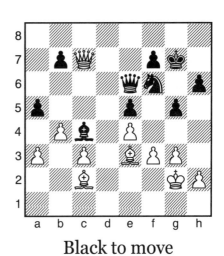

Black to move

Chapter 11

Diagram 349

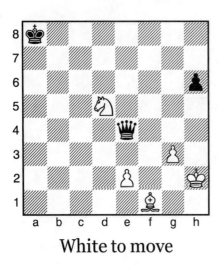

White to move

Diagram 350

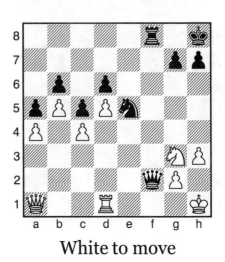

White to move

Diagram 351

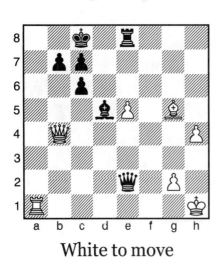

White to move

Diagram 352

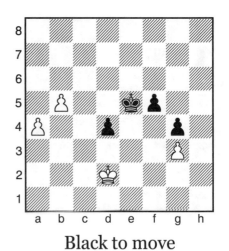

Black to move

Diagram 353

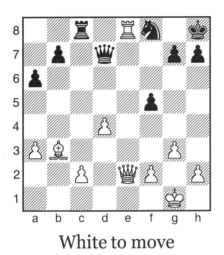

White to move

Diagram 354

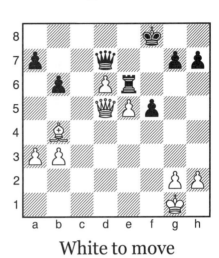

White to move

Diagram 355

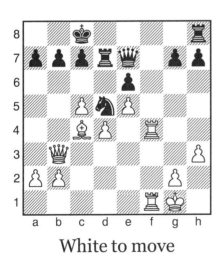

White to move

Diagram 356

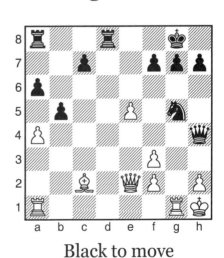

Black to move

Diagram 357

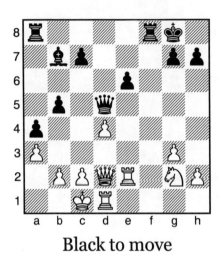

Black to move

Diagram 358

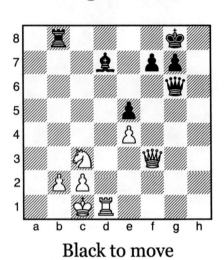

Black to move

Diagram 359

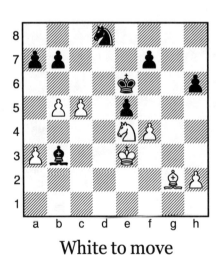

White to move

Diagram 360

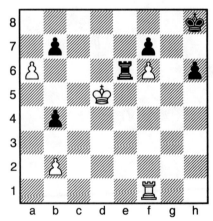

Analyze White's move 1.axb7.

Diagram 361

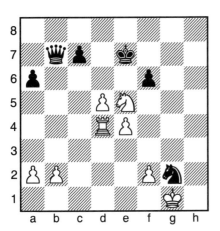

White to move. Tricky!
White traps the queen.

Diagram 362

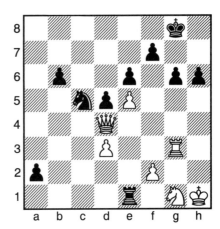

Can White draw this game?

Diagram 363

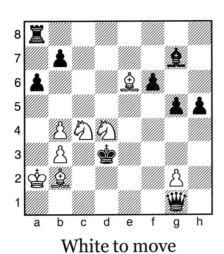

White to move

Diagram 364

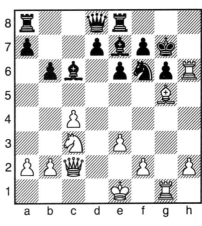

White to move

Diagram 365

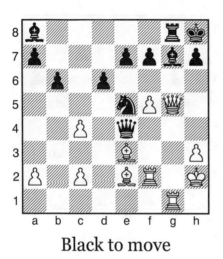

Black to move

Diagram 366

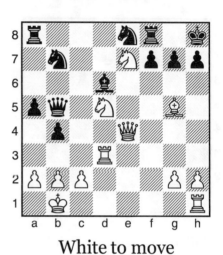

White to move

Diagram 367

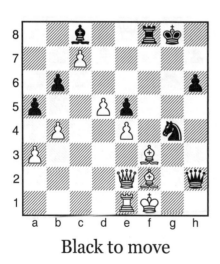

Black to move

Diagram 368

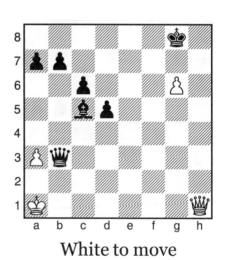

White to move

Diagram 369

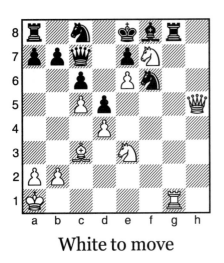

White to move

Diagram 370

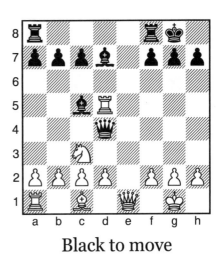

Black to move

Diagram 371

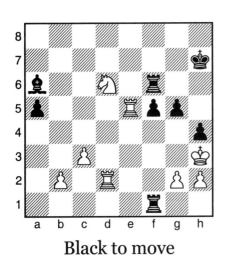

Black to move

Diagram 372

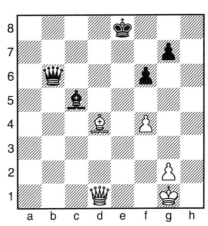

Should White play 1.Bxc5 ?

Diagram 373

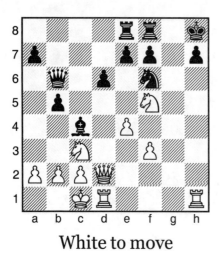

White to move

Diagram 374

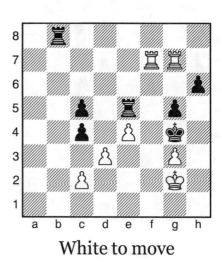

White to move

Diagram 375

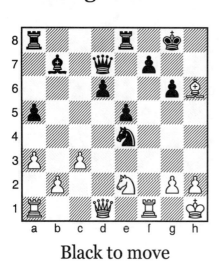

Black to move

Diagram 376

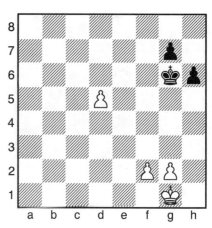

White to move:
1.g4 or 1.f4 ? Why?

Diagram 377

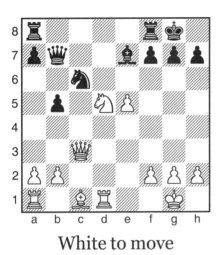

White to move

Diagram 378

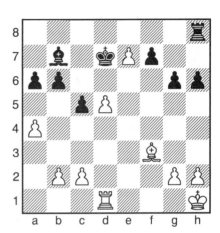

Active King Study 3:
White to move

Diagram 379

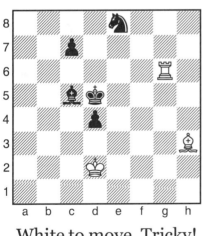

White to move. Tricky!

Diagram 380

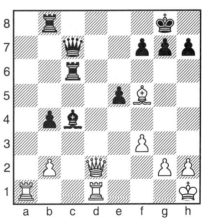

White to move

Diagram 381

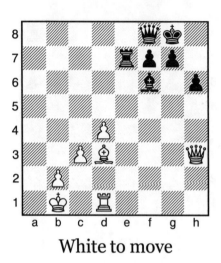

White to move

Diagram 382

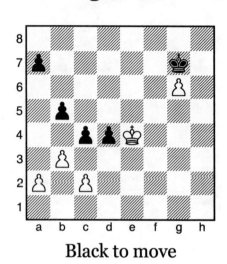

Black to move

Diagram 383

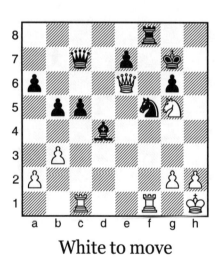

White to move

Diagram 384

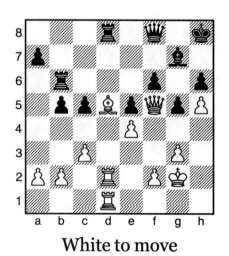

White to move

Diagram 385

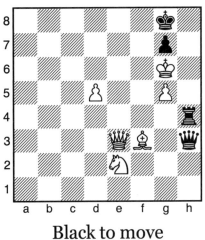

Black to move

Diagram 386

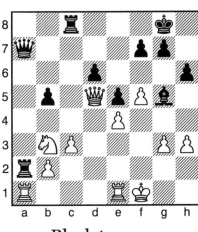

Black to move

Diagram 387

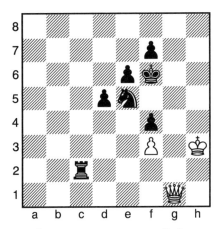

White to move and draw

Diagram 388

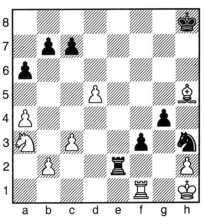

Black to move

Diagram 389

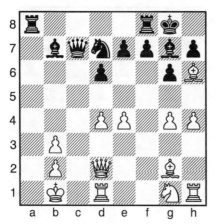

Is 1...Bxd4 a good
move for Black?

Diagram 390

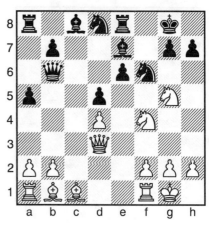

White to move

Diagram 391

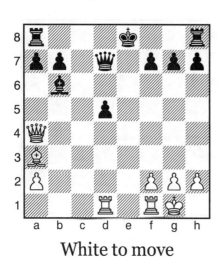

White to move

Diagram 392

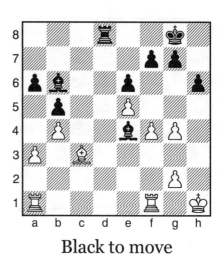

Black to move

Diagram 393

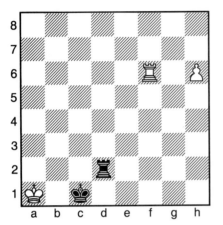

What happens after 1.h7 ?

Diagram 394

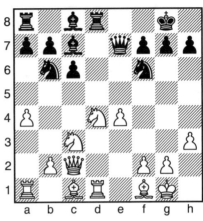

Black to move

Diagram 395

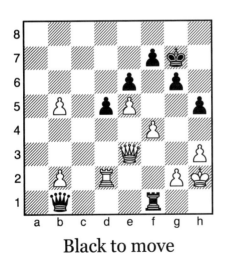

Black to move

Diagram 396

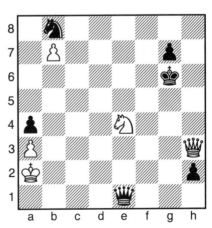

Is 1.Qh2 White's best move?

Diagram 397

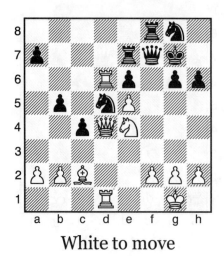

White to move

Diagram 398

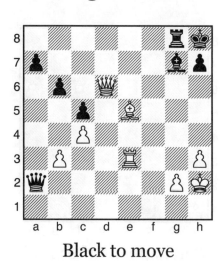

Black to move

Diagram 399

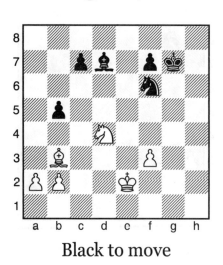

Black to move

Diagram 400

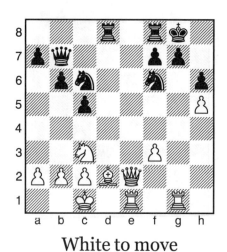

White to move

Diagram 401

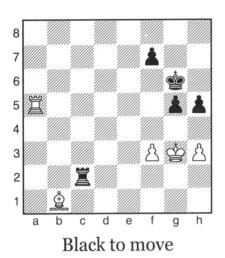

Black to move

Diagram 402

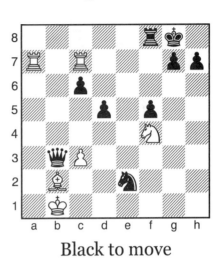

Black to move

Diagram 403

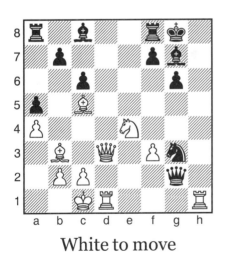

White to move

Diagram 404

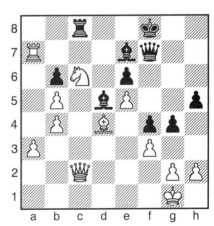

Is 1.Re7 a good move for White?

Diagram 405

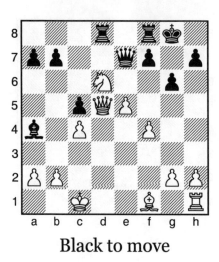

Black to move

Diagram 406

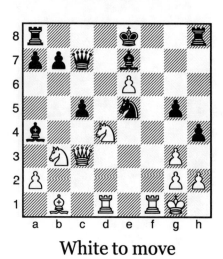

White to move

Diagram 407

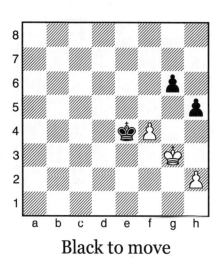

Black to move

Diagram 408

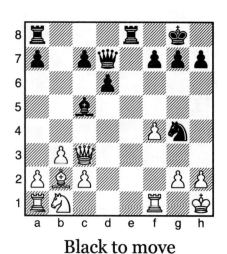

Black to move

Diagram 409

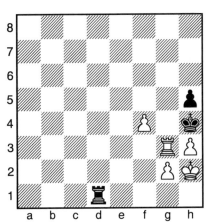

Black to move and draw

Diagram 410

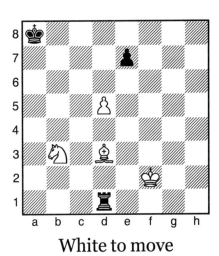

White to move

Diagram 411

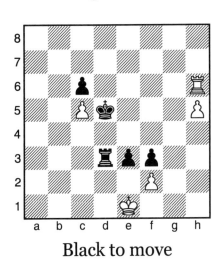

Black to move

Diagram 412

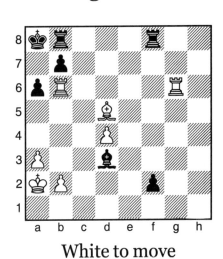

White to move

Diagram 413

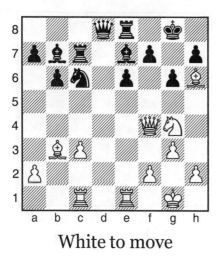

White to move

Diagram 414

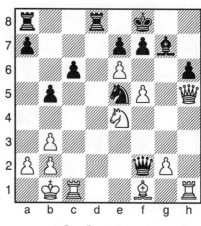

Black to move

Diagram 415

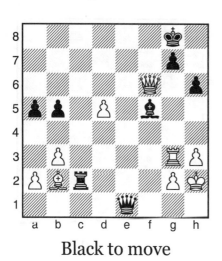

Black to move

Diagram 416

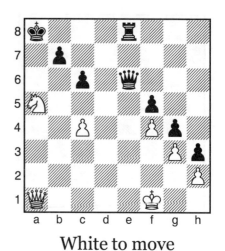

White to move

Diagram 417

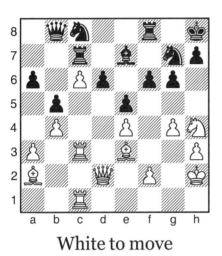

White to move

Diagram 418

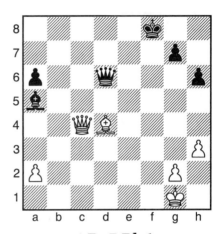

1.Bc5 Bb6.
What does White do now?

Diagram 419

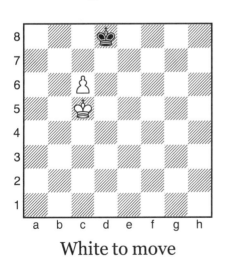

White to move

Diagram 420

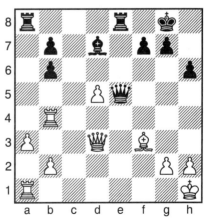

Black to move. A classic!

Diagram 421

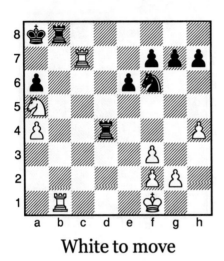

White to move

Diagram 422

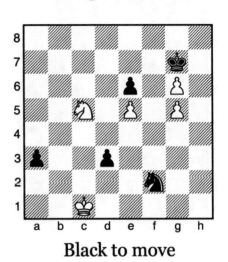

Black to move

Diagram 423

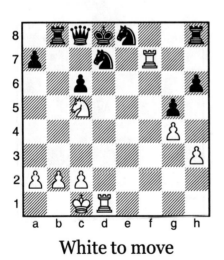

White to move

Diagram 424

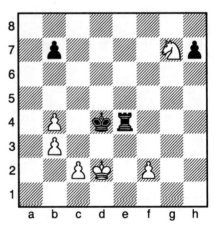

White to move. Trap the rook.

Diagram 425

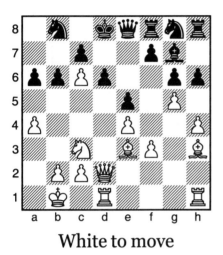

White to move

Diagram 426

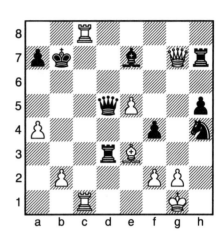

Should Black play 1...Rxg7 ?

Diagram 427

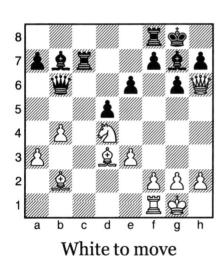

White to move

Diagram 428

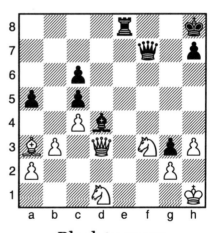

Black to move

Diagram 429

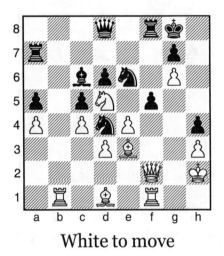

White to move

Diagram 430

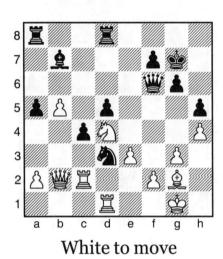

White to move

Diagram 431

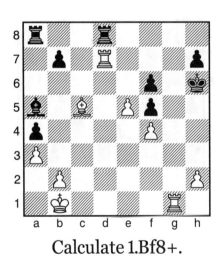

Calculate 1.Bf8+.

Diagram 432

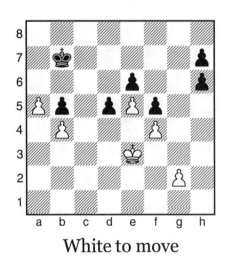

White to move

Diagram 433

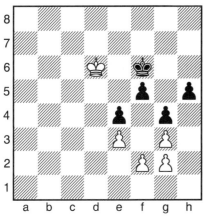

Black to move and draw

Diagram 434

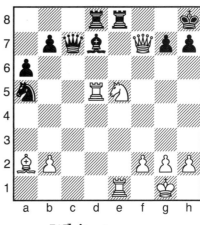

White to move

Diagram 435

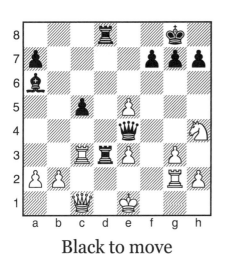

Black to move

Diagram 436

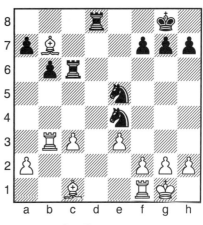

Black to move

Answers

Diagram 137

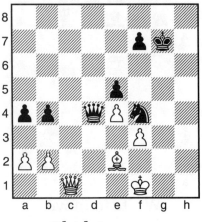

Black to move

Sometimes the goal of a chess problem is checkmate, and sometimes it is winning material. There is no checkmate here, but we can win a piece. 1...Qg1+ 2.Kxg1 (the only move) 2...Nxe2+ and then 3...Nxc1. Black ends up a piece ahead.

Diagram 138

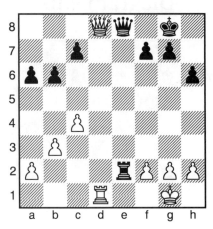

Black to move

1...Re1+ forces White to play 2.Rxe1 and then Black plays 2...Qxd8. If White had the h2-pawn on h3, then 2.Kh2 would have saved the game. The problem was that there was no flight square.

Diagram 139

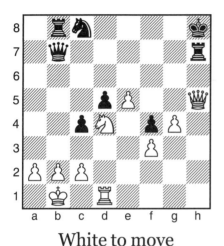

White to move

Two-move checkmate with no options: 1.Qe8+ Kg7 2.Nf5#.

Diagram 140

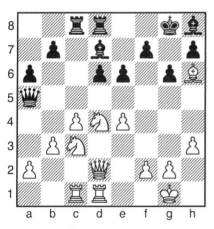

White to move

The key to this problem is that Black's king has no moves. How can White take advantage of that? 1.Nd5 makes two threats: 2.Qxa5 and 2.Ne7#. There is nothing Black can do. If this was you, give up your queen and fight on.

Diagram 141

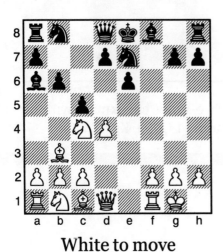

White to move

1.Nd6#, game over.

Diagram 142

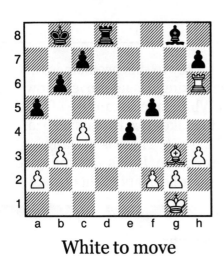

White to move

See the bishop on g3. What does it do? It pins the pawn on c7. 1.Rxb6+ wins the b-pawn because Black cannot take the rook. Winning even one pawn is very important.

Diagram 143

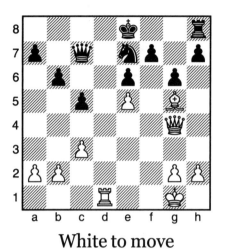

White to move

This one is a little tricky. 1.Qa4+ Qc6 (1...Kf8 2.Bh6+ Kg8 3.Qe8#) 2.Rd8+! Kxd8, and now 3.Qxc6 and the knight cannot take back because it is pinned to the king.

Diagram 144

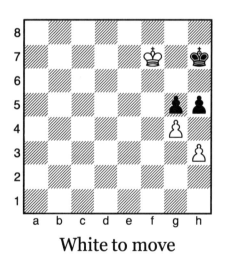

White to move

If White is careless, he might play 1.gxh5 but then Black can reply 1....Kh6 and 2...Kxh5, and if White's king follows along, the game should end in a draw.

However, there is 1.h4!:

If 1...gxh4 2.g5 h3 3.g6+ Kh6 4.g7 h2 5.g8Q h1Q 6.Qg6#.

If 1...hxg4 2.hxg5 g3 3.g6+ Kh6 4.g7 g2 5.g8Q wins.

Diagram 145

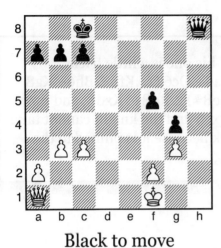

Black to move

1...Qh1+ 2.Ke2 Qxa1. This is a skewer.

Diagram 146

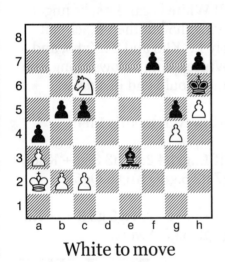

White to move

After 1.Ne7, Black cannot stop 2.Nf5+.

Diagram 147

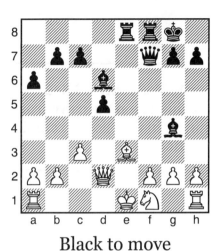

Black to move

This is like Problem 143. The first move will set up the second move. Did you notice that the bishop on e3 is pinned?

1...d4 forces White to play 2.cxd4. If the queen takes the pawn, Black plays 2...Qf2#.

1...d4 2.cxd4 Bb4! 3.Qxb4 Qf2#.

You could give up your queen and keep playing.

Diagram 148

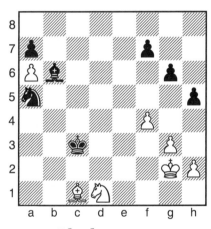

Black to move

1...Kc2 with a king fork, and Black will win one of White's pieces.

Diagram 149

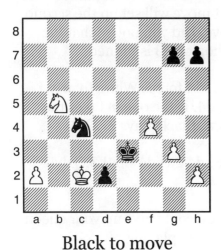

Black to move

After 1...Na3+ 2.Nxa3 Ke2, White cannot stop the pawn from queening. This is a good example of deflection.

Diagram 150

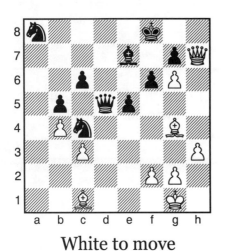

White to move

1.Bh6! Qg8 (1...gxh6 2.g7+ and the pawn queens) 2.Be6! Qxe6 3.Qxg7+ Ke8 4.Qh8+ wins (4... Kd7 5.g7 and 6.g8Q). Or 3.Qh8+ Qg8 4.Bxg7+ forcing the king to abandon the queen.

Diagram 151

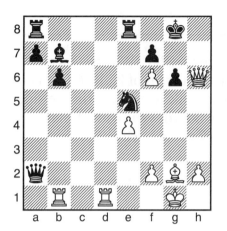

Yes! 1...Qxf2+ and if 2.Kxf2, then 2...Ng4+ forks the king and queen. If 2.Kh1, then 2...Qxf6 stops the threat.

Can Black stop 1.Qg7# ?

Diagram 152

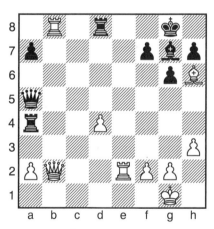

1.Re8+ Rxe8 2.Rxe8+ Bf8 3.Rxf8# is checkmate. Black was weak on the back rank.

White to move

Diagram 153

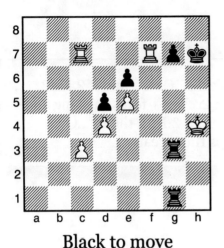

Black to move

After 1...Rg6, White is faced with the threat of 2...Rh6#. It is a "back-rank" weakness on the side of the board. White must play 2.Rxg7+ Rxg7, when Black wins a rook.

Diagram 154

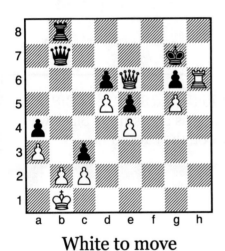

White to move

White is in trouble if the right move isn't found. 1.Qf6+ Kg8 2.Rh8#. When kings are castled on opposite sides, it's a race to get at your opponent's king.

Diagram 155

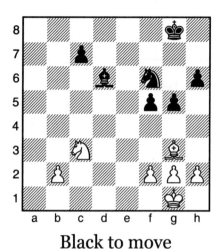

Black to move

After 1...f4, White's bishop is trapped.

Diagram 156

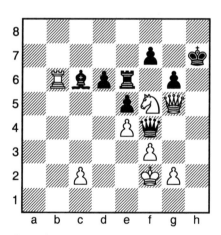

Should White trade queens?

The answer is – *yes!* 1.Qxf4 exf4 2.Nd4 forks the rook and bishop, and Black must lose at least the exchange.

Diagram 157

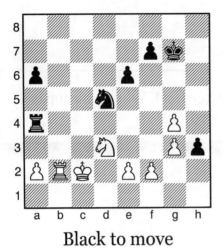

Black to move

This is like Problem 149. The idea is to queen the h-pawn. How? 1...Rc4+ 2.Kd2 Rc1!. After 3. Kxc1 h2, the pawn will queen.

Diagram 158

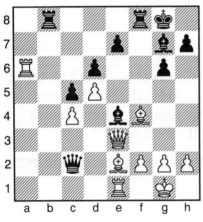

Black to move

1...Rxf4 2.Qxf4 Qxe2. White cannot take Black's queen because, after ...Rb1+, White will get checkmated. White's pieces can interpose, but they cannot stop checkmate.

Diagram 159

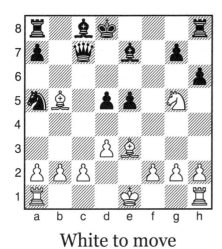

White to move

1.Nf7#.

Diagram 160

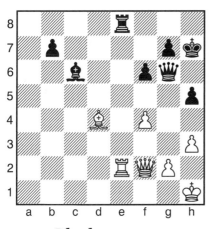

Black to move

After 1...Qxg2+ 2.Qxg2 Rxe2, White is stuck. The rook cannot be taken because of the pin. The only move is 3.Qxc6 bxc6, leaving White down the exchange and two pawns.

Diagram 161

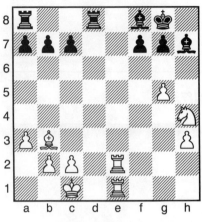

White to move

1.g6 and Black's bishop is trapped. Black can play 1...Bxg6, but after 2.Nxg6 Black cannot take the knight because the pawn on f7 is pinned by White's bishop.

Diagram 162

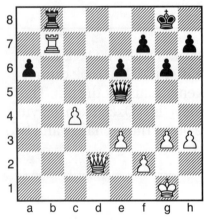

White to move

This is a little tricky to visualize. 1.Qd4 forces Black to make a bad choice. After 1...Qxd4, White will play 2.Rxb8+ first and then play 3.exd4.

If Black's queen moves off the h2-b8 diagonal, then White can take the rook for free.

Diagram 163

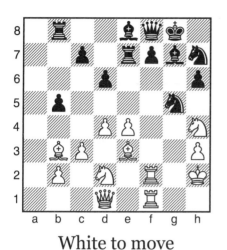

White to move

Remember Problem 161 and the bishop on b3 pinning the pawn on f7? Here it is again. 1.Ng6 wins the trapped black queen. The pawn is pinned and cannot take.

Diagram 164

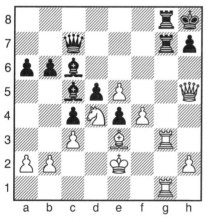

White to move

White plays 1.Qxh7+ and Black has two choices, both leading to checkmate: 1...Rxh7 2.Rxg8#, or 1...Kxh7 2.Rh3#.

Diagram 165

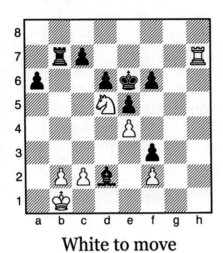

White to move

1.Re7#.

Diagram 166

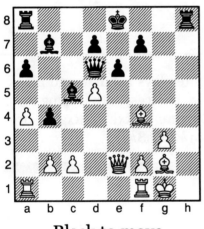

Black to move

I have a hard time visualizing this problem, but 1...Qxd5 and after 2.Bxd5 Bxd5 it is impossible to stop ...Rh1#.

Set up the position and try it. Notice the bishop on c5, what is it doing? Pinning the f2-pawn.

Diagram 167

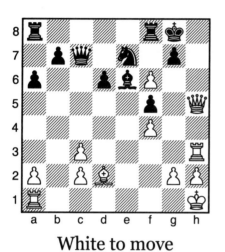

White to move

White can't play Qh7+ or Qh8+ because the black king will escape via f7. But after 1.f7+ Bxf7, 2.Qh8 is now checkmate.

Diagram 168

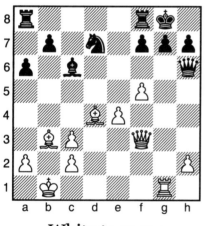

White to move

Following 1.Qh3, Black has only bad options. 1...Qxh3 2.Rxg7+ Kh8 3.Rxf7+ Kg8 4.Rg7+ Kh8 5.Rxd7+ Rf6 6.Bxf6#. Memorize these types of checkmate patterns.

Diagram 169

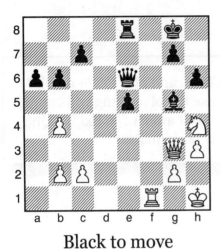

Black to move

You can look at this one awhile and miss the simplicity of it. 1... Qc4 attacks the knight twice and the unprotected rook once. White must lose something.

Diagram 170

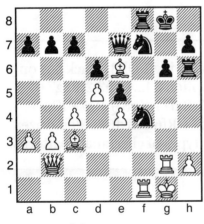

White to move

One of the keys to this position is the bishop on e6 that pins the knight. 1.Rxf4, and after 1...exf4 2.Bh8, 3.Qg7 is an unstoppable checkmate.

Diagram 171

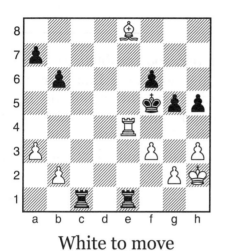

White to move

1.g4+ hxg4 2.hxg4#. Remember that pawns can sometimes give check and even checkmate!

Diagram 172

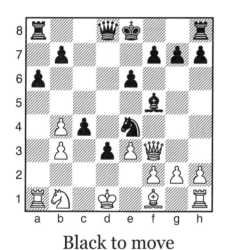

Black to move

This is a good problem to try to explain to a friend. 1...Bg4! 2.Qxg4 Nf2+ forks the king and queen. What words would you use to describe that?

Diagram 173

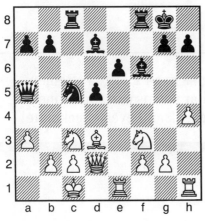

Black to move

Another good problem to explain to someone. 1...d4 drives the knight on c3 away, but why is that important? 1...d4 2.Ne2 Nb3 forks the king and queen, and the c2-pawn is pinned by Black's rook.

Diagram 174

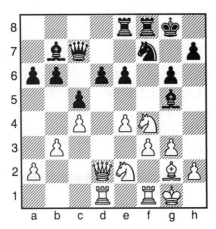

Black to move

The key to this problem is the bishop on g5 pinning the knight on f4. When a piece is pinned like this, we want to attack it. How? 1...e5: if the knight moves, the queen is lost, and it would be better for White just to lose the knight.

Diagram 175

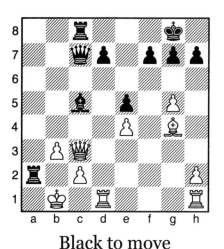

Black to move

1...Bd4 puts White in a tough spot. After 2.Qxc7 Black will play 2...Ra1#, while after 2.Kxa2, Black will play 2...Bxc3 and checkmate White anyway.

Diagram 176

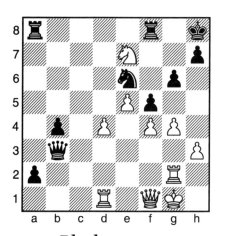

Black to move

It is true that Black is winning, but what is the fastest way to win? 1...Qxd1 2.Qxd1 and then 2...a1Q. Black is a rook ahead, with another pawn ready to queen.

Diagram 177

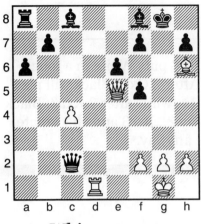

White to move

White is losing by a bishop, but is there any weakness on Black's back rank? 1.Qg7+! Bxg7 2.Rd8+ Bf8 3.Rxf8#.

This pattern happens a lot.

Diagram 178

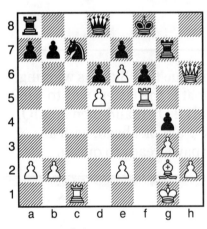

White to move

After 1.Rg5!, Black has to play 1...fxg5, opening up the f-file. White comes back with 2.Qh8+ Rg8, and then 3.Rf1+ Ke8 4.Qxg8#.

Diagram 179

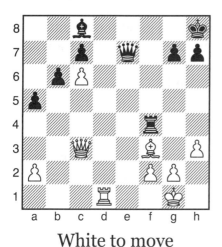

White to move

Black has a back-rank weakness, but how can White take advantage of it? 1.Qe5, and now 1...Qxe5 2.Rd8+ leads to mate. If Black tries 1...Qf6 to protect the rook and guard the d8 square, White can capture the rook for free.

Diagram 180

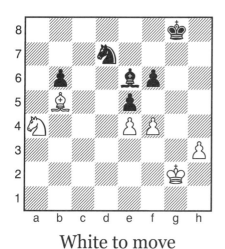

White to move

After 1.f5, the black bishop has to leave the protection of the knight. White will then play 2.Bxd7.

Diagram 181

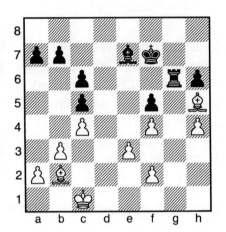

Is 1.Bxg6+ White's best move?

No!! It is a good move, but there is a better one. The rook is not going anywhere and the king is stuck on f7. Can we attack the rook twice? 1.e4 fxe4 2.f5 wins a whole rook.

When you have a good move, take your time and look for a better one.

Diagram 182

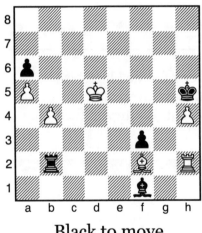

Black to move

This is an easy one to overlook: 1...Bg2.

Suddenly White's bishop is under attack and the rook is trapped. If the bishop moves, then 2...f2+ and the pawn queens.

Diagram 183

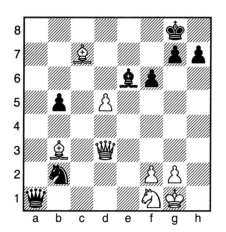

No! 1.dxe6 Nxd3 and now 2.e7+ Kh8 3.e8Q#.

Should White move the queen?

Diagram 184

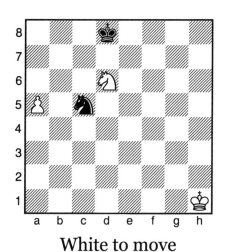

Another deflection problem. 1.Nb7+ Nxb7 2.a6 and Black cannot stop the pawn from queening.

White to move

Diagram 185

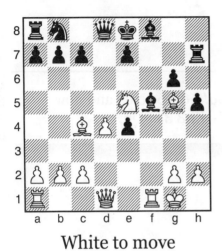

1.Rxf5 gxf5 2.Qh5+! Rxh5 3.Bf7#.

White to move

Diagram 186

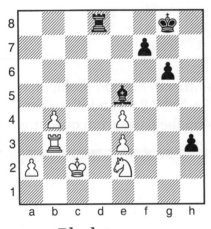

You have probably guessed that this is about queening the h-pawn. 1...Rd1 and now 2.Kxd1 h2. White's own king blocks the rook from controlling the queening square. The pawn queens.

Black to move

Diagram 187

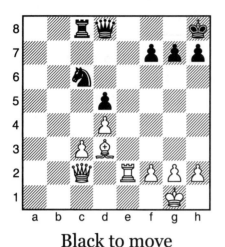

Black to move

Black can play 1...Nxd4 and win the pawn and the exchange (rook for knight).

If White is careless and plays 2.cxd4, then 2...Rxc2. The c3-pawn is pinned.

Diagram 188

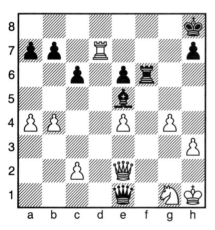

Black to move

The bishop on e5 controls h2, but how can Black use that? 1...Rf2! 2.Qxe1 Rh2#.

Black should at least have had this thought: What about White's rook checking me on d8? Does it accomplish anything? 2.Rd8+ Kg7 3.Rd7+ Kg6, and there are no more checks. It is important to look at it anyway.

Diagram 189

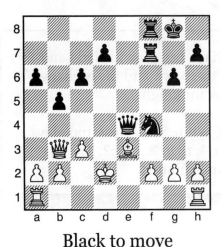

Black to move

1...Qd3+, and on 2.Kc1 Ne2#, while on 2.Ke1 Qe2#. This is a simple checkmate, but there are two possible king moves. Make sure you look at all the possible replies.

Diagram 190

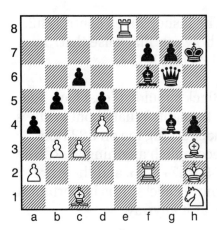

Is 1...Bxh3 Black's best move?

Yes!! But did you see why? 1...Bxh3 2.Kxh3 and now 2...Qg1 attacks two unprotected pieces. White loses either the knight or the bishop.

Black had to think, "What does the board look like after 1...Bxh3 ?"

Diagram 191

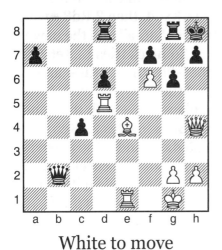

White to move

Checkmate: 1.Qxh7+ Kxh7 2.Rh5#. The pawn on g6 cannot take because it is pinned.

Diagram 192

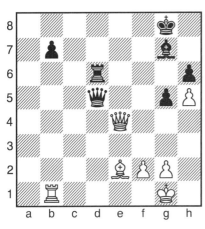

White to move

1.Bc4 pins the queen to the king.

Diagram 193

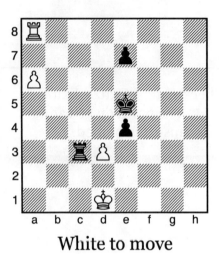

White to move

After 1.d4+, Black is in trouble. If 1...Kxd4, then 2.Rd8+ with the threat of a6-a7 and the pawn queens. So Black tries 1...Ke6 (if K to the f-file, then 2.Rf8+ and 3.a7 and the pawn queens). Now White plays 2.d5+ with the same threats. Black moves 2...Ke5 3.a7 Ra3 4.d6, and if the pawn is taken, the rook will check and the a-pawn queens, while if it isn't taken then 5.d7 and it's the d-pawn that queens.

Diagram 194

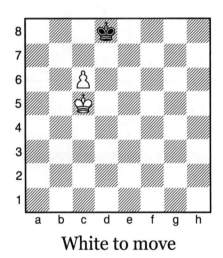

White to move

After 1.Kd6 Kc8 2.c7, Black's king must move to b7, when White plays 3.Kd7 and the pawn will queen.

Diagram 195

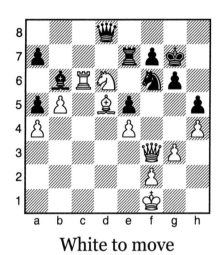

White to move

1.Qxf6++! Kxf6 2.Ne8#. Double check and mate.

Diagram 196

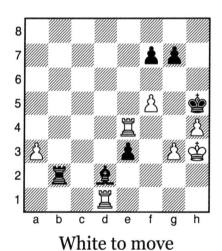

White to move

Interestingly, after 1.Re8 there is nothing Black can do about the threat of 2.Rh8#.

Diagram 197

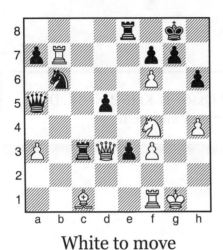

White to move

A classic position. 1.Qg6! and after 1...fxg6 2.Rg7+ K-any 3.Nxg6#.

Diagram 198

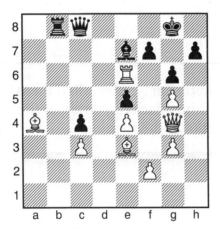

White to move.
Should White resign?

Things do seem a little grim for White: the rook is pinned and attacked by a pawn. Should White just give up and call it a day?

No! 1.Bd7! Qxd7 2.Rxg6+ and White wins a pawn and queen for a rook and bishop, and will win more material very soon.

Diagram 199

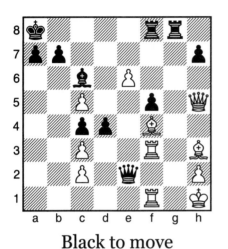

Black to move

The powerful 1...Rg4! completely destroys White's defenses. 2.Bxg4 Qxf1 is checkmate.

See the importance of the bishop on c6 and of the pin on the rook on f3.

Diagram 200

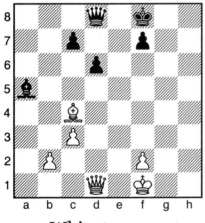

White to move

1.Qd5 makes two threats. The first threat is 2.Qf7# and the other is to take the bishop. Black should give up the bishop and fight on.

Diagram 201

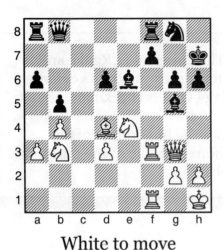

White to move

After 1.Qh3! (threatening Nxg5+) 1...Bxh3 2.Rxf7+ Rxf7 3.Rxf7#.

Diagram 202

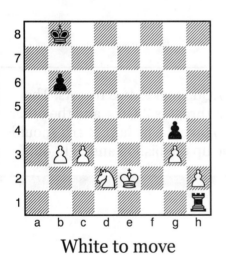

White to move

After 1.Nf1, Black's rook is trapped. White will play Kf2, Kg2, and Kxh1 and there is nothing Black can do to stop it. The best he can do is to give up the rook for the knight and play on two pawns down.

Diagram 203

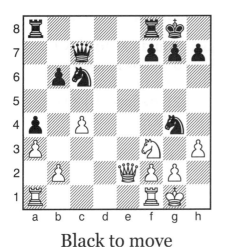

Black to move

Black plays 1...Nd4 and White must give up the queen. If the queen moves, Black can play ...Nxf3+ and ...Qh2#.

Diagram 204

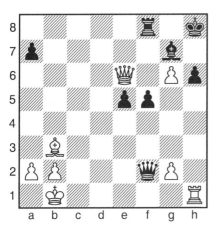

White to move

Always remember that queens can move backwards. 1.Rxh6+ Bxh6 2.Qxe5+ Bg7, and now 3.Qh2+ Bh6 4.Qxh6#.

Sometimes students get so focused on a position that they only look at the squares directly around the king. Remember to look at the entire board.

Diagram 205

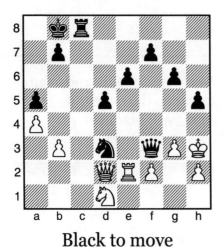

Black to move

Black would like to play 1... Nf4+ followed by 2...Qg4#, but can't because of White's queen. So, 1...Rc2! (deflection) 2.Qxc2 Nf4+ 3.Kh4 Qg4#.

If 2.Qe3, then 2...Qxe2 wins the rook.

Diagram 206

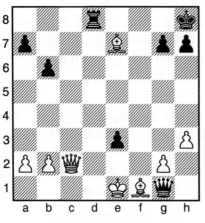

Black to move

Just like the last problem. 1... Rd1+ and White has two losing options: 2.Qxd1 Qf2#, or 2.Kxd1 Qxf1#. Check out each possibility before your start sacrificing pieces.

Diagram 207

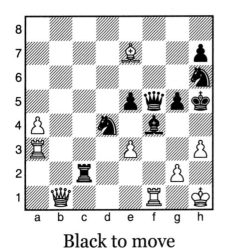

Black to move

1...Qxh3+! 2.gxh3 Rh2+ 3.Kg1 Ne2#.

Diagram 208

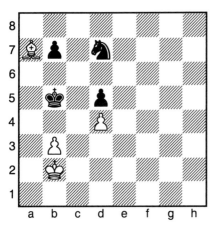

Black to move

It is easy to miss these: 1...b6 and the bishop is trapped. Black will play ...Ka6 and take the bishop next, and White can do nothing to stop it.

Diagram 209

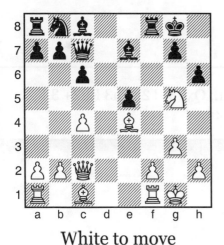

White to move

White would like to play Qh7# but can't because the bishop is in the way. So... 1.Bd5+ cxd5 2.Qh7#.

Black could try 1....Rf7, but then White plays 2.Qh7+ and 3.Qh8#.

Diagram 210

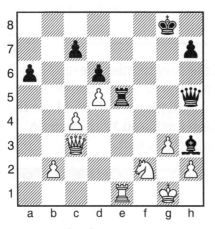

Black to move

You have thought, "I think White is weak on the back row, but how can I take advantage of that?'

1...Qf3! and if 2.Qxf3 then 2... Rxe1# or, on any other move, 2... Qg2#.

Diagram 211

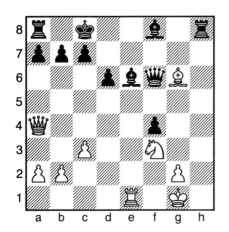

Yes!! 1.Rxe6 Qxe6 2.Bf5! Qxf5 is followed by 3.Qe8#.

Is 1.Rxe6 White's best move?

Diagram 212

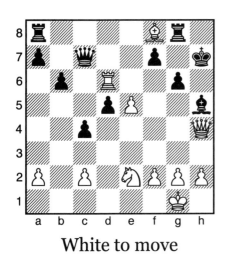

1.Qxh5 gxh5 2.Rh6#.

White to move

Diagram 213

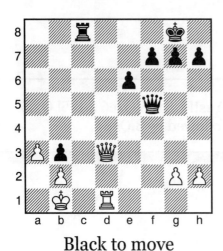

Black to move

After 1...Rd8, White is stuck. 2.Qxf5 Rxd1 is checkmate.

Diagram 214

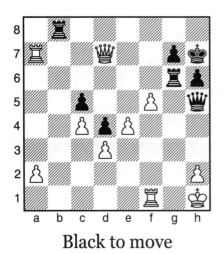

Black to move

White has serious threats and the game could go either way, but Black wins with the right move: 1...Qf3+ 2.Rxf3 (the only move) 2...Rb1+ 3.Rf1 Rxf1#.

Rooks belong on open files.

Diagram 215

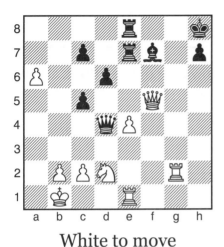

White to move

1.Qxh7+ Kxh7 2.Rh1+ Bh5 3.Rxh5#. Make sure you see moves like 2...Bh5. You don't want to sacrifice your queen and miss an interpose. This time it was harmless.

Diagram 216

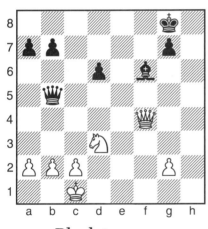

Black to move

1...Bg5 pins the queen to the king.

Diagram 217

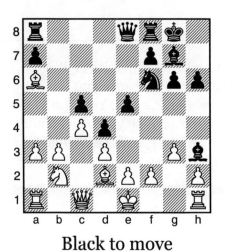

Black to move

How long did you think about this one?

1...Qc6 attacks two unprotected pieces.

Diagram 218

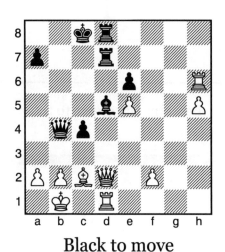

Black to move

1...Be4! 2.Qxb4 Rxd1#.

White has other moves, but they will all lose at least the queen.

Diagram 219

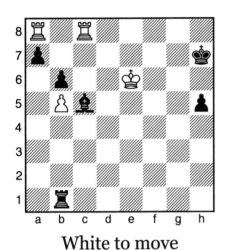

White to move

1.Rh8+ K-any 2.Rag8#.

Diagram 220

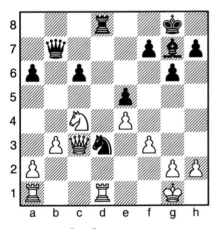

Black to move

It looks bad for Black. Black is behind and the knight seems lost. But... 1...Qa7+.2.Kh1 Nf2+ 3.Kg1 Nh3+ 4.Kh1 Qg1+ 5.Rxg1 Nf2# (smothered mate).

Diagram 221

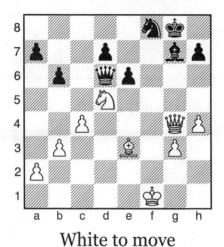

White to move

White wins a piece. How?
1.Nf6+ K-any 2.Qxg7+! Kxg7
3.Ne8+ followed by 4.Nxd6.

Diagram 222

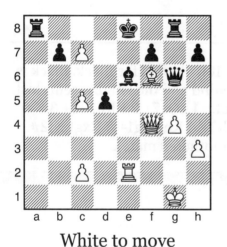

White to move

There are many things to look at. White's rook pins Black's bishop. The pawn on c7 is close to queening. What makes this work?

1.Qa4+ Rxa4 2.c8Q#.

Scan the whole board for moves!

Diagram 223

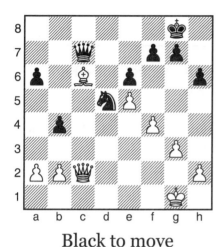

Black to move

How does Black take advantage of the pin on White's bishop? 1...b3 2.axb3 Nb4 attacks the bishop twice and wins it.

Diagram 224

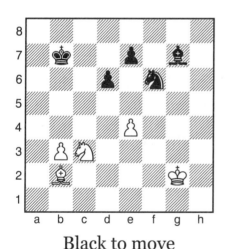

Black to move

1...Nxe4 2.Nxe4 Bxb2 wins a pawn. Pawns are very important in endgames and that one pawn could be the difference between a win and a draw.

Diagram 225

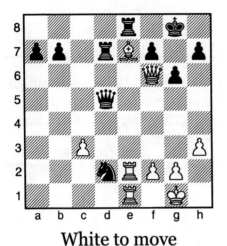

White to move

1.Qh8+ Kxh8 2.Bf6+ Kg8 3.Rxe8#.

Take advantage of back-rank weaknesses.

Diagram 226

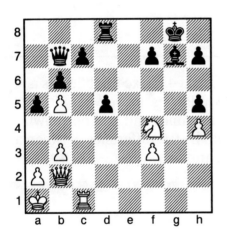

White to move.
Should White resign?

No! It looks bad, but White is actually winning: 1.Rg1 and now the bishop is pinned. Black can block with 1...d4, but then 2.Nxh5 wins the bishop.

Diagram 227

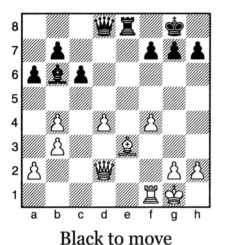

Black to move

After 1...Rxe3, White should not take back because of 2.Qxe3 Bxd4 and the queen is pinned to the king.

Diagram 228

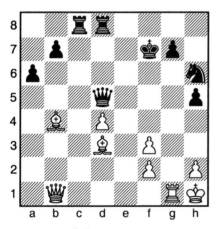

White to move

This is like Problem 209. How? If White could put the queen on g6, it would soon be checkmate. The bishop is in the way. So... 1.Bc4! Qxc4 2.Qg6+ Kg8 3.Qxg7#.

Diagram 229

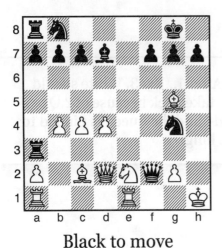

Black to move

For this problem, you need to look at the entire board: 1...Rh3+ 2.gxh3 Qh2#.

Diagram 230

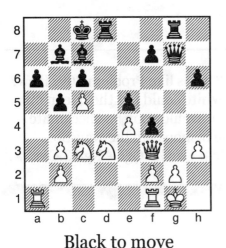

Black to move

Black would like to play ...Qg2# but can't, so... 1...Rxd3! 2.Qxd3 Qxg2#.

White can sacrifice the queen and play on a queen down.

Diagram 231

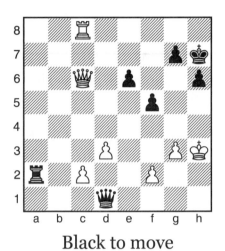

Black to move

1...Rxc2! and if 2.Qxc2 Qh1#, or 2. Q-anywhere else Rxc8.

Diagram 232

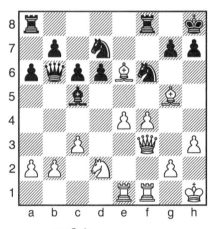

White to move

Did this one take more than 5 minutes?

1.b4 traps Black's bishop.

Diagram 233

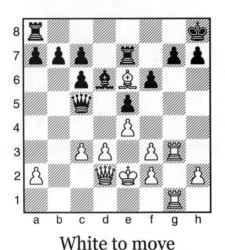

White to move

After 1.Qh6 Black has two losing options:

1...gxh6 2.Rg8+ Rxg8 3.Rxg8#;
or 1...Rg8 2.Qxh7+ Kxh7 3.Rh3#.

Diagram 234

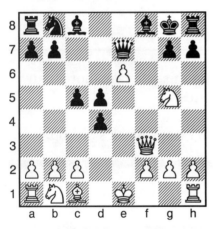

White to move

1.Qf7+ Qxf7 2.exf7#.

Diagram 235

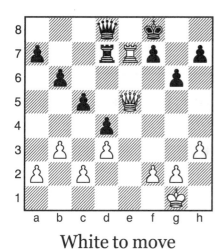

White to move

1.Qf6 and Black is in a hopeless position. If 1...Qxe7 or 1...Rxe7, then 2.Qh8#. On 1...Kg8, 2.Qxf7+ and 3.Qxh7#.

Diagram 236

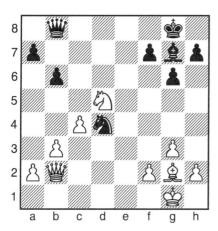

Which is better, 1...Ne2+ or 1...Nf3+ ?

What is the difference? 1...Ne2+ loses because White can play 2.Qxe2, but with 1...Nf3+ Black wins White's queen.

Be careful and look at your opponent's pieces and where they can go before you make a move. It is the difference between winning and losing.

Diagram 237

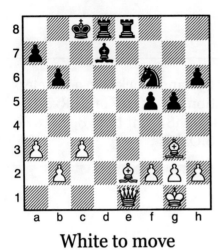

White to move

1.Ba6#. Learn the cross-bishop pattern.

Diagram 238

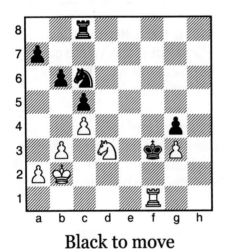

Black to move

1...Ke2. King fork. Remember that the king is a weapon in the endgame.

Diagram 239

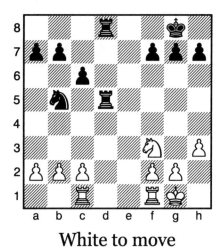

White to move

1.c4. Pawn fork.

Diagram 240

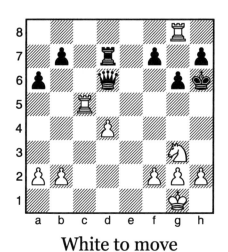

White to move

1.Rh5+ gxh5 2.Nf5#.

Diagram 241

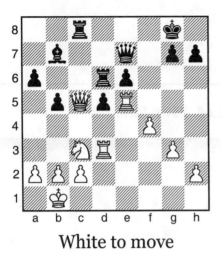

White to move

1.Nxd5. Black can take the knight three different ways: 1...Bxd5 2.Qxc8+; 1...Rxd5 2.Qxe7; or 1...exd5 2.Rxe7 Rxc5 3.Rxb7 and White ends up a piece ahead.

What about 1...Rxc5 ? There follows 2.Nxe7+ K-any 3.Rxc5 and White wins at least the exchange.

It is very important to make a habit of calculating all possibilities.

Diagram 242

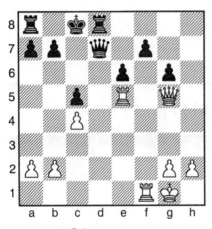

White to move

This idea has happened before, but it needs to be set up. 1.Rxc5+ Kb8 2.Qe5+ Qd6 3.Rd1! and the black queen cannot move forward to take the rook because of the pin. After 3...Qxe5, it's 4.Rxd8#.

Diagram 243

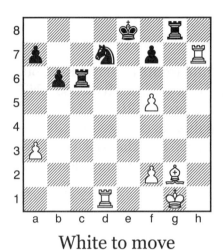

White to move

White would like to play 1.Bxc6, but can't because the bishop is pinned. So, 1.Rh8 Rxh8 and now 2.Bxc6, and Black's knight will also fall. White wins a piece.

Diagram 244

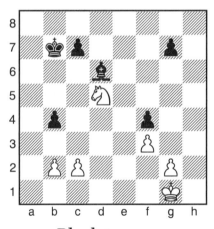

Black to move

This type of thing happens in endgames because many players aren't thinking about it happening: 1...c6. White's knight is under attack and it cannot make a safe move. The knight is lost and should give itself up for a pawn.

Diagram 245

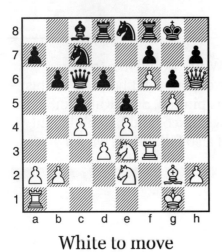

White to move

White wants to play 1.Rh3, but can't because of 1...Bxh3, so 1.Nf5 and if 1...gxf5 2.Rh3 and it's unstoppable checkmate. If 1...Bxf5, then 2.exf5 and the rook will move to h3 with checkmate to follow.

Diagram 246

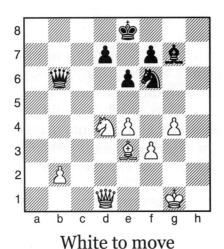

White to move

1.Nf5 and three things happen at once: First, the unprotected black bishop is under attack. Next, the knight protects White's bishop. And last, Black's queen is under attack.

Since the queen has no checks, Black will lose a piece.

Diagram 247

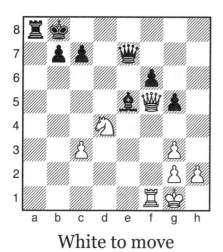

1.Nc6+ bxc6 2.Rb1+ Ka7
3.Qf2+ Ka6 4.Qa2+ Qa3 (forced)
5.Qxa3#.

The tough part of this problem
was picturing the queen going
from f2 to a2. Queens have the
unique ability to move backwards
and attack diagonally.

White to move

Diagram 248

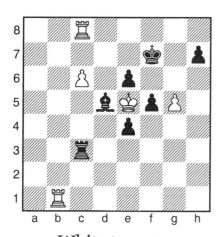

1.g6+ and Black has two losing
options: 1...hxg6 2.Rb7#, or 1...
Kxg6 2.Rg8+ Kf7 (2...Kh5 3.Rh1
leads to checkmate) 3.Rbg1 and
the threat is R1g7#, which Black is
powerless to stop.

White to move

Diagram 249

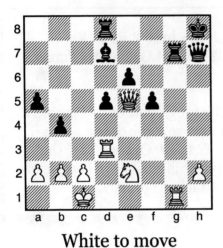

White to move

1.Rh3 and Black has a big problem. If Black tries 1...Qxh3 there is 2.Qxg7#, and on 1...Rg8 to protect the rook on g7, White just takes the queen.

Diagram 250

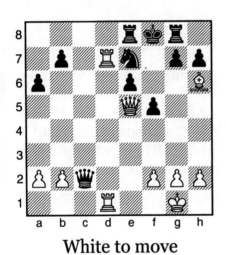

White to move

1.Qf6# game over.

Diagram 251

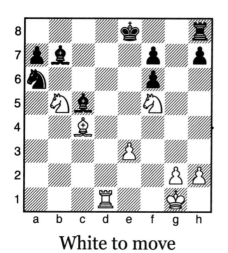

White to move

Sometimes you need to think two moves deep: 1.Nbd6+ Bxd6 2.Nxd6+ K-any 3.Nxb7 and you win a piece.

Diagram 252

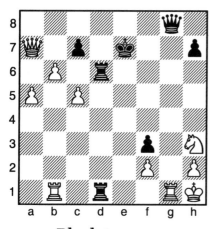

Black to move

1....Qg2# game over.

Diagram 253

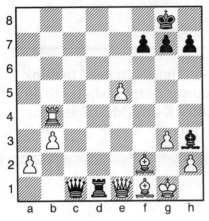

White to move

It looks bad for White, but...
1.Rd4! and suddenly Black is
completely lost. If 1...Rxe1 then
2.Rd8#, while on 1...Qc8 2.Qxd1
wins the rook.

Diagram 254

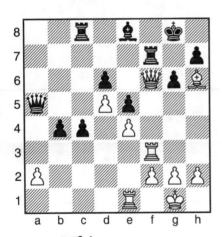

White to move

1.Qe7! and now if 1...Rxe7 then
2.Rf8#, or if 1...Rxf3 2.Qg7#.

Diagram 255

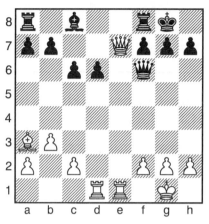

White to move

The power is discovered check. 1.Qxf8+ Kxf8 2.Rxd6.

This attacks the queen, but wherever the queen moves, the rook can move and attack it while the bishop gives check. More importantly, Rd8 is checkmate.

Diagram 256

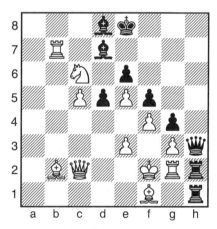

Black to move

Lots of black pieces on the h-file, but where is the breakthrough? 1...Qxg3+ 2.Kxg3 Bh4#.

Diagram 257

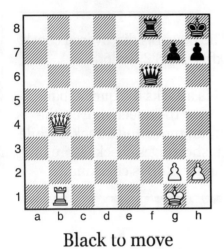

1...Qf2+ (pushes the king to h1) 2.Kh1 Qf1+ 3.Rxf1 Rxf1#.

Black to move

Diagram 258

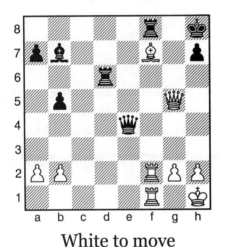

A very sharp position. However, 1.Bd5 does three things: it attacks the queen; Rxf8 with checkmate is being threatened; and if Black tries 1...Rxf2 then 2.Qg8 is checkmate.

White to move

Diagram 259

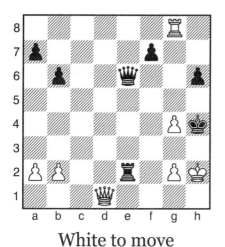

White to move

1.Qe1+ probably surprised Black, but after 1...Rxe1 (forced) White wins with 2.g3#.

Diagram 260

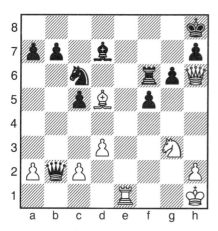

White to move

It seems like all the back rank is protected. But... 1.Nh5! (threatens 2.Qg7#) 1...gxh5 2.Rg1 with the threat of 3.Rg8#. There is no way out.

Diagram 261

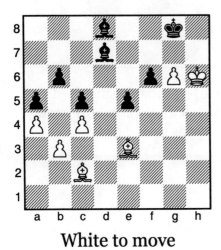

White to move

White would like to queen the pawn, but how? 1.g7 would be met by 1...f5. However, 1.Bg5 fxg5 2.g7 followed by 3.Bh7+ and the pawn queens.

Diagram 262

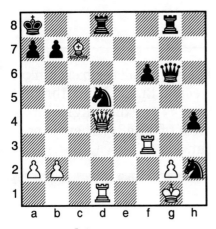

White to move

A typical checkmate pattern. 1.Qxa7+ Kxa7 2.Ra3#. These kinds of checkmates should become part of your chess thought process.

Diagram 263

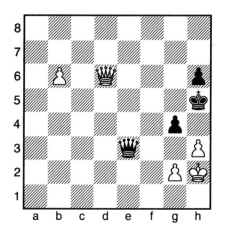

Black to move and draw

White's pawn will queen if Black doesn't do something. 1...g3+ 2.Qxg3 Qg1+ 3.Kxg1= (stalemate).

Diagram 264

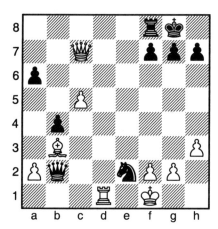

White to move

Another typical checkmate pattern: 1.Qxf7+ Rxf7 2.Rd8#.

Diagram 265

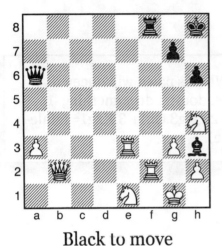

Black to move

Another pattern. Black is behind, but that's OK: 1...Qf1+ 2.Rxf1 Rxf1#.

Diagram 266

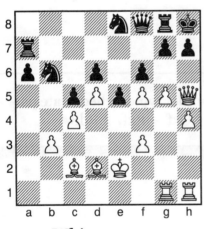

White to move

1.Qxh7+ Kxh7 2.g6+ Kh8 3.Rg5!. This threatens Rh5#, but if 3...fxg5 then 4.hxg5#.

Diagram 267

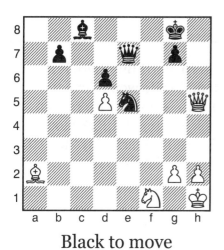

Black to move

How much time did you spend on this one? 1...Bg4 and the queen is trapped.

Diagram 268

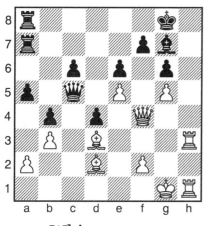

White to move

There are many power pieces aimed at Black, but how does White break through?

1.Qf6! threatens 2.Rh8+ Bxh8 3.Rxh8#.

Black can play 1...Bxf6, but after 2.gxf6 the threat of 3.Rh8# is unstoppable.

Diagram 269

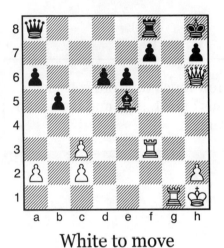

White to move

Pattern alert! But there is a problem. White would love to play 1.Qxh7+ Kxh7 2.Rh3#. But the rook is pinned. 1.Rg2 blocks the pin, and if Black plays 1...Qxf3 then White plays 2.Qxf8#.

Diagram 270

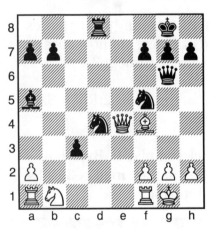

Black to move

Did you see this one or did you peek at the answer? 1...Ng3! and not only is Black threatening 2...Nde2#, but White's queen is under attack. There are no good options for White. If 2.Qxg6, now 2...Nde2 is checkmate.

Diagram 271

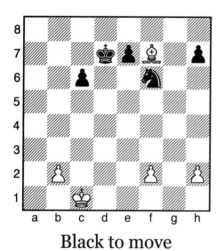

Black to move

After 1...e6, the bishop is trapped. Black will play ...Ke7 and take the bishop. The bishop should at least take the e-pawn.

Diagram 272

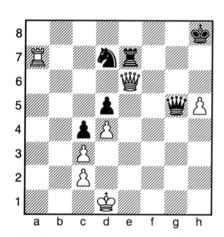

White to move and draw

A tricky one, but you will see the idea: 1.Ra8+ Kh7 2.Rh8+ Kxh8 and 3.Qh6+. Black has to take the queen, and after 3...Qxh6 it is stalemate.

Diagram 273

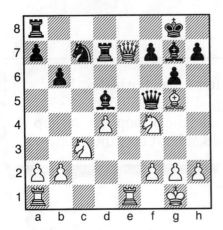

Yes! 1.Ncxd5 Rxe7 2.Nxe7+ and 3.Nxf5 wins material. Or 1...Nxd5 2.Qe8+! Rxe8 3.Rxe8+ Bf8 4.Bh6 and checkmate can't be stopped.

Is 1.Ncxd5 White's best move?

Diagram 274

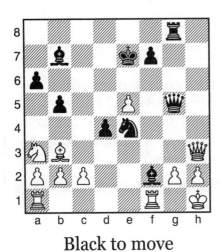

1...Qxg2+! 2.Qxg2 Ng3+ 3.hxg3 Rh8#. Notice how the bishop on b7 pins the queen.

Black to move

Diagram 275

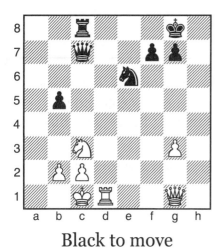

Black to move

1...b4 and if White moves the knight, then 2...Qc2#. White loses a piece.

Diagram 276

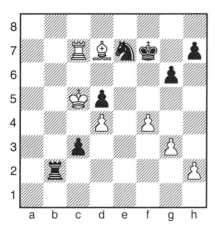

Is 1...Rb7 Black's best move?

Yes! After 1...Rb7 2.Rxb7 c2, there is no way for White to stop the pawn from queening. White's king is in the way again.

Diagram 277

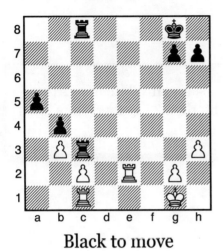

Black to move

In an even ending, every pawn is important. 1...Rxb3 and if 2.cxb3 then 2...Rxc1+, and Black has won a pawn.

Diagram 278

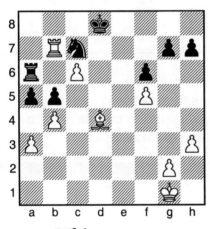

White to move

1.Rb8+ Ke7 2.Bc5+ Kf7 3.Rf8#.

Diagram 279

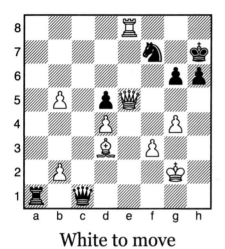

White to move

1.Bg6+ Kg6 2.Rg8+ Kh7 3.Qg7#.

Diagram 280

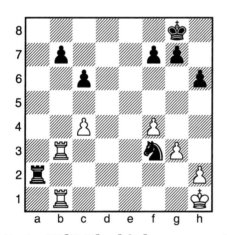

Is 1...Nd2 Black's best move?

No! 1...Rh2# is the best move. Remember: when you find a good move, take your time and try to find a better one.

Diagram 281

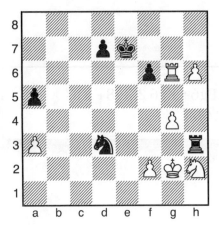

Is 1.Kxh3 White's best move?

No! 1.Kxh3 Nf4+ 2.K-any Nxg6 and Black is still in the game.

All White needs to do is to play 1.Rg7+ first and only then take the rook. That way, you come out a whole rook ahead.

Diagram 282

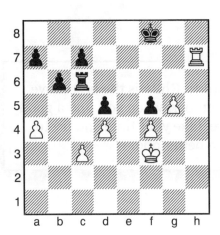

Active King Study 1:
White to move

1.Kg3! Rxc3+ 2.Kh4 Rf3 3.g6 Rxf4+ (so far it seems like White is just giving away pawns) 4.Kg5 Re4 5.Kf6 Kg8 6.Rg7+ Kh8 7.Rxc7 Re8 8.Kxf5 Re4 9.Kf6 Rf4+ 10.Ke5 Rg4 11.g7+ Kg8 12.Rxa7 Rg1 13.Kxd5 Rc1 14.Kd6 Rc2 15.d5 Rc1 16.Rc7 Ra1 17.Kc6 Rxa4 18.d6, Black resigns (Capablanca vs. Tartakower, New York 1924).

White's king simply ran all over the board, while Black's king was stuck. The king is a weapon in the endgame.

Diagram 283

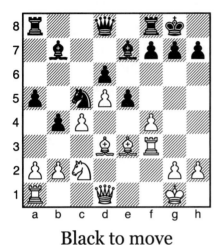

Black to move

There are many pieces on the board and so it's important to look at all of them, including the pawns. 1...e4 with a pawn fork (the knight protects the pawn).

Diagram 284

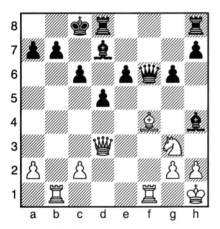

White to move

One key to this position is the bishop on f4. White takes advantage of that with 1.Qa6. The threat is 2.Qb7#, but can't Black just play 1...bxa6? No, because of 2.Rb8#. It's hopeless.

Diagram 285

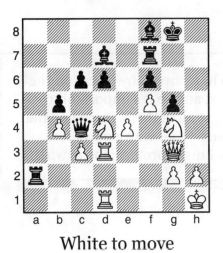

White to move

How long did you spend looking at this one? Are you peeking at the answer? There are many pieces on the board, However, 1.Ne3 traps Black's queen.

My experience is that trapping pieces is one of the hardest tactics to see.

Diagram 286

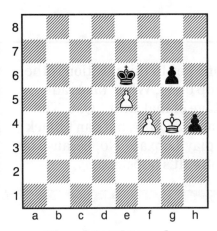

Should White play
1.Kxh4 or 1.Kh3 ?

Let's look at each move:

1.Kxh4 Kf5 2.Kg3(h3) g5 3.fxg5 Kxg5 and Black's king takes the e-pawn, with a draw.

1.Kh3 Kf5 2.Kxh4 g5+ 3.fxg5 Kxe5 4.Kh5 and the king will help the pawn to queen.

Diagram 287

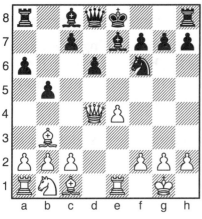

Black to move

This problem requires you to see two moves ahead. The target you are eyeing is the bishop on b3. 1...c5 2.Q-any 2.c4 and the bishop is trapped.

Trapping pieces and putting your opponent's pieces on bad squares is really important.

Diagram 288

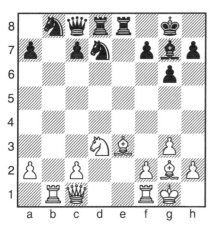

White to move

You should see this one: 1.Bb7 traps the queen.

Diagram 289

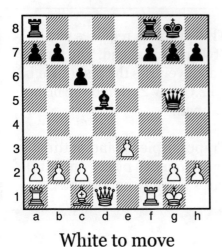

White to move

Black is threatening ...Qg2#; what is the best way to stop it? 1.e4. Now the queen and bishop are both under attack.

Sometimes the best defense is a good offense.

Diagram 290

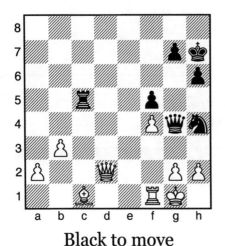

Black to move

A tricky one. 1...Rxc1 and White has two losing options, 2.Qxc1 Qg2# and 2.Rxc1 Nf3+ (knight fork) winning the queen.

White's rook was guarding the f3 square.

Diagram 291

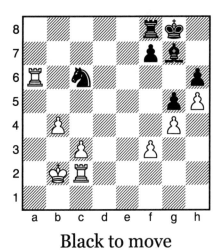

Black to move

Did you notice the bishop on g7? What is it doing? It is pinning the pawn on c3.

1...Nxb4 forks the rooks and will win one of them. When you can combine tactics like a pin and a fork, they can be very powerful.

Diagram 292

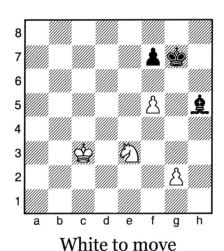

White to move

You should be seeing these kinds of problems fairly quickly. 1.g4 traps the bishop.

Diagram 293

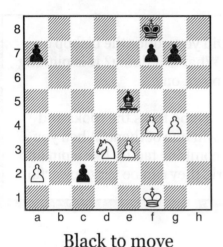

Black to move

Black cannot queen the pawn right now, but after 1...Bb2 Black forces White to give up the knight to stop the pawn.

Diagram 294

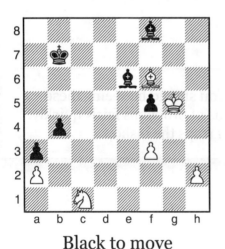

Black to move

There is an emphasis on queening a pawn in some of these problems. What is the fastest way for Black to win? 1...Bxa2, and after 2.Nxa2 b3 White's knight and bishop cannot stop one of the pawns from queening (3.Nc1 b2, or 3.Nc3 b2 and if Black needs it, ...Bb4 will force the knight to move and a pawn queens).

Diagram 295

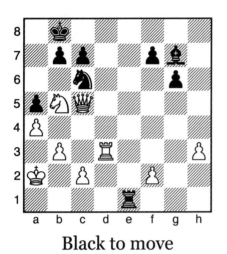

Black to move

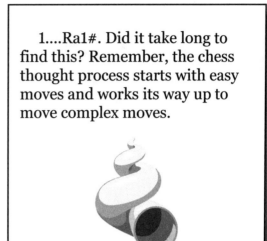

1....Ra1#. Did it take long to find this? Remember, the chess thought process starts with easy moves and works its way up to move complex moves.

Diagram 296

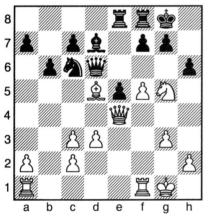

White to move

Notice how the bishop on d5 pins the f7-pawn? 1.f6 hxg5 (2.Qh7# was threatened) and now 2.Qg6, and the only way Black can stop 3.Qg7# is with 2...Qf6, when White can play 3.Rxf6. Black's position is in a shambles.

Diagram 297

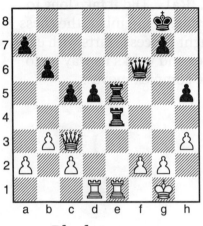

Black to move

Sometimes there is a "setup" move for a tactic. First, Black moves 1...Rxe1+ 2.Rxe1. So far, nothing too dramatic. But now Black plays 2...Re2!.

This threatens ...Qxf2+ followed by ...Qxg2# as well as ...Qxc3. If White tries to trade queens with 3.Qxf6, Black will reply with 3...Rxe1+ first and then play 4...gxf6, ending up a rook ahead.

Diagram 298

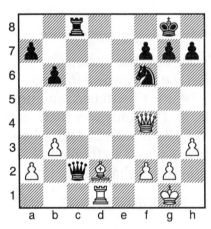

White to move

1.Rc1 and suddenly Black is either losing the queen or getting checkmated.

Diagram 299

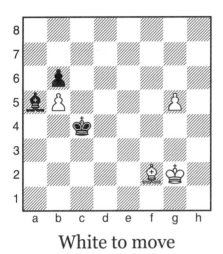

White to move

White wants to queen a pawn, but how?

1.Bxb6! Bxb6 2.g6 Bd4 3.b6 and Black will have to give up the bishop to stop one of the pawns while the other one queens (3... Bxb6 4.g7; or 3...Kb5 4.b7 Be5 5.g7).

Diagram 300

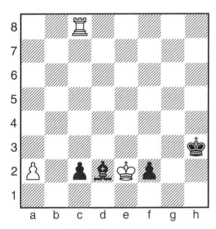

Black to move

Trying to queen a pawn: 1... Bc3 2.Rxc3+ Kg2 and the f-pawn queens.

Diagram 301

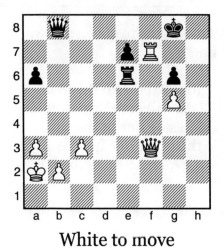

White to move

1.Qh3!. There are two threats. First, 2.Qh7#, and second, if 1...Kxf7, then 2.Qh7+ K-any and now 3.Qh8+ skewers the king and wins the queen.

Diagram 302

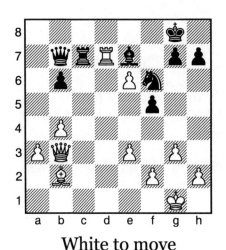

White to move

Another pawn queening adventure: 1.Rd8+ Bxd8 2.e7+ and then exd8Q.

Diagram 303

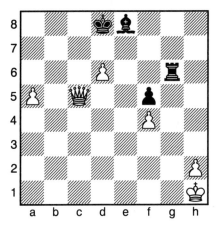

Black to move and draw

Try to create a stalemate. 1...Bc6+ 2.Qxc6 Rg1+! 3.Kxg1, stalemate.

Diagram 304

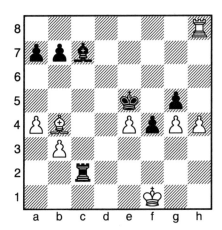

Active King Study 2:
Black to move

1....Kd4 (using the e-pawn as protection from White's rook) 2.hxg5 Ke3 3.Rh3+ f3 4.Ba3 (stops checkmate) 4...Bd6 5.b4 a5 6.Rh6 Bxb4 7.Bxb4 axb4 8.Kg1 b3 9.Rb6 b2 10.g6 Ke2 11.g7 f2+ 12.Kh2 f1Q 13.g8Q Kf3# (Schlage vs. Reti, Berlin 1928).

Diagram 305

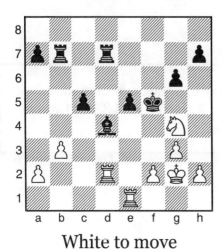

White to move

> 1.Rxd4 cxd4 (or 1...Rxd4)
> 2.Rxe5+ Kxg4 3.h3#.

Diagram 306

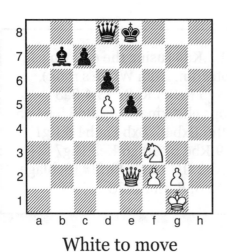

White to move

> 1.Qb5+ and then 2.Qxb7.

Diagram 307

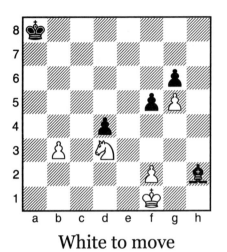

White to move

1.f4 and the bishop gets trapped. Black can try 1...Bg3, but after 2.Kg2 the bishop has no useful squares to go to.

Diagram 308

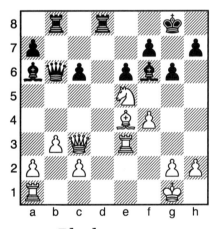

Black to move

After 1...Bd3 White can take the bishop four different ways, but they all lose at least an exchange:

2.cxd3 Qxe3+.
2.Bxd3 Qxe3+.
2.Nxd3 Qxe3+.
2.Qxd3 Rxd3.

Diagram 309

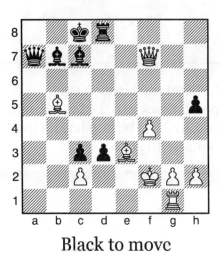

Black to move

1...Qxe3+ 2.Kxe3 Bb6#. Does this one surprise you? The king is in the middle of the board and Black had all the right pieces in all the right places.

Diagram 310

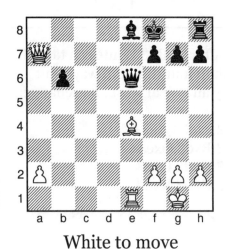

White to move

Remember that queens can move backwards: 1.Qa3+ Qe7 2.Bc6 Qxa3 3.Re8#; or 1...Kg8 2.Bxh7+ winning the queen.

Diagram 311

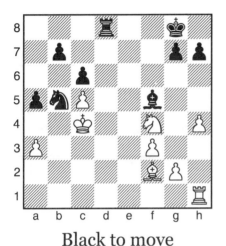

Black to move

This is a tough one. 1...Rd3!.
The threat is Rc3# so White plays
2.Nxd3 and now 2...Be6#.

Chess Tip:

Study checkmates where there
are no queens on the board.

Diagram 312

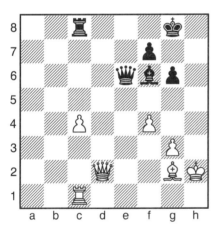

White to move

And the answer is... 1.Bh3,
skewering the queen and rook.
White wins the exchange.

Remember: start with the simple
moves. The queen and rook are
on the same diagonal.

Diagram 313

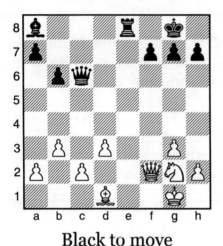

Black to move

Think "deflection." 1...Re1+ and White has two losing options, 2.Qxe1 Qg2+# and 2.Nxe1 Qh1#.

Diagram 314

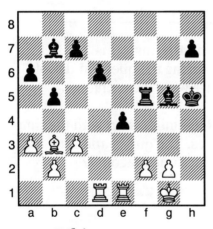

White to move

This tactic requires an interesting setup move: 1.g4+ Kxg4 and 2.Be6, pinning the rook to the king. White wins the exchange.

Diagram 315

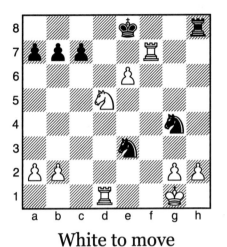

White to move

1.Nxc7#. Sadly for White, this move was missed and (along with many other bad moves) White went on to lose.

Diagram 316

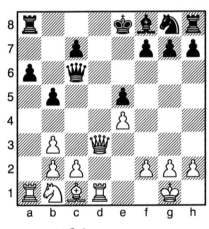

White to move

1.Rxa6! and again Black has two losing options: 1...Qxa6 2.Qd7# or 1...Rxa6 2.Qd8#.

Diagram 317

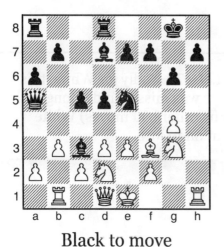

Black to move

White's knight on d2 can't move and the queen is doing double duty guarding the bishop and knight. 1...Nxf3+ 2.Qxf3 Bxd2+. White loses a piece.

Diagram 318

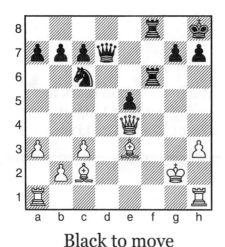

Black to move

Black has to stop checkmate and comes up with 1...Rg6+ 2.Kh2. Now there comes 2.... Qd2+ (deflection) 3.Bxd2 Rf2+ 4.Qg2 and R(either)xg2#.

Diagram 319

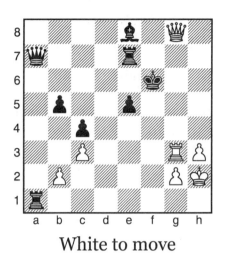

White to move

1.Rf3#.

Start simple. ☺

Diagram 320

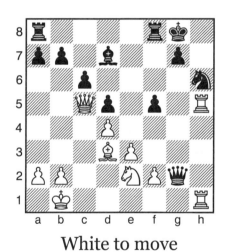

White to move

1.Rxh6 gxh6 2.Rg1 pins the queen to the king.

Diagram 321

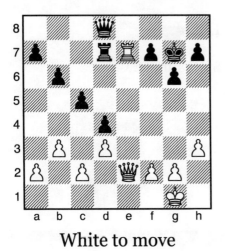

White to move

1.Qe5+ Kf8 (after 1...Kg8 2.Re8+ Black drops the queen and then the rook) 2.Qf6. If Black takes the rook with the queen or rook, then 2.Qh8#.

Diagram 322

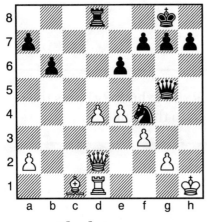

Black to move

Black seems to be in trouble, but 1...Rxd4 must have been a surprise for White:

2.Qxd4 Qg2#; or
2.Qxf4 Rxd1+ 3.Kh2 Qxf4 and Black is an exchange ahead.

Diagram 323

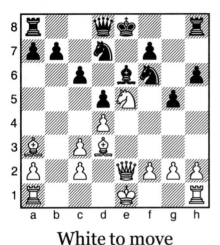

White to move

1.Nxc6 bxc6 2.Qxe6!+ fxe6 3.Bg6#. Another example of the cross-bishop checkmate.

Diagram 324

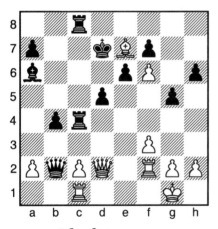

Black to move

1...Rxc2 2.Rxc2 Qb1+ 3.Rc1 Rxc1+ 4.Qd1 Rxd1 5.Rf1 Rxf1#.

One of the keys to this problem is the bishop on a6. It targets f1. Combine that with the active position of the queen and rooks, and Black must have something.

Diagram 325

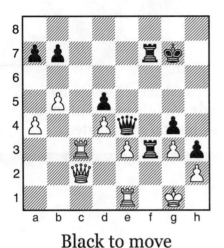

Black to move

1...Rf1+ 2.Rxf1 and now the surprising 2...Qh1+ 3.Kxh1 Rxf1#.

Noticed the doubled rooks on the open file and the aggressively placed queen.

Diagram 326

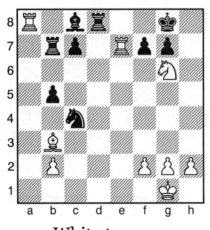

White to move

White's pieces are very active, but the knight is hanging.

1.Rd7, and now 1...Bxd7 2.Rxd8+ Kh7 3.Nf8+ and 4.Nxd7.

Or 1...Rxd7 2.Rxc8+ Kh7 3.Nf8+ and 4.Nxd7.

Diagram 327

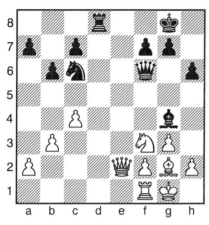

Black to move

You have seen a problem like this.

1...Nd4 and now three pieces attack White's knight. The knight will be lost.

Diagram 328

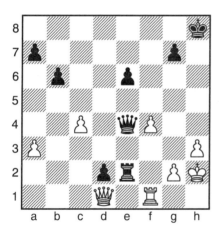

White to move and draw

After 1.Rf2, Black can try 1...Rxf2 and then White plays 2.Qh5+ and 3.Qe8+. The queen can check the black king forever, and that is perpetual check.

Diagram 329

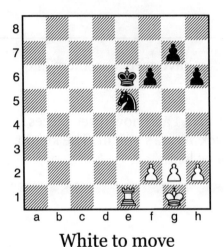

White to move

The black knight is pinned to the king. What should White do? 1.f4 and the knight is lost.

Attack pinned pieces!

Diagram 330

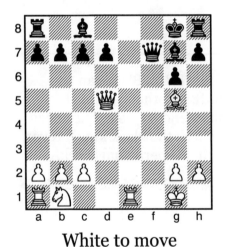

White to move

There are some back-rank weaknesses here. After 1.Re8+ Bf8 2.Bh6, it is unstoppable checkmate.

Diagram 331

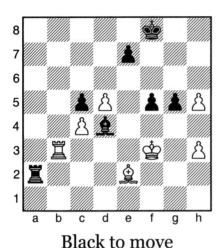

Black to move

Deflection: 1...g4+ 2.hxg4 fxg4+ and the king has to move away from protecting the bishop. Black wins a piece.

Diagram 332

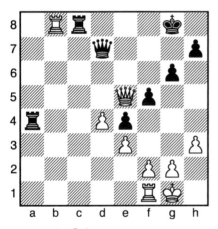

White to move

After 1.Rc1 Rxb8 2.Qxb8+ K-moves and 3.Rc7 pins the queen to the king.

What makes this idea work? White has a flight square. If White's pawn were on h2, White could not play Rc7 as then Black would checkmate after ...Ra1+.

Diagram 333

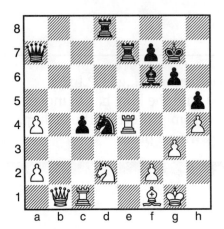

Should Black play 1...Rxe4 ?

No! 1...Rb8 hitting the queen is much stronger. If 2.Qa1, then 2...Ne2+ or 2...Nf3+ wins the queen.

White can only play 2.Nb3 and lose the knight instead (2...cxb3).

Diagram 334

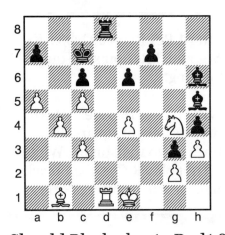

Should Black play 1...Rxd1 ?

Yes! Why? Now Black can queen a pawn:

1...Rxd1 2.Kxd1 Bxg4+ 3.hxg4 and after 3...h3 a pawn will queen.

Diagram 335

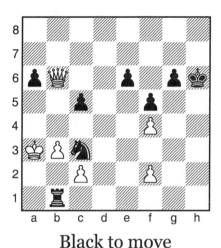

Black to move

You might think White is winning because White has a queen. But after 1...Na4 Black is threatening 2...Ra1# and 2.Kxa4 still loses to 2...Ra1#. White can only play 2.bxa4, giving up the queen.

Diagram 336

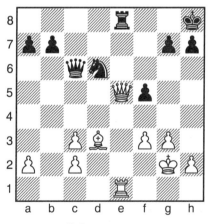

White to move

Black has a back-rank weakness, but how can White exploit it? 1.Qxd6, and if 1...Qxd6 2.Rxe8+ will lead to mate next move, while 1...Rxe1 2.Qf8# is mate right away. Black's position is hopeless.

Diagram 337

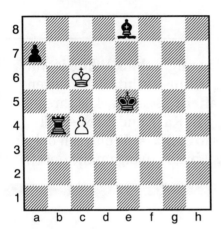

White to move and draw

1.Kc5. Black has to make a choice. Any rook move will be stalemate. What about giving the rook away for free? Shouldn't Black be able to win with bishop and pawn? Most of the time the answer is yes. Here, though, if Black plays something like 1...Bd7 2.Kxb4, White's king can head to the a1 corner and the pawn, king, and bishop are helpless. With an a- or h-pawn, you need to have the bishop which controls the queening square. If you don't, the game is a draw. Try it and see.

Diagram 338

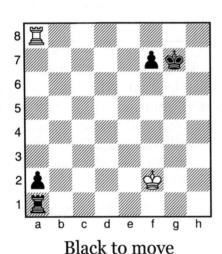

Black to move

After 1...Rh1, White is lost. 2.Rxa2 Rh2+ skewers the king and wins the rook. On any other move, 2...a1Q wins.

Diagram 339

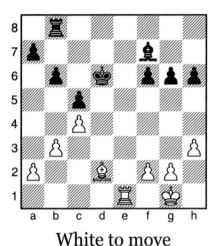

White to move

Start simple and find 1.Bf4+ and you skewer the king and win the rook.

Diagram 340

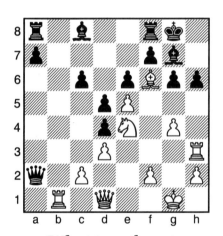

What two threats does 1.Qc1 make?

The first threat is Qxh6. If ...Bxh6, then after Rxh6 it is unstoppable checkmate. What is the other threat? Imagine that Black sees the threat on h6 and plays 1...g5. Now 2.Ra1 traps the queen.

It is much harder for an opponent to see threats coming from all directions.

Diagram 341

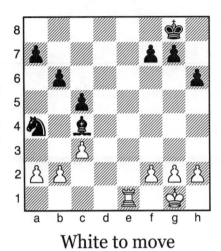

White to move

Pawn fork: 1.b3 and Black loses a piece.

Diagram 342

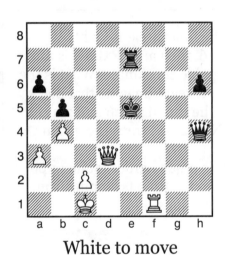

White to move

After 1.Rf5+ Ke6, White wins with 2.Qd5#.

Diagram 343

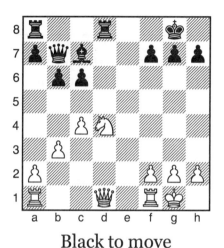

Black to move

Attack a pinned piece! 1...c5 will win the knight.

Diagram 344

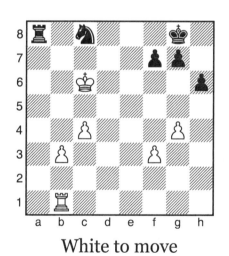

White to move

King fork: 1.Kb7 and White will win a piece.

Diagram 345

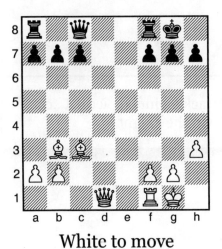

White to move

What is the key to this position? The bishop on b3 pins the f7-pawn.

What is the move? 1.Qd4 and it's unstoppable checkmate.

Diagram 346

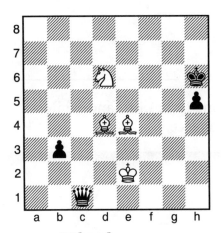

What happens
after Black plays 1...Qc7 ?

After 1...Qc7, White can play 2.Be3+. This forces Black to play 2...Kg7, and then 3.Ne8+ forks the king and queen.

If Black had played 1...Qa3 to be safe, then there was 2.Nf7#.

Diagram 347

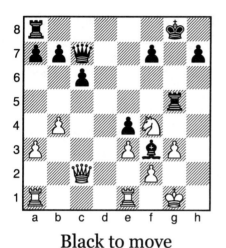

Black to move

Notice the bishop on f3 and how the rook has been lifted to g5. The rook wants to get to h1, but the knight holds h5. So 1...Qxf4 2.exf4 Rh5 and it is unstoppable checkmate on h1.

Diagram 348

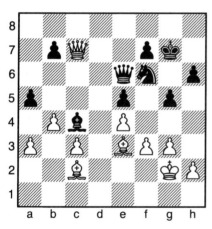

Black to move

Black is a pawn down, but that doesn't matter: 1...Qh3+ 2.Kxh3 Bf1#.

Diagram 349

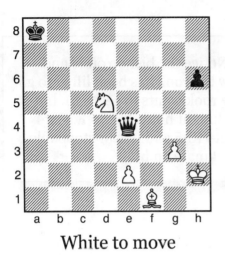

White to move

After 1.Bg2 the queen is under attack, but strangely enough there is not a single safe square on the board anywhere:

1...Qh7 2.Nf6+ wins the queen.
1...Qb1 2.Nc3+ wins the queen.
1...Qe5 2.Ne7+ K-any 3.Nc6+ forks.
1...Qd4 2.Nb4+ K-any 3.Nc6+ forks.

Diagram 350

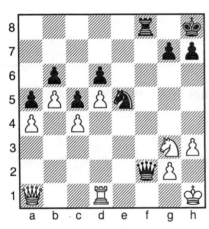

White to move

1.Rf1 and if the queen moves, then 2.Rxf8# is checkmate. Otherwise Black loses the queen.

Diagram 351

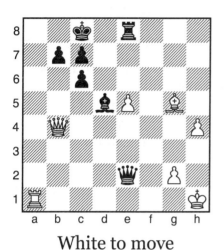

White to move

This is a hard one to visualize, but play through it a couple of times: 1.Ra8+ Kd7 2.Rd8+! Rxd8 3.Qe7+ Kc8 4.Qxd8#.

Diagram 352

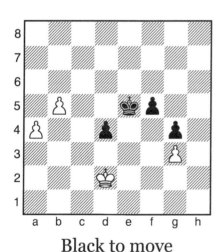

Black to move

Black will try to create two passed pawns and stop White's pawns. How? 1...f4 2.gxf4+ Kd6!!. Black's king stays an equal distance between White's b- and f-pawns, but the white king cannot stop Black's pawns. 3.f5 g3 4.Ke2 d3+ 5.Kxd3 g2 and the pawn queens.

If Black had played 2...Kxf4, then 3.b6 would queen.

Diagram 353

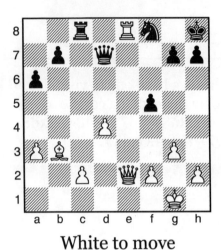

White to move

You should sense that Black has a back-rank weakness. How do you take advantage of it? 1.Qc4!. This threatens 2.Qg8#. It looks like Black could play 1...Rxc4, but then there's 2.Rxf8#.

Diagram 354

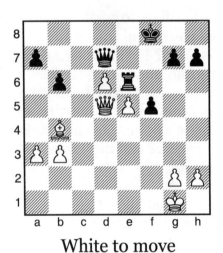

White to move

After 1.Qxe6 Qxe6 2.d7+, the pawn queens.

Diagram 355

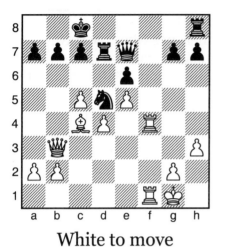

White to move

After 1.c6, White is threatening Qxb7+ and then Qb8#. However, after 1...bxc6 White has 2.Ba6+ Kd8 3.Qb8#.

1.c6 is a strong move which breaks open the opposing king's position.

Diagram 356

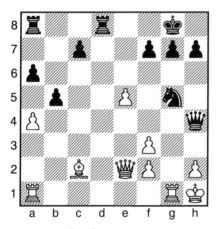

Black to move

Deflection time! 1...Rd2 2.Qxd2 Nxf3 attacks the queen and threatens checkmate on h2. It is true that the queen doesn't have to take, but after any other move Black continues either 2...Qxf2 or 2...Rxc2 depending on where White puts the queen.

Diagram 357

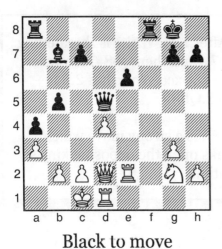

Black to move

Sometimes when we solve many chess problems, we start to overthink things. This is a simple problem with one idea: White's rooks are on the same diagonal. First 1...Qa2 threatening checkmate, and then 2...Bf3 attacking the rooks and winning one of them.

Diagram 358

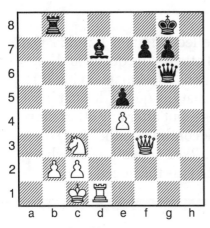

Black to move

Remember the last problem? 1...Bg4 and, after the queen moves away, 2...Bxd1. That is a skewer.

Diagram 359

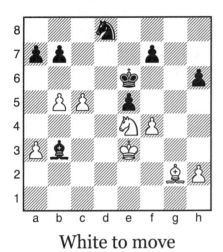

White to move

This is a deceptively simple problem. 1.c6 bxc6 2.Nc5+ forks the king and the bishop.

Diagram 360

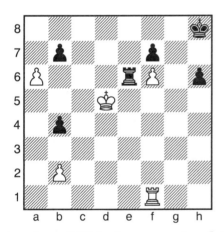

Analyze White's move 1.axb7.

After 1.axb7, Black must stop the pawn with 1...Rb6. Now 2.Ra1 threatening 3.Ra8+ and then queening the pawn. So 2...Rxb7, but now 3.Ra8+ Kh7 4.Kc6 and the rook is trapped.

Diagram 361

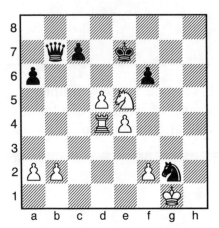

White to move. Tricky!
White traps the queen.

Watch how the knight and rook work together: 1.Rb4 Qc8 (1...Qxb4 2.Nc6+ forks) 2.Rb8 Qh3 (2...Qxb8 3.Nc6+ forks) 3.Rh8 Nh4 (3...Qxh8 4.Ng6+ forks) 4.Rxh4 Qc8 (4...Qxh4 5.Ng6+ forks) 5.Rh8 Qb7 6.Rb8, and the queen is trapped.

That is a complicated problem, but we have seen the rook and knight work together and while these problems may seem challenging now, if you practice them and learn the ideas, your chess will get better and you will be able to solve harder problems in the future.

Diagram 362

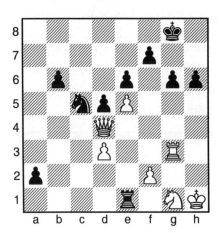

Can White draw this game?

Yes!! Black is about to queen and has some extra pawns. What can White do? 1.Qh4 a1Q 2.Rxg6+ fxg6 3.Qd8+ and the queen can play Qe7+ and Qd8+ forever, with perpetual check.

Diagram 363

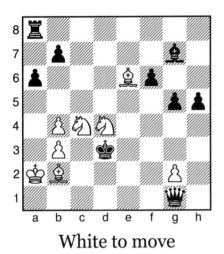

White to move

And... 1.Bf5# game over. Start simple and work outward from there.

Diagram 364

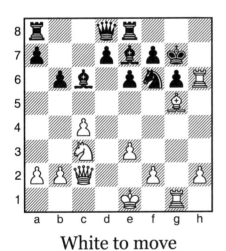

White to move

1.Rxg6+ fxg6 2.Bh6+ Kxh6 3.Qxg6#. Or 2...Kh8 3.Qxg6 Rg8 4.Bg7+ Rxg7 5.Qxg7#.

Diagram 365

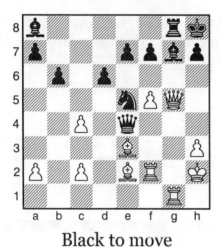

Black to move

After 1...Ng4+, no matter what White does Black follows up with 2...Be5+, when the discovered attack wins the queen.

Diagram 366

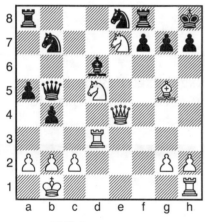

White to move

Pattern alert! 1.Qxh7+ Kxh7 2.Rh3#.

These things happen when you develop your pieces to effective squares and know what the targets are.

Diagram 367

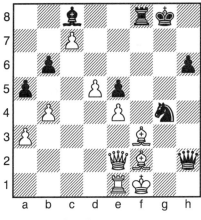

Black to move

Deflection alert: 1...Ba6 and now the queen is stuck. 2.Qxa6 Qf2#. What about 2.Bxg4 ? Now 2...Qf2# because the white queen is pinned and the black rook protects the black queen.

Diagram 368

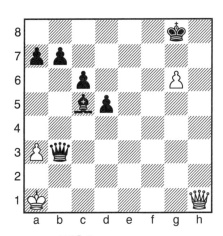

White to move

Easy one. 1.Qh7+ Kf8 2.Qf7#.

Remember that pawns can be very effective support points for pieces and for taking away flight squares.

Diagram 369

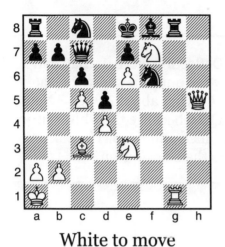

White to move

This is a smothered mate. Watch how it is done: 1.Nd6++ (double check) 1...Kd8 2.Qe8+ Nxe8 3.Nf7#.

Diagram 370

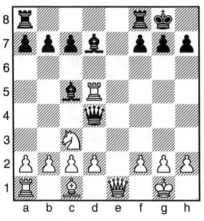

Black to move

It looks like Black might have some problems. White's rook is forking the queen and bishop, so... 1...Rfe8!. White's rook cannot do anything and the queen is under attack. 2.Qf1 Qxf2+ 3.Qxf2 Re1#. The bishop pin keeps popping up.

Diagram 371

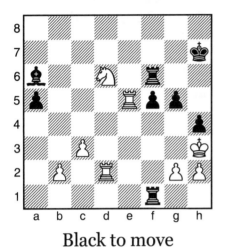

Black to move

After 1...Rf3+ the game ends with 2.gxf3 Bf1#.

Diagram 372

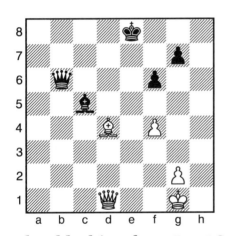

Should white play 1.Bxc5 ?

No! That leads just to an equal game.

After 1.Qh5+ the king is in check and the black bishop is attacked twice. White wins a piece.

Diagram 373

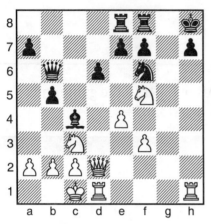

White to move

A good visualization problem. 1.Rxh7+ Nxh7 2.Qh6 Rg8 (Qg7# was threatened).

Now 3.Rh1 and it is impossible for Black to protect the knight on h7. Black is going to get check-mated.

When you try combinations like this in a game, you may miss a defensive possibility. Scanning the board and really analyzing is very important.

Diagram 374

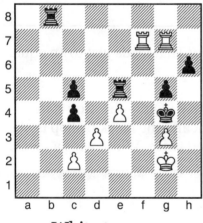

White to move

Another pattern: 1.Rf4+ Kh5 2.Rh4+! gxh4 (forced) and 3.g4#.

Checkmate with a pawn.

Diagram 375

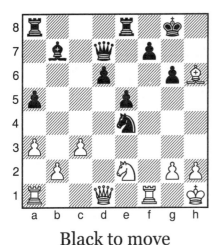

Black to move

Take note of Black's bishop.
1...Qh3! (threatening 2...Ng3+
3.Nxg3 Qg2#). So 2.gxh3 Nf2++
(double check) 3.Kg1 Nh3#.

Diagram 376

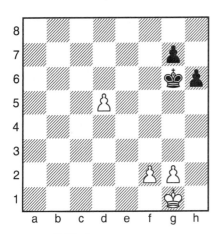

White to move:
1.g4 or 1.f4 ? Why?

The difference is between a win
and a draw. 1.g4 Kf6 2.Kg2 Ke5
and Black wins the d-pawn. Or
2.f4 Ke7 3.Kf2 Kd6, also winning
the pawn.

However, with 1.f4 Kf7 2.Kf2
Ke7 3.Ke3 Kd6 4.Kd4 White saves
the d-pawn and should win. After
1.f4, it took White three moves to
protect the pawn and three moves
for Black to get to the pawn.

Diagram 377

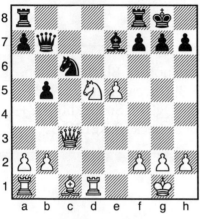

White to move

You have seen this tactic before: 1.Qxc6 Qxc6 2.Nxe7+ Kh8 3.Nxc6, and White is a piece ahead.

Diagram 378

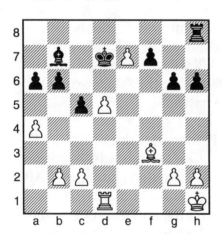

Active King Study 3:
White to move

1.d6 Bxf3 2.gxf3 Rc8 3.Kg2 g5 4.Rd5 Rg8 5.Kg3 f6 6.Kg4 Ke6 7.Kh5 a5 (7...Kxd5 8.d7 queening one of the pawns) 8.Kxh6 Kf7 9.Kh5 Rh8+ 10.Kg4 Rh4+ 11.Kg3 (11.Kf5 Rf4# – White needs to be careful) 11...Rh8 12.f4 gxf4+ 13.Kxf4 Ke6 14.d7 Kxe7 15.d8Q+ Rxd8 16.Rxd8 Kxd8 17.Kf5, and White will push the h-pawn, drawing Black's king to the h-file, and then grab all of Black's pawns (Botvinnik vs. Kan, Sverdlovsk 1943).

Diagram 379

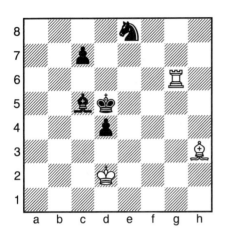

White to move. Tricky!

There is a lot going on in this problem.

1.Bd7 Nd6 (forced). White can make a very direct threat with the next move: 2.Kd3.

What is the threat? 3.Rg5+ and the knight will have to interpose and it will be lost.

After 2.Kd3, any knight move is followed by 3.Bc6#. If 2...c6, then 3.Rg5+ Nf5 4.Rxf5#.

Black is in a box and can't get out.

Diagram 380

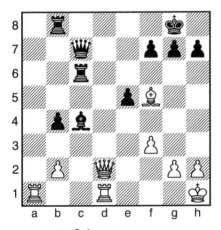

White to move

Black has back-rank weaknesses. How does White take advantage of them? 1.Ra7. Black cannot take because 2.Qd8+ leads to checkmate. After 1.Ra7 Qb6 2.Rb7!, Black must lose the queen to stop checkmate: 2...Rcc8 3.Rxb6. It's for free.

Diagram 381

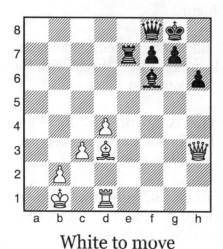

White to move

After 1.Qf5, Black must lose the bishop to stop checkmate: 1.Qf5 g6 2.Qxf6.

Diagram 382

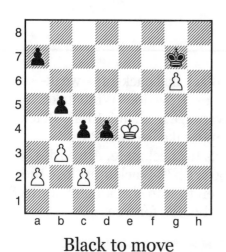

Black to move

It looks bad for Black, but there is something sneaky: 1...d3 2.cxd3 c3 and the pawn queens because White's king is stopped by its own d-pawn.

Diagram 383

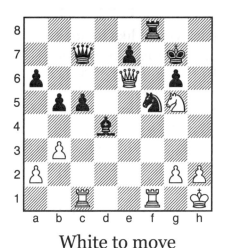

White to move

An idea we have seen before. 1.Qxf5 P or R takes Q and now 2.Ne6+ forks the king and queen. White wins a piece.

Diagram 384

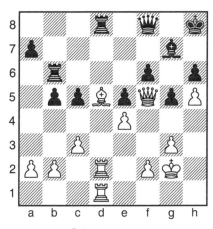

White to move

After 1.Bg8 there are too many threats for Black to meet: 1...Qxg8 2.Rxd8 and Black's queen is pinned, or 1...Rxd2 2.Qh7#.

The more threats you can make, the better your chances of winning.

Diagram 385

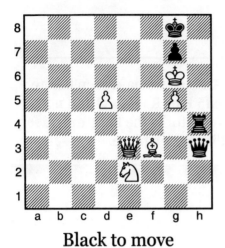

Black to move

Black would like to hop the queen over the rook and play ...Qh7#. If you hop over pieces with your queen, though, you will get in trouble. Do the next best thing, make a great move: 1... Re4 and now White must lose the queen in order to stop checkmate by playing 2.Bh5.

Diagram 386

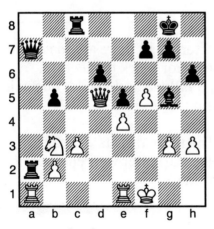

Black to move

How does Black crash through? 1...Rxc3 and if White plays 2.bxc3, then 2...Qf2#; or (on almost any other move) 2...Rf3+ and White soon gets mated.

Diagram 387

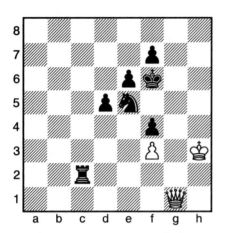

White to move and draw

After 1.Qg5+, 1...Kxg5 is stalemate.

You might look at the position and wonder why White wants a draw. In top-level chess, Black would be winning here. The passed d-pawn, combined with the knight and rook, will decide the game.

Diagram 388

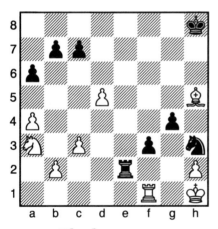

Black to move

It looks like Black is losing, but there is a nice combination: 1...Rg2 2.any Rg1+ 3.Rxg1 Nf2#.

It is very important to practice how checkmates happen without the queen and how the pieces work together.

Diagram 389

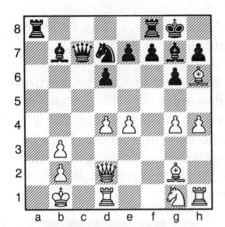

Is 1...Bxd4 a good
move for Black?

Yes! First you need to calculate what happens after 2.Qxd4. If you don't see it, don't play the move.

2...Ra1+! 3.Kxa1 Qc2 and now White cannot avoid losing to ...Ra8. The best White can try is 4.Bf3 Ra8+ 5.Qa4, Rxa4+ 6.bxa4, but Black wraps it up with 6...Qxa4+ 7.Kb1 Bxe4+ 8.Bxe4+ Qxe4+ and the h1-rook drops.

Take a look and try different things. ...Ra8 ends the game.

Diagram 390

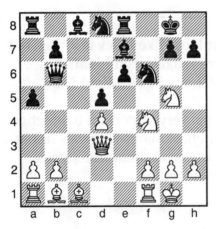

White to move

Pattern alert! 1.Qxh7+ Nxh7 2.Bxh7+ Kh8 (or 2...Kf8) 3.Ng6#.

Diagram 391

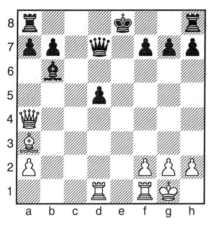

White to move

White's queen is under attack, but Black's king is in the center. What should White do? 1.Rxd5!. After 1...Qxa4 2.Re1+, mate follows after the bishop and queen interpose uselessly.

Chess tip:

Make sure your opponent's blocks are useless when you sacrifice your queen.

Diagram 392

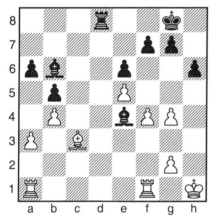

Black to move

I like the look of Black's bishops and the rook on the open file. 1...Rd3 attacks White's bishop and threatens ...Rh3#.

White must play 2.Rf3 and give up the rook. White will lose some pawns, too.

Diagram 393

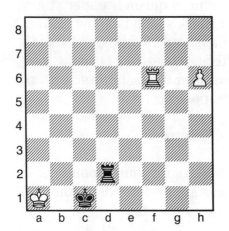

White should win. Black has two ways to try to stop the pawn:

1...Rh2 2.Rf1+ K-any 3.Rf2+ and the rook must move and then the pawn queens. Or:

1...Rd8 2.Rc6+ K-any 3.Rd6+ and the rook must move and then the pawn queens.

What happens after 1.h7 ?

Diagram 394

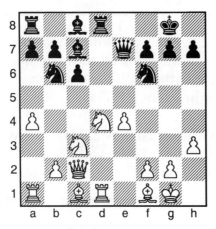

Play simple: 1...Rxd4 2.Rxd4, and now 2...Qe5 makes two threats, 3...Qh2# and 3...Qxd4. (White must prevent the mate and then Black's queen captures the undefended rook.)

Black to move

Diagram 395

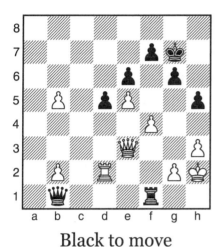

Black to move

White has a pawn that will queen, but Black controls the back rank. Which is more important? 1...h4 and now checkmate is unstoppable. If 2.g3, then 2...Rh1+ 3.Kg2 Qf1#.

White has more material, but Black's position is much stronger.

Diagram 396

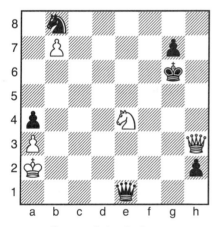

Is 1.Qxh2 White's best move?

No! The best move is 1.Qe6+, because it puts Black's king in a bad way. The king has to move 1...Kh7 which will be met by 2.Ng5+ and Black loses the queen, or 1...Kh5 2.Nf6+ and Black still loses the queen, plus the pawn is stopped from queening.

What's the tactic? Discovered check.

Diagram 397

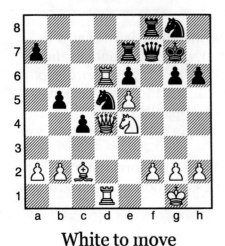

White to move

After 1.Rxd5 exd5 2.e6+, Black loses the queen.

Tactic? Discovered check.

Diagram 398

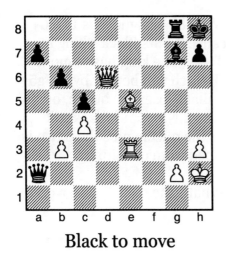

Black to move

White to move has 1.Bxg7+ and Black is in big trouble. What can Black do?

1...Qxg2+ 2.Kxg2 Bxe5+ 3.K-any Bxd6 and Black comes out a piece ahead.

Tactic? Discovered check.

(Author's note: the three discovered checks in a row were not intentional!)

Diagram 399

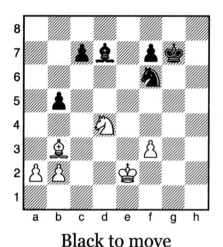

Black to move

This is a deceptively simple problem. The game looks even, and none of the pieces appear to be in trouble. *But...* 1...c5 attacks the knight. The knight has only one safe square: 2.Nc2, and then 2...c4 traps the bishop.

Diagram 400

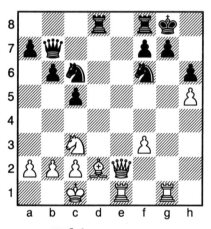

White to move

By now, you should see things such as how the rook on g1 is across from Black's king. What is in between them? A pawn.

1.Bxh6 wins a pawn and starts to open up Black's king.

Diagram 401

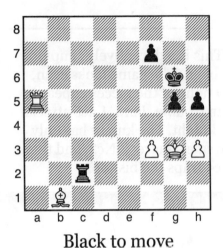

Black to move

White carelessly played 1.Bb1 to pin the rook. Sadly for White, the pin turns out to be useless: 1...h4+ 2.Kg4 f5+ 3.Rxf5 (forced and the pin disappears) 3...Rg2#.

White lost track of Black's potential threats.

Diagram 402

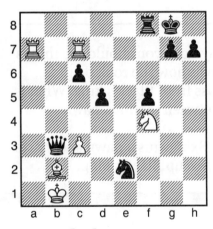

Black to move

Black's king is in trouble, but so is White's. 1...Nxc3+ 2.Ka1 Qd1+ 3.Bc1 (forced) 3...Qxc1#.

Diagram 403

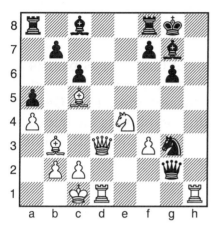

White to move

Pattern alert! Notice the bishop on b3 – it is doing something important. 1.Nf6+ Bxf6 2.Qxg6+ (the f7-pawn is pinned) 2...Bg7 3.Qh7#.

Diagram 404

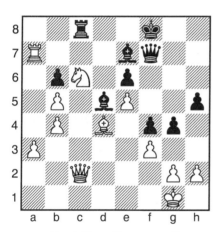

Is 1.Rxe7 a good move for White?

Yes! That is, if you can calculate what happens after that move. If you thought 1.Rxe7 Qxe7 2.Nxe7 Rxc2, you missed something and Black is winning.

You need to see 1.Rxe7 Qxe7 2.Bc5! and Black's queen is lost. It is true that Black has captured a rook and a bishop, but White has a huge edge here.

Diagram 405

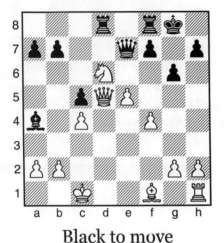

Black to move

Look at Black's bishop on a4 and watch how it gets involved: 1...Rxd6, and now 2.exd6 Qe1#, or 2.Qxd6 Rd8 pinning the queen to the checkmate square d1. White must lose the queen.

Diagram 406

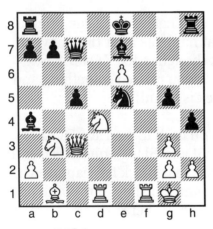

White to move

White's rooks on d1 and f1 keep Black's king in a box. What can White do? 1.Nb5 Bxb5 2.Qxe5, and if Black plays 2...Qxe5 then 3.Bg6 is checkmate. On almost all other moves, Black will get checkmated soon anyway.

Diagram 407

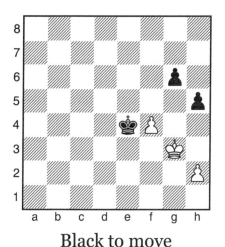

Black to move

Black might think the game is won after 1...Ke3, but after 2.h3 Ke4 3.Kh4, now with 3...Kxf4 it is stalemate.

Diagram 408

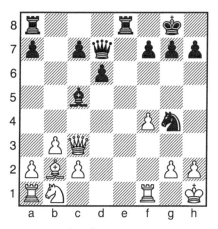

Black to move

This starts with 1...Nf2+ 2.Rxf2 (White drops the queen after 2.Kg1 Nd1+) 2...Bd4! and 3.Qxd4 Re1+ leads to checkmate. On any other queen move, 3...Bxb2 and then 4...Bxa1 will leave Black ahead in material.

Diagram 409

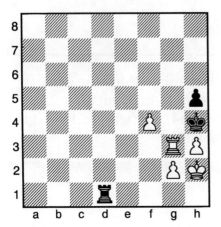

Black to move and draw

Since Black is two pawns down, a draw would be a good result (half a point is better than nothing): 1...Rd3 2.Rf3 (2.Rxd3 is stalemate) 2...Rxf3 3.gxf3, stalemate.

Diagram 410

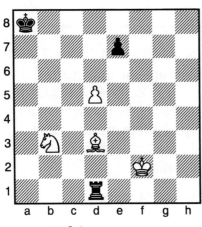

White to move

Many players starting out in chess would play something like 1.Be4 or 1.Nc5 and they might win, or they might not. 1.d6 exd6 2.Bc2 and the rook has just one "safe" move, 2...Rh1, but then 3.Be4+ wins the rook.

You might think, "What about 1...Rxd3?" There follows 2.dxe7 and Black cannot stop the pawn from queening.

Diagram 411

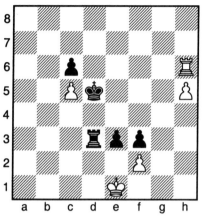

Black to move

How does Black queen a pawn? 1...Rd1+ 2.Kxd1 exf2 and there is no way to stop the pawn. (Notice that after 3.Rd6+ Kxc5, White's king blocks the rook from getting to d1.)

Diagram 412

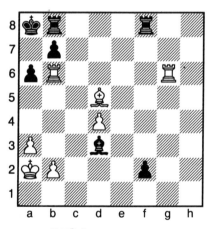

White to move

I see a bishop pinning a pawn. Something good must come of it: 1.Rxa6+ Bxa6 2.Rxa6# (the b7-pawn is pinned).

Diagram 413

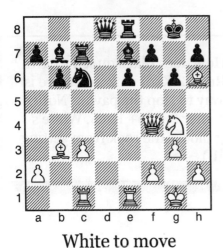

White to move

1.Qxf7+ Kxf7 2.Be6#.

Diagram 414

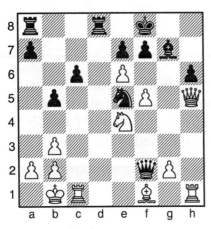

Black to move

This pattern has been seen before.

1...Qxb2+ 2.Kxb2 Nc4++ (double check) 3.Kb1 Na3#; or 3.Kc2 Na3#.

Diagram 415

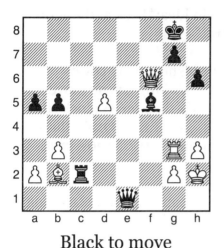

Black to move

It seems hopeless for Black. White is threatening Qg7# and the g-pawn is pinned. Should Black resign? *No!*

1...Qxg3+! 2.Kxg3 gxf6 and now Black is a rook ahead.

Diagram 416

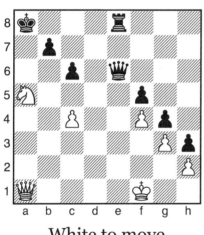

White to move

1.Nc6# (discovered checkmate). Learn the simple things quickly and you will get the more complex things faster.

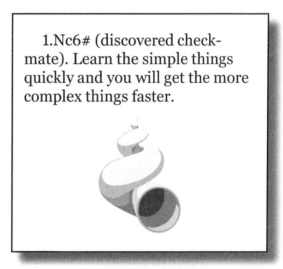

Chapter 11

Diagram 417

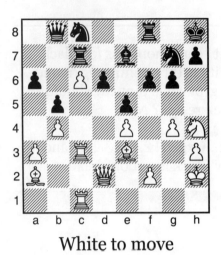

White to move

Main idea: "Look at the entire board."

The bishop on a2 covers g8. Black's king has no moves. White's bishop on e3 blocks the queen... so, 1.Ba7! Qxa7 (there is nothing else) 2.Nxg6+ hxg6 3.Qh6#.

The board saw pieces moving everywhere.

Diagram 418

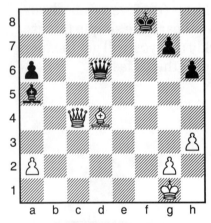

White 1.Bc5,
Black 1...Bb6. White?

1.Bc5 pins the queen. Then 1...Bb6 pins the bishop... and now 2.Qf4+ wins a piece.

Diagram 419

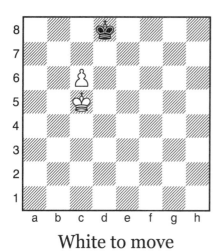

White to move

Very simple but very important. When the white king plays 1.Kd6, it forces Black to move 1...Kc8, then 2.c7 Kb7 3.Kd7 and the pawn will queen. Now imagine that the black king was on c8: 1.Kd6 Kd8 2.c7 Kc8 3.Kc6, stalemate (or White can lose the pawn).

1.Kd6 gives White the opposition.

Diagram 420

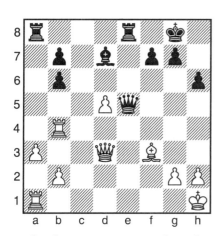

Black to move. A classic!

A move which has been seen many times and it deserves to be seen many times.

1...Rxa3!. White can take back three different ways and loses in all of them:

2.Rxa3 Qe1+ will mate.
2.bxa3 Qxa1+ 3.Qd1 Re1+ will mate.
2.Qxa3 Qe1+ will mate.

Diagram 421

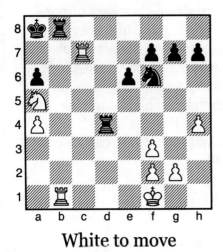

White to move

A very double-edged position:

1.Ra7+! Kxa7 2.Nc6+ Ka8 3.Rxb8#.

Diagram 422

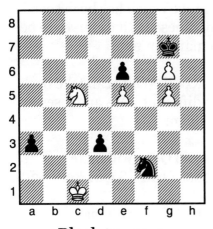

Black to move

Hopefully your brain is thinking, "A pawn will queen and there may be a deflection".

1...d2+ 2.Kxd2 Ne4+ (deflection) 3.Nxe4 a2 and the a-pawn will queen.

Diagram 423

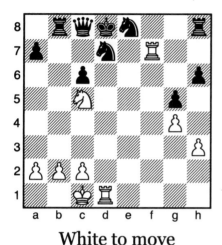

White to move

How fast did you find this one? 1.Ne6#.

Diagram 424

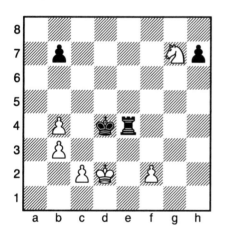

White to move. Trap the rook.

A tough one, but this position is about looking at all the squares your opponent's pieces can move to. 1.f3 Re5 (the only safe move) 2.c4 then any pawn move 3.f4 and the rook has no moves – if the rook moves along the e-file, then 4.Nf5#. This is a visualization problem involving thinking of what squares the pawns control and what squares the knight controls.

Diagram 425

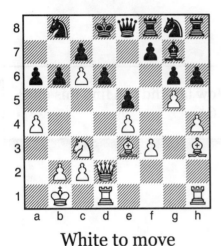

White to move

It's mate after 1.Qxd6+ cxd6 2.Bxb6+ Ke7 3.Nd5#.

Diagram 426

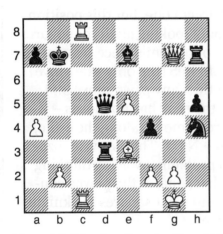

Should Black play 1...Rxg7 ?

NO!! NO!! NO!!! NO!! NO!! NO!! NO!! NO!!NO!! NO!!

After the terrible 1...Rxg7??? 2.R1c7+ Ka6 3.Rxa7#, Black turns a win into a loss.

Correct is 1...Nf3+ 2.gxf3 and only now 2...Rxg7+. On 2.Kf1 or 2.Kh1, Black finishes things with 2...Rd1+ 3.Rxd1 Qxd1#.

Diagram 427

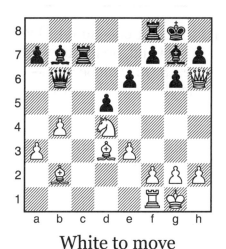

White to move

Pattern alert: 1.Qxg7+ Kxg7 2.Nf5++ Kg8 3.Nh6#.

Diagram 428

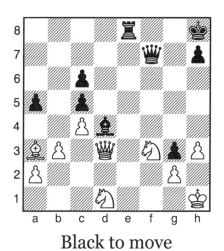

Black to move

White is weak on the back rank, but what should Black do?

After 1...Qxf3, White has two losing options:

2.Qxf3 Re1+ 3.Qf1 Rxf1#.
2.gxf3 Re1+ 3.Kg2 Rg1#.

Diagram 429

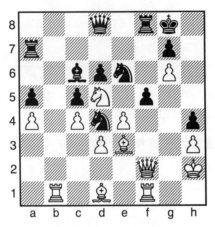

White to move

Tactic used? Deflection! 1.Rb8 Qxb8 2.Qxh4 and, no matter what Black does, 3.Qh7 will be checkmate or lead to a quick checkmate.

Think about it this way. White's getting to the h4 square was more important than an entire rook.

Diagram 430

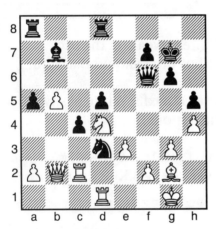

White to move

This is a tricky one. 1.Rxd3 cxd3 2.Ne6+ fxe6 and 3.Rc7+ and Black's king must leave its protection of the queen. 4.Qxf6 then wins easily.

Diagram 431

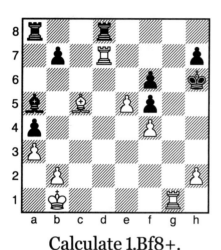

Calculate 1.Bf8+.

After 1.Bf8+, Black has a couple of options:

1...Kh5 2.Rxh7#.
1...Rxf8 2.Rd3 Be1 3.Rh3+ Bh4 4.Rxh4#.

Most of the time, there are multiple possibilities and you need to think through each one.

Diagram 432

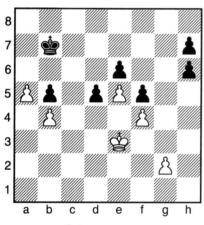

White to move

The idea here is for White to get pawns rolling up the board which are far enough apart that Black's king cannot stop them all. 1.g4 fxg4 2.f5 exf5 3.e6 and either the a- or the e-pawn queens.

If 1.g4 d4+ 2.Kxd4 fxg4 3.f5 exf5 4.e6 g3, then 5.Ke3 g2 6.Kf2 stops the black pawn.

Diagram 433

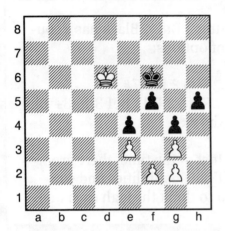

Black to move and draw

Breakthrough! 1...f4 and there are several options:

2.exf4 h4 3.gxh4 g3 4.fxg3 e3 queens.
2.gxf4 h4 3.any h3 queens.
2.Kd5 h4 3.Kxe4 f3 4.gxf3 h3 queens.

Diagram 434

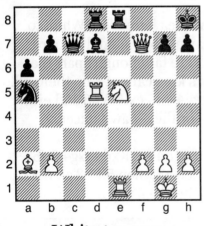

White to move

After 1.Rxd7 (of course you ruled out 1.Nxd7 because of 1...Rxe1#) 1...Qxd7 2.Qxd7 Rxd7, 3.Nf7+ wins for White.

Diagram 435

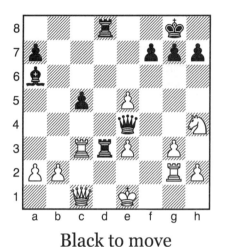

Black to move

One of the keys to this position is the bishop on a6.

Black starts with 1...Qxe3+ 2.Qxe3 Rd1+ 3.Kf2 Rf1#.

Diagram 436

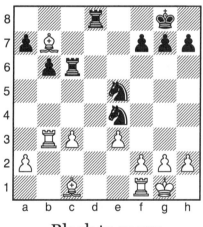

Black to move

It looks like Black is in trouble. However, after 1...Nf3+! White has two losing options:

2.gxf3 Rg6+ 3.Kh1 Nxf2+! 4.Rxf2 Rd1+ 5.Rf1 Rxf1#.
2.Kh1 Nxf2+ 3.Rxf2 Rd1+ 4.Rf1 Rxf1#.

Practice checkmates where the queen isn't involved.

Glossary

Pins

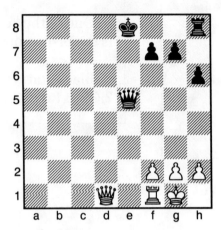

1.Re1 *pins* the queen to the king.

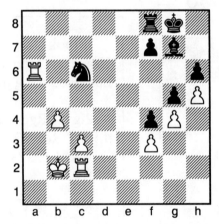

1...Nxb4 is a knight fork and the pawn on c3 can't take the **knight because** it's pinned. The king can never move into check.

Glossary

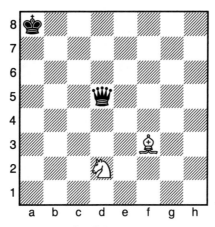

The bishop pins the queen to the king.

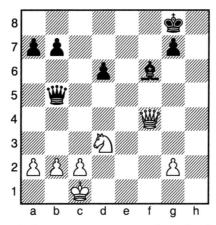

Black plays 1...Bg5 and the queen is pinned to the king.

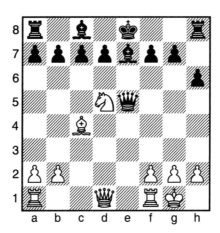

White plays 1.Nxe7 and, no matter which piece Black recaptures with, White will play 2.Re1 and pin the queen to the king.

Knight forks

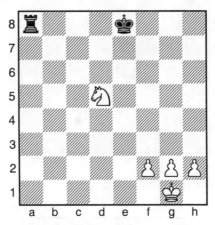

White plays 1.Nc7+ and *forks* the king and rook.

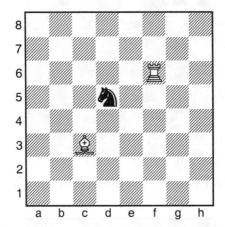

Black has a choice: 1...Nxf6 will win 2 points because the bishop will take you back, while 1...Nxc3 will win 3 points. Take the bishop!

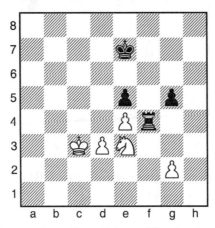

1.Nd5+ forks the king and rook. White will win 2 points.

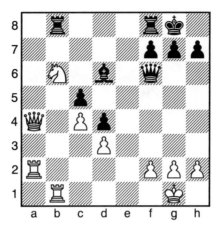

See the knight fork 1.Nd7 ? It's a terrible move this time. Black will play 1...Rxb1+ and you will get checkmated. Ask yourself, "What will my opponent do after I make my move?"

Discovered attack

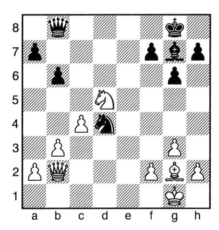

Black has a choice of 1...Ne2+ or 1...Nf3+. Which is better? If Black plays 1...Ne2+, the queen can take the knight. After 1...Nf3+, White plays 2.Bxf3 and then Black plays 2...Bxb2.

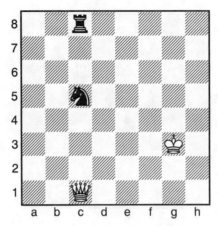

1...Ne4+. White's king moves and then 2...Rxc1.

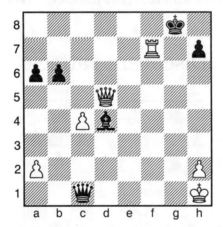

White is in check. 1.Rf1 blocks the check and puts Black's king in check. You win Black's queen.

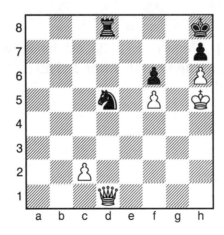

Glossary

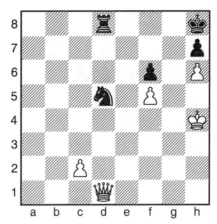

Look at the two diagrams above. In one, 1.c4 is a great move and in the other it's a terrible one. In the position on the left, 1.c4 is terrible. Why? Because of 1...Nf4+ with *discovered check* and White loses his queen. On the right, 1.c4 (attacking a pinned piece) will win a knight or rook.

Deflection

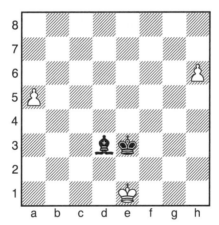

White plays 1.a6 and the bishop must take it. Next, White will play 2.h7 and queen his other pawn.

The Learning Spiral

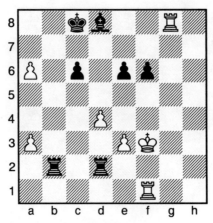

After 1.Rxd8+ Kxd8, White's pawn queens.

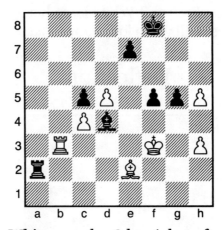

Black plays 1...g4+. White can play 2.hxg4, but after Black replies 2...fxg4+ White's king must leave his protection of the bishop. Black will then take the bishop.

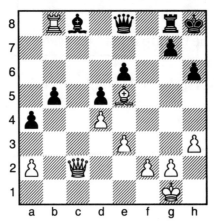

This is a tough one. White plays 1.Rxc8. Why? Because after 1...Qxc8 White can play 2.Qg6 and threaten 3.Qxh6#.

Black's queen was deflected from protecting the g6 square. Often times, tactics work in combination with each other.

Silent move

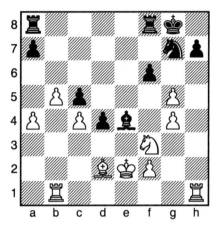

1...Bxb1 with a +2 for Black looks obvious. However, it is not even close to the best move, as 1...Rae8 with a +6 for Black is much stronger. How did Carlsen (who was playing Black) "see" that?

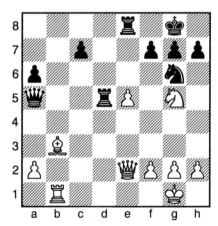

White plays 1.Qf3. It's not check. Most players would play 1.Bxd5 immediately. 1.Qf3 waits and makes additional threats. Patience is a virtue.

Zugzwang

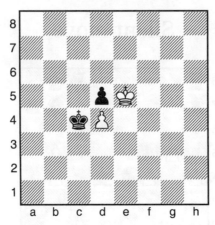

Whoever has to move loses.

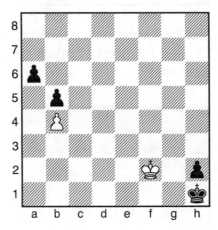

Black to move. Black must play 1...a5. He has to play a losing move. White will take the pawn and then queen on a8 with checkmate.

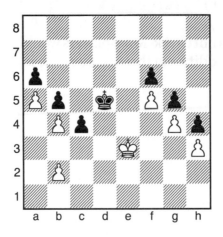

Glossary

After Black plays 1...Ke5, White must give ground.

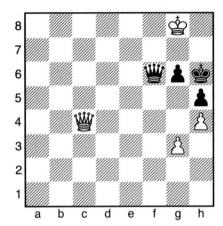

Should White play 1.Qf4+ ? After trading queens, the position would look like this:

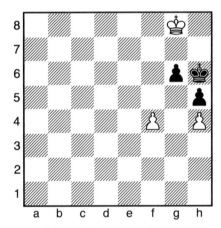

Black has to play 1...g5. After 2.fxg5+, he loses.

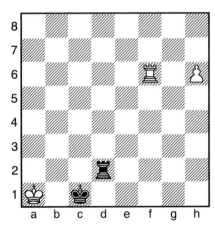

After White plays 1.h7, Black is in *Zugwang*.

If he plays 1...Rh2 to stop the pawn, White plays 2.Rf1+ Kc2(d2) 3.Rf2+ (deflection) and the pawn will queen. But if Black plays 1...Rd8 to stop the pawn, White will play 2.Rc6+ Kd1(d2) and White will play 3.Rd6+ (deflection) and again the pawn will queen.

In-between move

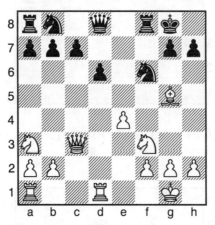

Black plays 1...Nxe4, thinking 2.Bxd8 Nxc3. But instead White plays 2.Qb3+ *(in-between move)* and then takes the queen.

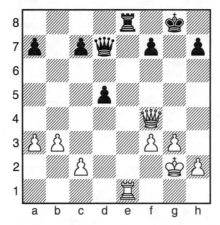

White plays 1.Qg4+, then 1...Qxg4. Instead of retaking the queen immediately with the pawn, White plays 2.Rxe8 (check!) and only then takes the queen.

Glossary

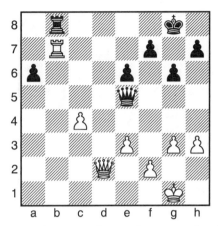

White plays 1.Qd4. Black has no choice but to take the queen with 1...Qxd4. But now instead of taking back with the pawn, White plays 2.Rxb8+ and only then takes the queen.

Opposition

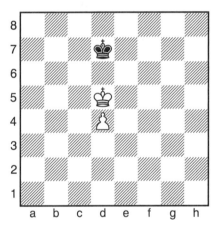

White has the opposition if it's Black's turn to move. Black's king moves away, and then White's king moves like this:

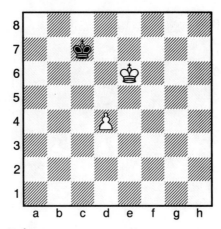

Black has to move again.

If he plays 2...Kc6, White will play 3.d5+, Black goes back to c7 and White's king plays 4.Ke7. Then he just pushes the pawn.

On the second move, if Black's king goes to c8, White goes to the other side with 3.e7. Now if Black plays 5...Kc7, the pawn queens.

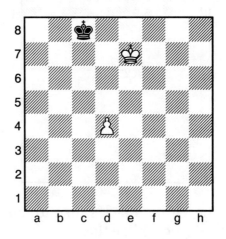

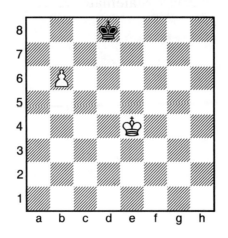

White plays 1.Kd5. The goal is to make the following position happen:

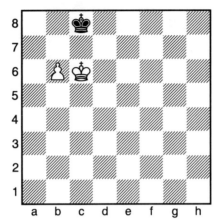

Black to move, Black loses. White to move, draw. Practice this a lot.

Stalemate

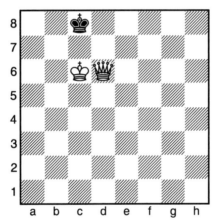

White is trying to checkmate with the king and queen. Sadly, Black's king has no moves and isn't in check. Stalemate. ½-½

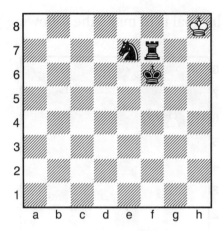

Stalemate!

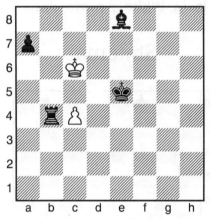

1.Kc5 and it's either stalemate or Black will have to give up his rook, after which White's king will head to a1 and it's a draw.

Trapped pieces

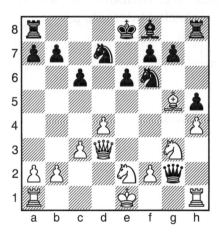

Glossary

1.Nf4 and the queen is trapped.

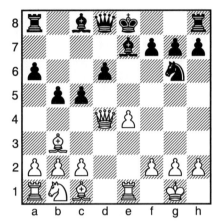

After White's queen moves, Black can play 1...c4 trapping the bishop.

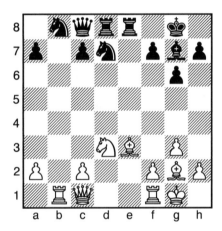

White plays1.Bb7 and the black queen is trapped.

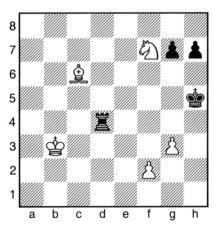

White plays 1.Kc3 and the rook is trapped.

Pawn majorities

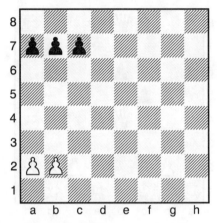

In many games, the strategy involves managing pawns on one side of the board.

If Black gets the pawns rolling forward, this can happen:

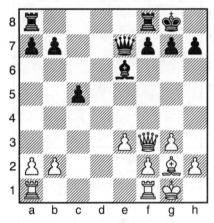

...which turns into this:

Glossary

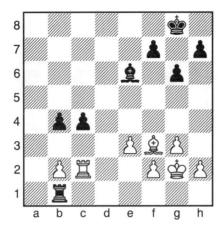

If the two white pawns move forward, this can happen:

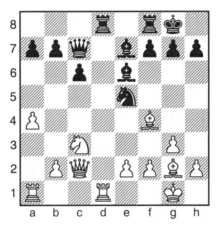

...which turns into this:

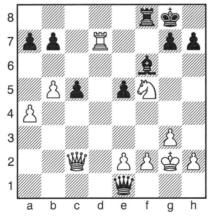

The two pawns have weakened the three pawns. Look at the game Alekhine vs. Euwe (p. 240).

Rooks on the seventh/second rank

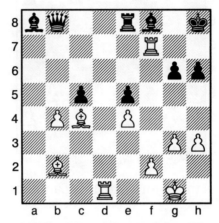

White plays 1.Rdd7 and it's over. The rooks dominate the game.

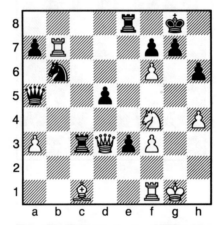

After White plays 1.Qg6, Black must take the queen or else be checkmated. Then 2.Rg7+ and 3.Ng6#.

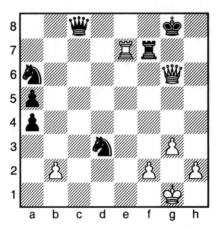

The rook on the seventh helps the queen. It will be mate in three moves.